On Her Own

Also by Ruth Sidel

WOMEN AND CHILDREN LAST:
THE PLIGHT OF POOR WOMEN IN
AFFLUENT AMERICA

URBAN SURVIVAL:
THE WORLD OF
WORKING CLASS WOMEN

FAMILIES OF FENGSHENG:
URBAN LIFE IN CHINA

WOMEN AND CHILD CARE IN CHINA:
A FIRSTHAND REPORT

RUTH SIDEL

On Her Own

GROWING UP IN THE SHADOW OF THE AMERICAN DREAM

VIKING

VIKING
Published by the Penguin Group
Viking Penguin, a division of Penguin Books USA Inc.,
40 West 23rd Street, New York, New York 10010, U.S.A.
Penguin Books Ltd, 27 Wrights Lane, London W8 5TZ, England
Penguin Books Australia Ltd, Ringwood, Victoria, Australia
Penguin Books Canada Ltd, 2801 John Street,
Markham, Ontario, Canada L3R 1B4
Penguin Books (N.Z.) Ltd, 182–190 Wairau Road,
Auckland 10, New Zealand

Penguin Books Ltd, Registered Offices:
Harmondsworth, Middlesex, England

First published in 1990 by Viking Penguin,
a division of Penguin Books USA Inc.

1 3 5 7 9 10 8 6 4 2

Grateful acknowledgment is made for permission to reprint excerpts
from the following copyrighted works:
Teenage Pregnancy in Industrialized Countries, by Elise F. Jones
et al. By permission of Yale University Press.
"For Bronx Nurses in Protest, Staying Home Is Painful," by
Stacey Okun, *The New York Times,* February 20, 1988. Copyright
© 1988 by The New York Times Company. Reprinted by permission.
"Is 'Quality' Time Really as Good as a Good Time?" from Anna
Quindlen's "Life in the 30's" column, *The New York Times,* June 9,
1988. Copyright © 1988 by The New York Times Company. Reprinted by permission.

LIBRARY OF CONGRESS CATALOGING IN PUBLICATION DATA
Sidel, Ruth.
On her own: growing up in the shadow
of the American dream / Ruth Sidel.
p. cm.
Includes bibliographical references.
ISBN 0-670-83154-9
1. Young women—United States—Attitudes. 2. Women—United
States—Social conditions. I. Title.
HQ1421.S59 1990
305.42'0973—dc20   89-40354

Set in Sabon
Printed in the United States of America

To Flora Donham and Marilyn Grossman-Jackson,
whose lives, both public and private,
help lead the way

CONTENTS

ACKNOWLEDGMENTS

This book has truly been a collaborative effort. The words, experiences, hopes, and dreams of the young women who so readily, so enthusiastically, and so generously talked with me make up the heart of the book. Without their participation the book literally would not exist. In order to protect their anonymity, I cannot thank them individually here, but they have my deep appreciation and my warm wishes for the future. My appreciation also to the somewhat older women who took time out of very busy lives to share with me their personal experiences, their thoughts, and their perspectives around the role of women in contemporary American society. While they, too, cannot be acknowledged individually, I want them to know that I am most grateful.

In the course of interviewing for this book I spoke with dozens of concerned, caring professionals who also gave of themselves and their time unstintingly. I am particularly grateful to Lynn Barnhardt, Terri L. Bartlett, Gwendolyn Boyd, Penelope R. Brazile, Barbara Brody, Charlotte Brody, Marilyn Cate, Naomi F. Chase, Kathleen Cherwinski, Theresa Cullen, Mary Curry, Eva Deykin, Michael A. Drake, Ellen Dreskin, William Dreskin, Joy Dryfoos, Linda Flanagan, Josephine Foulks, Judith Gorbach, Mary Ellen Grossman, Eileen Hayes, Loretta N. Jones, Neela Josbi, Sally Kohn, Ethel L. Levine, Suzanne Michael, Deborah Prothrow-Stith, Dena Romero, Lisa Rubenstein, Michelle A. Saint-Germain, Claire E. Schwartz, Eve Shapiro, Barbara Strumstad, Georgia Vancza, Deborah Walker, Barbara H. Warren, Catherine Riley Wineburg, Sara Winter, Virginia L. Yrun, and Sandra Zubkoff.

Many of these people, particularly Marilyn Cate, Kathleen Cherwinski, Theresa Cullen, Michael Drake, Ellen and William Dreskin, Linda Flanagan, Josephine Foulks, Loretta Jones, Dena Romero,

Claire Schwartz, and Barbara Warren, went out of their way to locate young women for me to interview and to facilitate the interviewing process. My gratitude to them and to Toni Harlan, Robbin Harvey, Ruth Heifetz, Marilyn Grossman-Jackson, Christine Oakley, and Robert J. Wineburg for their interest and their critical help in identifying a broad spectrum of young women for in-depth interviews.

To Lynn Chancer and Janet Poppendieck, my appreciation for administering the questionnaire to their students at Hunter College. I am particularly grateful to Lynn Chancer for reading drafts of several chapters, for helping to clarify the major themes of this book, and for her warm support and encouragement.

Many others have demonstrated their support and interest. My thanks to Mimi Abramovitz for graciously sharing my time with this book long after I should have moved on to our joint efforts; to Flora Donham for reading the entire manuscript and telling me what she really thought; to Barbara Grossman for her concern even while she was trying to finish her own book; and to Margot Haas my gratitude for always being there.

Data gathering for this project was supported in part by the WorldWorks Foundation. I am grateful to the foundation for enabling me to travel to various parts of the United States in order to interview a diverse group of young women.

To my editor, Mindy Werner, my deep appreciation for her warmth, her flexibility and availability, her concern about the lives and future of young women, and her unfailing editorial insight and skill. To Janine Steel, my thanks for all she does to help make working with Viking Penguin such a pleasure. To Patrick Dillon, my appreciation for his thoughtful and meticulous copyediting of the manuscript.

And to Vic—who hears every doubt, reads every word, is always upbeat, and, above all, shares my hopes for a better world—all my love.

On Her Own

INTRODUCTION

Throughout American history the idea of progress has persisted as a national destiny and a personal dream. The story of American life often resembles a Hollywood narrative, a miraculous metamorphosis in which people of humble origins, using simple implements, ascend to a "city on a hill." Through the elixirs of *virgin land, streets of gold, industry, enterprise,* and *opportunity,* common folk become comfortable residents in paradise. The past is left behind. A new world is born.

Until recently that vision, that quintessentially American vision, was for the most part a male dream. While over the centuries women have shared the dream and worked to make it a reality for themselves and for their families, men have been perceived by women and men alike as the primary players, the central characters in the struggle toward success and affluence. But over the past two decades significant changes within American society, within the family, and in women's perceptions of their roles, their rights, and their responsibilities have altered in a fundamental way many women's image of themselves and their relationship to the American Dream.

In recent years it has become increasingly clear to many women in the United States that the old rules no longer apply. Conventional wisdom once held that if a woman married wisely, played her role as caregiver to husband, children, and possibly other family members as well, and was lucky enough to avoid disasters such as incapacitating illness or premature widowhood, she was likely to be cared for economically by her husband or her children for the remainder of her life. "Till death do us part" was not thought of as an empty phrase or as a cliché but rather as the natural order of life.

We now know, after years of meticulous research by historians, economists, sociologists, and other scholars concerned with women's and family issues, that this vision of the lives of American women was deeply flawed. We know that significant numbers of women have always worked outside the home, not simply for "self-fulfillment" or for "pin money" but out of economic necessity. We also know that since colonial times significant numbers of women have not been cared for by family members and indeed have lived in poverty and near-poverty. What has changed in recent years is that increasing numbers of women no longer accept and believe in what one researcher has termed the "industrial family ethic," the ideology that made "reproduction rather than production the centerpiece of women's life."

Recent developments such as the accelerating dependence of families on two incomes, the high rates of divorce and separation, the disturbing phenomenon of teenage pregnancy, the explosive rise in the number of female-headed families, and the growing number of women—and their children—who are living in poverty are clear indications that even if the old rules once applied to some segments of society, they surely are not relevant to most women today. In the course of my research for my recent book *Women and Children Last: The Plight of Poor Women in Affluent America*, it became clear that while societal conditions were changing rapidly for women, often leaving them simultaneously overburdened with family responsibilities and economically vulnerable, the majority of women were still playing by the old rules. In the early-to-mid-1980s women in their twenties, thirties, and forties told me repeatedly, "I was taught that my husband would take care of me," "It was clear that if you're not attached to a man, something must be wrong with you," or "I thought Prince Charming was going to come down the pike and we would live happily ever after." By the time these women talked with me, after their lives had fallen apart and they and their children had fallen into poverty, they knew that their assumptions had been tragically flawed. Some regretted not acquiring more education and training, others regretted marrying and having children so young, and still others regretted that they had been socialized for subservience and dependency. Some picked up the pieces of their lives as best they could; others had too many children, were too mired in poverty or too depressed to do more than try to survive from day to day.

But low-income women are not the only group questioning the old rules and the old expectations. Over the past twenty-five years women of disparate backgrounds and life experiences have been questioning traditional attitudes toward work and family, dependence and independence, ways of balancing public roles and private lives. Many, spurred on by the women's movement, have taken the giant leap of discarding their original life scenarios and developing new ones; others have been forced by circumstance to do so. Whatever the impetus, many women have found that while the traditional role of women may indeed be obsolete, a new order has yet to be put into place. The society simply has not been transformed to the extent that their expectations had been transformed; although they might be playing by new rules, much of society was still playing by the old ones. Trade-offs had to be made. Some women who had entered demanding, time-consuming professions decided not to have children at all; others decided that they would not even try to make it to the top of their fields—at least while their children were small. Still others made the decision to leave much of the child rearing to other caregivers. Yet another group found themselves coming to the end of their child-bearing years without either a partner or a child. While many women were living full, exciting lives their mothers could never have imagined, for others the promise of "having it all" often gave way to chronic fatigue, constant compromise, and, in some instances, a sense of missed opportunities.

The question that began to interest me was "What about the next generation?" What about women in their teens and early twenties? What are their hopes and dreams? How do they see the fabric of their lives in the future? After decades of writing by thinkers such as Simone de Beauvoir, Betty Friedan, Germaine Greer, Alice Kessler Harris, Ann Oakley, Marian Wright Edelman,

Barbara Ehrenreich, Gloria Naylor, Toni Morrison, and many others have left their mark on our culture, what are young women thinking about family, work, and women's roles? How are young women planning for their future after decades of activism around the status of women, of closely researched and well-publicized studies of the economic consequences of divorce, the epidemic of teenage pregnancy, and the problems of balancing work and family? In short, how have young women been affected by a quarter-century of feminism?

In an attempt to understand the key issues involved in growing up female in the United States during the waning years of the twentieth century, I conducted over one hundred and fifty open-ended interviews in many parts of the country with three groups of people: young women between the ages of twelve and twenty-five; professionals who work with these young women; and older women in their twenties, thirties, and early forties. While the main group of interviewees, teenagers and young adults, in no way represents a random sample, every effort has been made to ensure its diversity—diversity of class, of race, of ethnic background, of educational level, and of geography. The group includes blacks, whites, Hispanics, Asian-Americans, and Native Americans. The young women come from the Northeast, the South, the Southwest, the Far West, and the Middle West, from the inner cities, from the suburbs, and a small number from rural America. Defining "class" by the traditional criteria of income, education, and occupation, the majority of young women come from middle-class families; some, however, come from the upper middle class, from the working class, or from families living in poverty. Many were college students; some were going on to college; yet others were simply planning to finish high school or had dropped out of school. I have tried insofar as possible to describe their backgrounds while preserving their anonymity. All the women who discuss their personal lives have been given pseudonyms; all the professionals whom I quote are identified by their real names.

The young women I interviewed were selected through an intermediary, usually a professional actively involved with a large number of young people—for example, a health worker, a social worker, a member of the clergy, or a community activist. By visiting many different communities and speaking with a wide variety of professionals I was able to interview a varied group of young women.

The "older" women, most of whom are in their thirties, are part of the "baby boom" generation. Born between the late 1940s and the late 1950s, they came of age during the late 1960s and early 1970s, experienced some of the turbulence and reassessment of values and priorities that took place during that era, and have since tried to make lives for themselves that in many cases are fundamentally different from the lives of their mothers. They are in a real sense the path breakers, often trying to put into practice the changing views of women and of women's relationship to society. I spoke with this "older" group in order to understand with greater clarity and precision the reality and complexity of women's lives in the late 1980s and 1990s.

Women in both groups were eager to talk about their lives, their priorities, their conflicts and concerns. No one refused to be interviewed; in fact, all were vitally interested in the topic and pleased to contribute to a greater understanding of women's attitudes and day-to-day lives.

What emerged from the interviewing process was almost totally unexpected. I had assumed that young women today, those of high-school and college age, would surely have somewhat different attitudes from their mothers' and even from their "older sisters'." They are, after all, growing up during the 1980s, a time of emphasis on the individual and on materialism; they are growing up in an era of AIDS, an era of danger and of frankness about sex unparalleled in American history; and they are growing up in an era of wide acceptance of certain elements of feminist thinking but one in which feminism as a movement seems to be in retrenchment. In fact, of all the young women I interviewed, only one professed to be a feminist; several others actively claimed they were not. I surely expected young women today to be more knowledgeable about sex than we who came of age in the fifties or than those who grew up in the sixties and early seventies, more aware of the many dangers that awaited them in the larger society, more in control of their lives. If the availability of the pill and the legalization of abortion meant anything, it must mean, I assumed, that young women could finally take greater control over the most intimate aspects of their lives.

I was, of course, aware of the incredibly high rate of unplanned teenage pregnancy in the United States and therefore immensely curious about the seeming discrepancy between the opportunities for greater control and the evident lack of use of that control. Why were all these young women getting pregnant? What did *they* think about these issues? What is *their* analysis of the epidemic of teen pregnancy and birth in this country?

I assumed, moreover, that young women might have different expectations in terms of work and career. High-school and college students could not help being affected by the increasing numbers of women entering and remaining in the labor force and the increasing numbers going into prestigious occupations. But exactly how did they see themselves in terms of work and career, in terms of marriage and motherhood? Were they going to try to be "superwomen," or had they given up on that dream? Were they planning their lives sequentially or were they retreating from the dreams of public life of the earlier generation and returning to the private life of hearth and home?

What became clear after these in-depth interviews is that the American Dream—indeed, a female version of the American Dream—is alive and well. Despite the national deficit, the decline of the middle class, the increasing need for two wage earners in the family, the vast numbers of poor Americans, particularly women and children, and the until recently unimaginable increase in the hungry and the homeless, the American Dream lives on. In a time in which many analysts seem to have accepted the notion that the "American era" is ending, that we are no longer preeminent in the world's marketplace and that we are floundering in solving many of our critical social and economic problems, many young women hold on to that quintessentially American ideology of success, of upward mobility, of almost unlimited possibilities.

By singling out young women I do not mean to suggest that young men do not also share a commitment to the ideology of the American Dream. I focus on the attitudes of women because they have been my primary research interest for the past two decades and because their ideology in some ways seems to have undergone a dramatic shift during that same period of time. This study is in no way intended to diminish the role of men or to suggest that they are not also imbued with traditional American values; it attempts, rather, to explore the recent transformation of the attitudes and values of young American women. Young women cannot, of course, be understood separately from young men. I have attempted to demonstrate the interplay between the two, the impact of male attitudes and behavior on female attitudes and behavior; but, nonetheless, the primary focus here is young women.

The American dream has been an essential component of American ideology since the first settlers crossed the Atlantic. From the early colonists of the mid-1600s to the yuppies of the 1980s, this nation has fostered the worship of success. Over the years success has surely meant making money, but perhaps equally important it has meant rising from a relatively lowly status to a significantly higher one. "Rags to riches," "poor boy to President," "making something of oneself" have been the essence of the American Dream.

From the Puritan preacher Cotton Mather, who reminded his flock of "what we are told in Deuteronomy 8:18, 'Thou shalt remember the Lord thy God, for 'tis he that gives thee power to get wealth,' " to Benjamin Franklin, the epitome of the self-made man, who personified what many have felt to be the "most important thing about America: the chance for the individual to get ahead on his own initiative," a central component of the belief in success has been the belief in the power of the individual (usually the male) to dramatically alter the course of his life. The Horatio Alger hero, memorialized in nearly one hundred novels written during the last thirty years of the nineteenth century, symbolized the "poor boy of lower-class origins, with no advantages except his own sterling character, who rose to the top by his own abilities and efforts." Alger's fictional heroes, usually teenage boys, "started poor and finished rich." While luck often played a significant part in the transformation of the hero's life, it was clear that "the boy deserved the break, [and] that he had prepared himself through goodness, hard work, and perseverance."

For the immigrants of the nineteenth and twentieth centuries, belief in the American Dream was often the force that propelled

them to leave family, home, country—indeed, all that was familiar—to venture to "the promised land across the sea, a land of
freedom, gold and safety." To the "old" immigrants of the mid-
1800s (those from Northern and Western Europe), to the "new"
immigrants who came from the 1880s through the early 1920s (the
Italians, Russians, Poles, Hungarians, Czechs, Greeks, Jews from
all over Eastern Europe, and many other nationalities), to the West
Indians who have emigrated during this century, and to the newest
wave, those from Central America, Latin America, and Asia, America has been seen as a land of freedom from religious and political
persecution. Above all, it has been perceived as "a place of gold,
where anybody could move from poverty to riches, where a person's place in life wasn't irrevocably fixed at the moment of birth."

Thus, for the colonists, for those who migrated from country to
city, for those who pushed back the frontier traveling from east to
west amidst great hardship, and finally for the millions of immigrants during the nineteenth and twentieth centuries, the ideology
was clear: the individual, with enough hard work, perseverance,
and a bit of luck, could make his fortune in America—or if he
didn't quite make his fortune, he could at least significantly improve
his income and social status. And, of course, the pronoun "he" is
apt and accurate. It was, for the most part, the male who was
expected to make his way in American society, while the female
was expected to improve her social status by marrying well, or at
least wisely, and by helping her husband to succeed.

Many of these patterns, however, have changed in recent years:
women have entered the labor force in vast numbers; previously
male-dominated professions have become viable options for women
seeking challenge, status, and a decent income; and women of
different backgrounds have come to realize that they can succeed
in the world of work. Young women all over the United States
have witnessed profound change in the very nature of family life
during their childhood, and their attitudes have clearly been affected by transformations both within the family and in the larger
society. This book attempts to explore the effects of these rapid
societal changes on the attitudes of young women.

Several months after I began interviewing, it became clear that what I was hearing from young women was quite different from what older generations of women have been saying. The young women seemed to fall into three general groups of approximately equal size: those whom I began to call "New American Dreamers"; those whom I call "Neotraditionalists"; and a third group, the "Outsiders."

The most striking theme to emerge from my interviewing is the belief on the part of many young women that they can and must make their own way in life, can and must provide for themselves materially, can and must take control of their own lives. Many of these young women are optimistic, adventurous, and, above all, individualistic. They see the future as bright and full of promise. They focus on career, on upward mobility, and on the need to be independent. They believe success is there for the taking; all they need do is figure out the right pathway and work hard. Above all, they believe that they must be prepared to go it alone. These young women are the New American Dreamers.

Yet another group of young women can be termed Neotraditionalists. These women often plan to have careers, or at the very least recognize that they will probably need to work; but they have a strong, often primary, commitment to their future roles within the family. They see their domestic roles in more traditional terms, imbue them with greater importance, and articulate more concern about balancing the various aspects of their lives than do the New American Dreamers.

The third group are young women whom I have termed Outsiders. These young women can barely see beyond tomorrow. When asked what they hope for the future, they indicate with a wave of the hand and a word or two that they cannot envision a future, cannot plan or dream about any aspect of their lives. They describe themselves as outside the larger society, outside the mainstream of their community, and often outside their family unit. They may be middle-class teenagers who have had a baby and now feel trapped in a life they never intended; they may be nonwhites who feel denigrated and stigmatized by white society. For some, "outsiderness" is a temporary phenomenon rooted in adolescence; these young women feel transiently alienated from the culture as they grope their way to adulthood. For others, being Outsiders may be in part a developmental phenomenon, but many come to feel so alienated and isolated and act on those feelings in such a way that their outsider-ness becomes a permanent way of life. If the New American Dreamers see few limits to their potential achievements and future success, and the Neotraditionalists hope to combine in somewhat equal proportion both public and private roles, the Outsiders see few choices or options for the future at all.

Some young women seemed to belong to more than one group— to identify, for example, with both the New American Dreamers and the Neotraditionalists or with the Outsiders and the New American Dreamers. This overlap was sometimes due to the women's ambivalence about goals and priorities; at other times, fantasy or wishful thinking came to the fore during an interview otherwise firmly grounded in day-to-day reality. Perhaps the most poignant moments occurred when Outsiders yearned for the rewards of the American Dream. It is noteworthy, moreover, that while many of the New American Dreamers are upper middle class, many of the Neotraditionalists are middle class, and many Outsiders are working class or poor, each ideological grouping includes women from all socioeconomic levels.

The book is divided into three parts. The first, "Dreams," describes the attitudes and values, hopes and dreams, conflicts and concerns of the young women I interviewed. Once again, as in my previous books, I have attempted to present their views largely through their own voices. The second part, "Realities," attempts to examine the social, economic, and cultural context in which these women have grown up and in which they are likely to live in the foreseeable future—the mixed messages of popular American culture, the current attitudes and data about sexuality, particularly in relation to young women, the yearning for intimacy on the part of many women, the reality of women's work experience in the United States today, and some of the crucial issues around child rearing. The third part, "Choices," explores the meaning of the American Dream for women today and suggests some of the societal changes that are necessary if we are indeed going to make it possible for the next generation to live full, productive, caring lives.

Felix Greene, a British journalist, has written that we must strive toward a more humane society, one that "doesn't divide us from one another . . . releases us from the prison, the small boring world of me, which allows us to be members of a community . . . [part of] a world in which we can be really human." Perhaps this examination of the hopes and dreams of young women can move us a bit closer to that goal.

PART I

Dreams

CHAPTER 1

The New American Dreamers

It's your life. You have to live it yourself . . . If you work hard enough, you will get there. You must be in control of your life, and then somehow it will all work out.

ANGELA DAWSON
high-school junior, Southern California

She is the prototype of today's young woman—confident, outgoing, knowledgeable, involved. She is active in her school, church, or community. She may have a wide circle of friends or simply a few close ones, but she is committed to them and to their friendship. She is sophisticated about the central issues facing young people today—planning for the future, intimacy, sex, drugs, and alcohol—and discusses them seriously, thoughtfully, and forthrightly. She wants to take control of her life and is trying to figure out how to get from where she is to where she wants to go. Above all, she is convinced that if she plans carefully, works hard, and makes the right decisions, she will be a success in her chosen field; have the material goods she desires; in time, marry if she wishes; and, in all probability, have children. She plans, as the expression goes, to "have it all."

She lives in and around the major cities of the United States, in the towns of New England, in the smaller cities of the South and Midwest, and along the West Coast. She comes from an upper-middle-class family, from the middle class, from the working class,

15

and even sometimes from the poor. What is clear is that she has heard the message that women today should be the heroines of their own lives. She looks toward the future, seeing herself as the central character, planning her career, her apartment, her own success story. These young women do not see themselves as playing supporting roles in someone else's life script; it is their own journeys they are planning. They see their lives in terms of *their* aspirations, *their* hopes, *their* dreams.

Beth Conant is a sixteen-year-old high-school junior who lives with her mother and stepfather in an affluent New England college town. She has five brothers, four older and one several years younger. Her mother is a librarian, and her stepfather is a stock-broker. A junior at a top-notch public high school, she hopes to study drama in college, possibly at Yale, "like Meryl Streep." She would like to live and act in England for a time, possibly doing Shakespeare. She hopes to be living in New York by the age of twenty-five, in her own apartment or condo, starting on her acting career while working at another job by which she supports herself. She wants to have "a great life," be "really independent," and have "everything that's mine—crazy furniture, everything my own style."

By the time she's thirty ("that's so boring"), she feels, she will need to be sensible, because soon she will be "tied down." She hopes that by then her career will be "starting to go forth" and that she will be getting good roles. By thirty-five she'll have a child ("probably be married beforehand"), be working in New York and have a house in the country. How will she manage all this? Her husband will share responsibilities. She's not going to be a "su-permom." They'll both do child care. He won't do it as a favor; it will be their joint responsibility. Moreover, if she doesn't have the time to give to a child, she won't have one. If necessary, she'll work for a while, then have children, and after that "make one movie a year."

Amy Morrison is a petite, black, fifteen-year-old high-school sophomore who lives in Ohio. Her mother works part-time, and her father works for a local art museum. She plans to go to medical school and hopes to become a surgeon. She doesn't want to marry until she has a good, secure job but indicates that she might be living with someone. She's not sure about having children but says emphatically that she wants to be successful, to make money, to have cars. In fact, originally she wanted to become a doctor "primarily for the money," but now she claims other factors are drawing her to medicine.

Jacqueline Gonzalez is a quiet, self-possessed, nineteen-year-old Mexican-American woman who is a sophomore at a community college in southern California. She describes her father as a "self-employed contractor" and her mother as a "housewife." Jacqueline, the second-youngest of six children, is the first in her family to go to college. Among her four brothers and one sister, only her sister has finished high school. Jacqueline's goal is to go to law school and then to go into private practice. While she sees herself as eventually married with "one or two children," work, professional achievement, and an upper-middle-class life-style are central to her plans for her future.

If in the past, and to a considerable extent still today, women have hoped to find their identity through marriage, have sought to find "validation of . . . [their] uniqueness and importance by being singled out among all other women by a man," the New American Dreamers are setting out on a very different quest for self-realization. They are, in their plans for the future, separating identity from intimacy, saying that they must first figure out who they are and that then and only then will they form a partnership with a man. Among the young women I interviewed, the New American Dreamers stand apart in their intention to make their own way in the world and determine their own destiny prior to forming a significant and lasting intimate relationship.

Young women today do not need to come from upper-middle-class homes such as Beth's or middle-class homes such as Amy's or working-class homes such as Jacqueline's to dream of "the good life." Even young women with several strikes against them see material success as a key prize at the end of the rainbow. Some seem to feel that success is out there for the taking. Generally, the most prestigious, best-paying careers are mentioned; few women of any class mention traditional women's professions such as teaching or nursing. A sixteen-year-old unmarried Arizona mother of a four-and-a-half-month-old baby looks forward to a "professional career either in a bank or with a computer company," a "house that belongs to me," a "nice car," and the ability to buy her son "good clothes." She sees herself in the future as dating but not married. "There is not so much stress on marriage these days," she says.

Yet another young woman, a seventeen-year-old black unmarried mother of an infant, hopes to be a "professional model," have "lots of cash," be "rich," maybe have another child. When asked if a man will be part of the picture, she responds, "I don't know."

An eighteen-year-old Hispanic unmarried mother hopes to "be my own boss" in a large company, have a "beautiful home," send her daughter to "the best schools." She wants, in her words, to "do it, make it, have money."

These young women are bright, thoughtful, personable. And they are quintessentially American: they believe that with enough hard work they will "make it" in American society. No matter what class they come from, their fantasies are of upward mobility, a comfortable life filled with personal choice and material possessions. The upper-middle-class women fantasize a life even more upper-middle-class; middle-class and working-class women look toward a life of high status in which they have virtually everything they want; and some young women who come from families with significant financial deprivation and numerous other problems dream of a life straight out of "Dallas," "Dynasty," or "L.A. Law." According to one young woman, some of her friends are so determined to be successful that they are "fearful that there will be a nuclear war and that they will die before they have a chance to live their lives. If there is a nuclear war," she explained, "they won't live long enough to be successful."

Young women are our latest true believers. They have bought into the image of a bright future. Many of them see themselves as professional women, dressed in handsome clothes, carrying a briefcase to work, and coming home to a comfortable house or condo, possibly to a loving, caring husband and a couple of well-behaved children. How widespread is the dream? How realistic is it? What is the function of this latest American dream? What about those young women who cling to a more traditional dream? What about those who feel their dreams must be deferred? What about those with no dream at all? And what about those who "share the fantasy," as the Chanel No. 5 perfume advertisement used to say, but have little or no chance of achieving it?

Perhaps the most poignant example of the impossible dream is Simone Baker, a dynamic, bright, eighteen-year-old black woman from Louisiana. Simone's mother is a seamstress who has been off and on welfare over the years, and her father is a drug addict. Simone herself has been addicted to drugs of one kind or another since she was five. She has been in and out of drug-abuse facilities, and although she attended school for many years and was passed from grade to grade, she can barely read and write. When I met her in a drug rehabilitation center, she was struggling to become drug free so that she could join the Job Corps, finish high school, and obtain some vocational training. Her dream of the future is so extraordinary, given her background, that she seems to epitomize the Horatio Alger myth of another era. When asked what she would like her life to be like in the future, Simone replies instantly, her eyes shining: "I want to be a model. I want to have a Jacuzzi. I want to have a *big*, BIG house and a BIG family—three girls and two boys."

"And what about the man?" I ask her.

"He'll be a lawyer. He'll be responsible, hardworking, and sensitive to my feelings. Everything will be fifty-fifty. And he'll take the little boys out to play football and I'll have the girls inside cooking. That would be a dream come true!"

Simone's dream is an incredible mixture of the old and the new—a Dick-and-Jane reader updated. And she's even mouthing the supreme hope of so many women in this age of the therapeutic solution to personal problems—that she'll find a man who is "sensitive" to her "feelings." She has lived a life far from the traditional middle class and yet has the quintessential image of the good life as it has been formulated in the last quarter of the twentieth century. But for Simone, it is virtually an impossible dream. One wishes that that were not so; listening to her, watching her excitement and hope at the mere thought of such a life, one gets caught up and wants desperately for it all to happen. The image is clear: the white house in the suburbs with the brass knocker on the front door, the leaves on the lawn in the fall, the boys playing football

with this incredibly wonderful husband/father, and Simone sometimes the successful model, other times at home, cooking with her
daughters. But we know how very unlikely it is that this particular
dream will come true. And yet, maybe . . .

How have young women come to take on the American Dream
as their own? That this is a relatively new dream for women is
clear. Until recent years women, for the most part, did not perceive
themselves as separate, independent entities with their own needs
and agendas. Women fit themselves into other people's lives,
molded their needs to fit the needs of others. For the full-time
homemaker the day began early enough to enable husband and
children to get to work and school on time. Chores had to be done
between breakfast and lunch or between lunch and the end of
school. Dinnertime was when the man of the house returned from
work. When a woman worked outside of the home, her work hours
were often those that fit into the schedules of other family members.
Her needs were determined by the needs of others, as often her
identity rested on her affiliation with them.

What some women seem to be saying now is that they will form
their own identities, develop their own styles, and meet their own
needs. They will be the central characters in their stories. They will
work at jobs men work at, earn the money men earn; but many
of them also plan at the same time to play all the roles women
have traditionally played.

What has become clear in talking with young women throughout
the country is that many of them are planning for their future in
terms of their "public" roles as well as their "domestic" roles, that
they are "laying claim to significant and satisfying work . . . as a
normal part of their lives and laying claim also to the authority,
prestige, power, and salary that . . . [that] work commands." Historically, women have been confined primarily to the "domestic"
sphere of life, particularly to child rearing and homemaking, and
men, for the most part, have participated in the "public" sphere—
that is, in social, economic, and political institutions and forms of
association in the broader social structure. This dichotomy between
"public" and "domestic" has led to "an asymmetry in the cultural
evaluation of male and female that appears to be universal." Margaret Mead noted this asymmetry when she observed that "what-

ever the arrangements in regard to descent or ownership of property, and even if these formal outward arrangements are reflected in the temperamental relations between the sexes, the prestige values always attach to the activities of men."

In New Guinea, women grow sweet potatoes and men grow yams; yams are the prestige food. In societies where women grow rice, the staple food, and men hunt for meat, meat is the most valued food. Traditionally, the more exclusively male the activity, the more cultural value is attached to it. Because male activities have been valued over female activities and women have become "absorbed primarily in domestic activities because of their role as mothers," women's work of caring has traditionally been devalued. However, as political scientist Joan Tronto has pointed out, it is not simply the dichotomy between the public and the private that results in the devaluation of the female but the immense difference in power between the two spheres. So long as men have a monopoly on the public sphere and it in turn wields great power within society, women, identified with the private sphere, which is seen as relatively powerless, will be devalued.

Since the emergence of the women's movement in the 1960s, women in the U.S. as well as in many other parts of the world have been questioning the traditional asymmetry between men and women, seeking to understand its roots, its causes, and its consequences, and attempting to modify the male monopoly of power. Many strategies have developed toward this end: laws have been passed in an attempt to eliminate discrimination; groups have formed to elect more women to positions of power; those already in power have been urged to appoint more women to administrative roles; dominant, high-status, high-income professions have been pressured to admit more women to their hallowed ranks; and strategies to bring greater equity to male and female salaries have been developed.

Great stress has been placed on raising the consciousness of both women and men concerning this imbalance of power, but particular attention has been devoted to raising the consciousness of women. Discussion about the relative powerlessness of the non-wage-earning "housewife" has been widespread. Books and articles about the impoverishment of the divorced woman, the problems of the displaced homemaker, and the often desperate plight of the single, female head of household have been directed at women. During the 1970s and 1980s, the message suddenly became clear to many women: perhaps they are entitled to play roles formerly reserved for men; perhaps they would enjoy these challenges; perhaps they have something special to offer and can make a difference in the practice of medicine or law or in running the country. Moreover, it became clear that if women want power, prestige, and paychecks similar to those men receive, if they want to lessen the asymmetry between male and female, then perhaps they must enter those spheres traditionally reserved for men. If men grow yams, must women grow yams? If men hunt and women gather, must women purchase a bow and arrow? If men are in the public sphere while women are at home caring for children and doing the laundry, the consensus seems to say that women must enter the public sphere. If men are doctors and lawyers and earn great rewards while women are nurses and teachers and earn meager rewards, then women see what they obviously must do. If men have focused on doing while women have focused on caring, then clearly women must become doers.

It is not sufficient, however, to become a doer in a traditionally female occupation, for, as we know, these occupations are notoriously underpaid and underesteemed. Women must become *real* doers in the arena that counts: they must learn to play hardball, or, as Mary Lou Retton says in her breakfast-cereal advertisements, "eat what the big boys eat." For real power, status, money, and "success," it's law, medicine, and finance—also, possibly, acting, modeling, or working in the media, if one is very lucky.

An illustration of the current emphasis on male-dominated careers as the road to success for young women are the career goals of *Glamour* magazine's "Top Ten College Women '88." One woman hopes to become an astronaut; a second plans to work in the area of public policy, another to be a biologist, another to obtain a degree in business administration, yet another to obtain a degree in acting; and one young woman is currently working in journalism. One college senior is undecided between journalism and law, and the last three are planning to go to law school. These young women, according to *Glamour,* "possess the talents and ambition necessary to shape tomorrow's society." It is noteworthy that none of the women *Glamour* chose to honor are entering any traditionally female occupation or any "helping" profession—not even medicine. Don't nurses, teachers, and social workers "possess the talents and ambition necessary to shape tomorrow's society"? The word has gone out and continues to go out that the way to "make it" in American society and the way to "shape tomorrow's society" is the traditional male route.

Once singled out, these young women play their part in spreading the ideology of the American Dream. Three of the ten honorees appeared on NBC's "Today" show. When asked about the significance of their being chosen, one woman replied without hesitation that if you work hard, you can do whatever you want to do. This statement was greeted by smiles and nods; she had clearly given the right message.

In addition to wanting to break out of the mold of a secondary worker receiving inferior wages and benefits and having little authority or opportunity for advancement, women have been motivated to make real money and to acquire valued skills and some semblance of security because of their relatively recent realization that women, even women with children, may well be forced to care for themselves or, at the very least, to participate in providing for the family unit. Women have come to realize that whether because of divorce (which leaves women on the average 73 percent poorer and men on the average 42 percent richer), childbearing outside of marriage, the inability of many men to earn an adequate "family wage," or their remaining single—either through design or through circumstance—they must be prepared to support themselves and anyone else for whom they feel responsible.

But what of all that caring women used to do—for children, for elderly parents, for sick family members, for the home? What about Sunday dinner, baking chocolate-chip cookies with the kids eating up half the batter, serving Kool-Aid in the backyard on a hot summer day? What about sitting with a child with a painful ear infection until the antibiotic takes effect, going with a four-year-old to nursery school the first week until the child feels comfortable letting you leave, being available when there's an accident at school and your second grader must be rushed to the emergency room?

Who's going to do the caring? Who is going to do the caring in a society in which few institutions have been developed to take up the slack, a society in which men have been far more reluctant to become carers than women have been to become doers. Members of the subordinate group may gain significantly in status, in self-image, and in material rewards when they take on the activities and characteristics of the dominant group, but there is little incentive for members of the dominant group to do the reverse.

Above all, how do young women today deal with these questions? How do they feel about doing and caring, about power, prestige, and parenting? What messages is society giving them about the roles they should play, and how are they sorting out these messages?

A key message the New American Dreamers are both receiving and sending is one of optimism—the sense that they can do whatever they want with their lives. Many Americans, of course—not just young people or young women—have a fundamentally optimistic attitude toward the future. Historically, Americans have believed that progress is likely, even inevitable, and that they have the ability to control their own destinies. A poll taken early in 1988 indicates that while the American public was concerned about the nation's future and indeed more pessimistic about "the way things [were] going in the United States" than they had been at any other time since the Carter presidency in the late 1970s, they nonetheless believed that they could "plan and regulate their own lives, even while the national economy and popular culture appear[ed] to be spinning out of control." As one would expect, those with higher incomes and more education are more optimistic than those with less; Republicans are more optimistic than Democrats or Independents; and, significantly, men are more hopeful than women. In looking toward the future, young men clearly dream of "the good life," of upward mobility and their share of material possessions. While young women historically have had far less control over their lives than men, for the past twenty-five years they have been urged to take greater control, both in the workplace and in their private lives, and they have clearly taken the message very much to heart.

Angela Dawson, a sixteen-year-old high-school junior from

southern California, sums up the views of the New American Dreamers: "It's your life. You have to live it yourself. You must decide what you want in high school, plan your college education, and from there you can basically get what you want. If you work hard enough, you will get there. You must be in control of your life, and then somehow it will all work out."

Angela is clearly reflecting widespread changes in young women's expectations. Recent studies indicate that over the past quarter-century there has been significant change in women's educational and career expectations. From 1960 to 1980, for example, the proportion of young women in their senior year of high school who expected to go on to college and complete a degree and the proportion who expected to follow "high level" professional careers increased significantly. Interestingly, the expectation for higher education and professional careers requiring an undergraduate degree rose more between 1960 and 1972, while the expectation of a professional career requiring a graduate degree rose most steeply between 1972 and 1980. Furthermore, some research indicates that by 1980 the notion of high achievement had become so widespread that even young women with lower academic achievement or without plans for going on to college expected to be able to enter a "high level" profession. One sociologist interprets these data as a fundamental shift in values among young women:

> This suggests less a form of rational calculation than an ideological surge to aim for the top of the career hierarchy, whatever one's chances. It seems that "career feminism"— achieving equality in the labor force for women—had made a major impact on young women by 1980. Instead of responding to a "pull" factor—increased opportunities drawing young women into institutions of higher education—the expectations of women for the highest level careers seem themselves to have represented a "push" factor. Propelled by the pressure to get out of the female job ghetto, by widespread media coverage of women entering male-dominated careers, by the discussion of new strategies and pressures (networking, mentoring) to break down sex segregation in careers, young women's plans to enter high level professions seem more an expression of the

new *values* [italics in original] of achieving job equality for women than of recognizing opportunities for such careers.

Other studies also indicate continuing and increasing "profeminist" views among women and men in the late 1970s and early-to-mid-1980s. Despite considerable media discussion of a backlash against feminism, General Social Survey data from the National Opinion Research Center indicate that between 1977 and 1985 an increased percentage of women and men supported women working and felt that "a working mother can establish just as warm and secure a relationship with her children as a mother who does not work." On this latter issue and on a question about working women and the well-being of preschool children ("A preschool child is likely to suffer if his or her mother works"), the percentage of men taking the "profeminist" view increased; nevertheless, men were considerably more traditional in their views than were women.

Thus, support for women entering the labor force, including women with children, has continued to grow. The idea of mothers working has gained such widespread acceptance that poor mothers who do *not* work, particularly those receiving Aid to Families with Dependent Children, are currently seen as deviant. Under so-called welfare reform legislation passed by the U.S. Congress during the fall of 1988, many of these mothers will be required to go out to work or at least to enter training programs and then to look for work. This action has been rationalized by the statement "It is now the norm for women to work. Why should poor women be any different?"

This increased commitment on the part of women to enter the "public" sphere and, in many cases, to aim for the most prestigious jobs, to reach for the top, to "go for it," is reflected in other aspects of their lives. One of these is young women's increased participation in athletic activities. A recent survey indicates that among a random sample of girls aged seven to eighteen, 82 percent said that they currently participate in sports. Eighty-seven percent of the parents polled believe that sports are as important for girls as for boys.

Young women clearly have a great deal to gain from intense athletic involvement: the confidence that comes with the development of skills, an understanding of the importance of teamwork, improved body image, and, of course, the friendships that can develop from continuous commitment to and participation in activities one cares about deeply. But perhaps the most important benefit was spelled out by the mother of a teenage female athlete: The "message of sports," she writes, is to "be aggressive . . . Go for the ball. Be intense." It must be noted that in this case it was the athlete's father who continuously counseled her to really "go for it," not to be content to "sit on the bench." The writer notes how girls have been trained for generations to "Be quiet, Be good, Be still . . . not to get dirty" and that being intense is "neither quiet nor good. And it's definitely not pretty." What participation in athletics can teach a young woman, and what she must learn if she is really to be a force in this society, is to not be "afraid to do her best." This is part of what Angela and some of the other young women seem to be saying—they are going to go out there and not be afraid to do their best.

These women have a commitment to career, to material well-being, to success, and to independence. To many of them, an affluent life-style is central to their dreams; they often describe their goals in terms of cars, homes, travel to Europe. In short, they want their piece of the American Dream. Many of them plan eventually to weave marriage and children into the superstructure; some of them are not so sure. But for now their priorities are to figure out who they are, get on with their education, and become successful in their chosen field.

What is new about the dreams of many young women today is not only that they are the central characters in their plans for the future but that they believe they must prepare themselves to go it alone. Young women of all classes talk about the need to be independent. Some quote their mothers and other female relatives who are urging them to organize their lives so that they can take care of themselves. A seventeen-year-old midwestern daughter of divorced parents reports, "My mom tells me I have to be self-secure. I don't want to have to depend on anyone." Another says, "My mother wants me to be happy and she wants me to be able to take care of myself." Yet another: "My grandmother says 'Have your own nest egg.' " Several young women in the Southwest agree.

A seventeen-year-old whose parents are divorced: "I want to be independent—financially and emotionally. I want to be stable and independent. I do not want to rely on anyone else," she says emphatically. A twelve-year-old agrees and says her friends talk about the need for women to be able to support themselves and their families. She was five months old when her parents divorced and freely admits she still wishes they would get back together. A sixteen-year-old whose mother is a "housewife" and whose father does "sales-type jobs" but is currently unemployed isn't sure what she wants to do but knows she wants a "decent job" and doesn't want "to end up dependent."

This perception on the part of young women that success is there for the taking, that affluence is a necessary ingredient in any life plan, and that they need to be able to stand on their own can be seen as a coming together of several strands of American thought: the American Dream promises upward mobility to those who plan and work sufficiently hard; the women's movement has taught at least two generations of women that they are entitled to play virtually any roles in society that they are capable of and that they are entitled to reap the appropriate rewards; and the ideology of the Reagan years has both stressed individualism and undermined Americans' belief in the necessity of creating a more humane and equitable environment in which all people can thrive. During the 1980s we have witnessed, I believe, the merging of these three lines of thought against a backdrop of ever-increasing disparities in wealth and well-being between rich and poor, black and white, and ever-increasing emphasis on materialism, often at any cost— what one social critic has called the "empty ostentation and narcissistic culture of the 1980s." Is it any wonder that young women feel they are on their own? The message that they must go it alone is being given to many Americans: the homeless; the hungry; the elderly nursing-home residents; the children who are essentially lost in the foster-care system; the millions who are uninsured for health care and those who do not have access to care because of inadequate or nonexistent services; the numbers of young people receiving inferior education that cannot possibly prepare them for living and working in the next century. Moreover, young women see on a personal level that individuals must be able to care for themselves. They see their divorced parents floundering; they hear the cautionary tales about relying too much on men; they are all too aware of the status and respect given in American society to those who embody the traditional male characteristics of autonomy and power, and know that to protect themselves they must have no less.

The feminist movement did not, of course, set out to bolster and extend to yet another group the ideology of individualism and the American Dream. With its appeal to "sisterhood" and its use of consciousness-raising groups, it set out, rather, on a far more collective course, encouraging women to see themselves not simply as individuals but as part of a long, international struggle for equality. But movements do not exist in a vacuum. The women's movement originated within a class system that drew largely middle- and upper-middle-class adherents and then was in part shaped by their concerns and their needs. It exists today within an individualistic, hierarchical system committed for the most part to private enterprise and profit making. Once it became clear that the movement was not going to disappear, elements of that structure began admitting "the best and the brightest" to their hallowed halls. Leaders of the movement might call for widely available day care, paid parental leave, larger welfare grants, and more money for prenatal care, but what was picked up by the media were the upper-middle-class women in the courtrooms, the board rooms, and the emergency rooms, often putting off marriage and children in order to go for the brass ring of success.

This ideology of independence and individualism can be seen to some degree in all three groups, but it is far more prevalent among the New American Dreamers, and adds significantly to the pressure these young women already feel. They feel pressure to succeed not only for the status and material rewards success bestows but because they recognize the likelihood that they may be the sole support of themselves and their children.

This sense of responsibility, of aloneness, brings a new intensity to the need to be "successful." Many young women see the choices as "making it" or "not making it," being "independent" versus being "dependent." Understood in those terms, the pressure is to work out a way for oneself to live the good life.

Nancy Delmonico exemplifies the young woman under pressure to achieve because she realizes she may well be out there on her own. She is a thoughtful, articulate, seventeen-year-old high-school senior who lives in Arizona. Nancy's parents are divorced; her father was raised on a farm and now has his own business, and her mother is an administrator of a community agency. Nancy feels considerable anxiety over both her choice of college and her choice of career. She is currently undecided between acting and criminal law. She says with obvious anxiety that she finds the decision "overwhelming."

Nancy expects to have an established career by the time she is in her mid-twenties, probably in law or in politics, and at some point to marry and have "a kid or two." She hopes eventually to be a "judge or a Supreme Court justice, travel a lot, see the world, and experience a lot of things." She sums up by saying, "Today you've got to be able to take care of yourself."

Some young women have an almost magical attitude about success—somehow they'll get there. Others have a clear picture of what they need to do to get where they want to go. These young women, with their dreams of achievement and success, recognize that they are under significant pressure to achieve. Not only must they get good grades and be accepted into a good college, but most of them anticipate graduate school as well.

"What is the key issue facing young women today?" I ask four high-school students as we sit around a table in the beautifully proportioned library on the third floor of an Episcopal church in the Midwest. The young women—a sophomore, two juniors, and a senior—reflect a minute; then the senior, a thoughtful, quiet, composed, articulate young black woman, responds: "College. That's what I'm worrying about. Everyone is worried about where they'll go, where they'll get the money." A fifteen-year-old junior chimes in, saying she is "hyper" about grades. She wants to get into a "good college"—she "wouldn't mind MIT." The fifteen-year-old sophomore, who hopes to go to medical school, worries about grades, too. She recognizes that it is going to take her a long time to pay for medical school and thinks she'll eventually specialize in some kind of surgery, an area of medicine known for its high income.

These young women are well aware that if they are going to be successful and independent, they need to start putting it together right now. One young woman from a New England college town states that the young people in her high school are *very* competitive about getting into college. She feels her school is not developing individuals but, rather, producing "Ivy League machines."

Billy Dreskin, a young rabbi who works with high-school students in a small community in Westchester County, outside New York City, comments on the pressures young people face today: "Their lives are consumed with doing well in school. They think they'll die if they don't make a good living, and school is their ticket to success. The pressures here are not so much economic as academic," he continues. "[There's] pressure to take AP [advanced placement] courses. They convey a certain status, and kids are taking them who shouldn't be. The kids can't do any of the things they want to do without money, and in order to earn the money, they need to succeed academically."

Several young women from Arizona describe some of the pressures they feel. Nancy Delmonico says, "Grades are a big pressure. I feel the pressure from teachers and from my parents. They are concerned about our being successful—about what we'll be doing with the rest of our lives." She states, moreover, that this enormous amount of pressure on young people is a key factor in adolescent alcohol and drug abuse. As a young woman who has attended both public and private schools, she feels that there is a much greater problem with drugs and alcohol among private-school kids, partly because they have the money to pay for the substances and partly because they are under such great pressure.

A high-school junior interjects, "I pressure myself! I get down on myself. I see a C as an F. And I feel I'm not worrying about college enough!" A twelve-year-old seventh grader says, "My mom and dad pressure me about grades. My sister is a gymnast—that's what she's good at, so lousy grades don't matter. I'm not good at anything special, so school has to be my thing." Another twelve-year-old says her greatest concern is choosing which of two high schools to attend. Her mother wants her to go to the more academically prestigious school. She's more concerned with where her friends are going. And she also worries about grades. Her father is a doctor, and her mother is a laywer; she feels she must get good grades for them.

Stacy Steinberg, a soft-spoken yet articulate seventeen-year-old high-school junior, whose mother is a school nurse and whose father is an auditor, analyzes the pressures young women feel: "It's so hard to be an adolescent today, and it's only going to get harder. Kids today have to worry about liquor, drugs, sex, *and* their academic work. And your parents want you to do better than they did, but it's harder to do better today than when they were growing up."

She goes on: "Guys have different pressures; they're more into sexual experiences. But it's harder to be a girl. You see models in ads and say, 'I don't look like that; how can I fit into that?' Parents say, 'When you lose a few more pounds, you can get a new outfit.' And the pressure about grades—the girls who cry if they don't do perfectly on a quiz!

"You want to be feminine but independent. What's an independent woman? Someone who if left on her own could fend for herself.

"The world is changing and it's hard to figure out where you belong. I have an anorexic friend; she just wants control over her life. What with competition, SATs, parents pressuring kids, and divorce, kids need their parents more than ever but they just can't communicate with them."

While the emphasis among the New American Dreamers is on doing, on career, on material rewards, these young women almost always include commitment to family as one of their central concerns. Although they have taken on the goals of high achievement, success, and independence, they have for the most part kept the values of caring for others. They now see a dual responsibility, at work and at home, both public and private. The New American Dreamers may at this time in their lives place their career goals first, but as they look ahead it becomes clear that many fully expect to care for family and children as well.

Alexandra Morgan, a black seventeen-year-old from the Midwest, whose mother is a high-school teacher and whose father is a chemist, hopes to be an oceanographer. She plans to "settle down" after she completes a B.S. and an M.S. in science and oceanography, but only when she finds the right person, one with whom she wants to "share the future." He must be "what I want in a guy"; what is important is "how he carries himself and if he knows what he wants out of life." She plans to have "no more than two children" and worries about "juggling work and coming home to the children—they need to know they are loved." She recalls that her mother always worked but was always there. But her mother had a work life based on the school calendar—Christmas and spring vacations, summers off. How will Alexandra manage to do both? In her plans for the future the doing is clear and concrete; the caring is hazier, harder to imagine.

Wendy Jackson has the dream, too. A twenty-year-old junior from one of the campuses of the University of North Carolina, Wendy is the youngest of three children and comes from a working-class family. Her father, now retired, was a supervisor in a local textile plant, and her mother still works as a winder in another textile plant. Wendy's dream seems in many ways to be at odds with the life she is leading. An undergraduate major in social work, she plans to work with handicapped people, probably as a school social worker. She is also engaged; her fiancé is studying, in her words, "ag ed"—agricultural education—and they plan to live in Raleigh. But Wendy does not see herself marrying until she is at least twenty-six. "The most important thing is independence," she says. "You have to be secure within yourself before making a connection with someone else. If something ever happens, you must be able to stand alone.

"I want to expand, to see things and meet people. I don't want to stay in one place. I don't want to hold back. I want to be released into a new world. I know social work might put me back because of the money; it might not allow me to do the things I want to do. I plan to go on and get an MSW so that I can make more money."

Wendy isn't sure whether she wants children. She does know that she wants to travel and that she wants a different kind of marriage than her mother had. "My father came home and lay on the couch." What kind of relationship does she want? "I'm selfish— call me greedy. I'm not going to come home and wash his clothes. I'd rather not get married than be someone's maid!"

Wendy is on course for a very different life than the one she says she wants. She's studying for a bachelor's degree in social work; as she comments, she is likely to be paid a meager salary and have few opportunities for promotion. Her professional options will improve somewhat with an MSW, but will these opportunities get her where she wants to go? She's engaged at the age of twenty and yet has an image of independence and adventure that seems at odds with the life of a married social worker living in a small city in North Carolina. Wendy's relatively unconventional ideas and dreams seem directly in conflict with her far more conventional life choices. It is almost as though Wendy's hopes for the future were taken from *Ms.* magazine while her real options were rooted in *Good Housekeeping*.

Other young women have this inner drive, this vision of what they want to become that impels them onward when others from similar backgrounds might choose more modest goals. Sandra Curran grew up in New York City, the youngest of four children. Her parents came to this country from Trinidad when Sandra was ten; they have both worked in a hospital for many years—her father as a security guard, her mother as a unit secretary. From the time she was a junior in college, Sandra has had a vision of her future life: she planned to get her master's degree in social work, work a couple of years, and then go on to law school. And she has done exactly that. Along the way she married a young man who is working in computers and also getting his master's degree; she is currently holding down a full-time, extremely demanding job in foster care while attending law school at night. Why is she doing all this? Where does the drive, the impetus come from? Sandra tries to explain:

"I have a picture of a certain life-style that I want. By the time I'm forty I want to be able to enjoy my family, live in the suburbs. I want to work by choice rather than out of necessity.

"Law will enable me to speak out—to advocate for individuals and families. I plan to practice either family or criminal law, and with my MSW and my law degree I can deal with counseling, advocating, and legal issues in a holistic way.

"I just have an image of how I see myself in the future, how I will be comfortable emotionally. I have always had high expectations."

Like many other New American Dreamers, Sandra is clear about how to develop her career but far less clear about how she will manage family and career. As with so many women who are firmly set on their quest, she sees what she must do to get where she wants to be professionally, but while she is also committed to children, to family, and to caring, that aspect of life is less mapped out, more sketchily drawn. One of the characteristics of the New American Dreamers is their focus on what they need to accomplish *before* they become emotionally involved. Their focus is on their professional lives, on doing; caring is part of the picture but less clearly visualized. Nonetheless it is always there, in the background, for though young women understand that they must be active participants in society, they also understand that new arrangements have yet to be worked out to provide the caring that women once provided. The New American Dreamers know that they want to be prepared to take on new roles and responsibilities even as they suspect they will still be expected to perform the old ones as well. The Neotraditionalists know the demands of the domestic role all too well.

CHAPTER 2

The Neotraditionalists

I want to be smart. I want to be somebody. I want to make money. I want to be a successful lawyer, but my personal life comes first. I want to be a lovely wife, do my husband's shirts, take Chinese cooking lessons, and have two children. . . . I want to have a briefcase in my hands. I want to look good and feel good and be happy in what I'm doing.

NICOLE DiMARCO
college senior, New York

While the New American Dreamers are focusing on career, on their "public" roles, and relegating "domestic" issues to a distant second place, another group of young women, whom I call Neotraditionalists, generally falls into two overlapping categories: they are either hoping to balance their public and private activities or are more focused on their "domestic" roles, preferring to mesh work with home rather than to fit home responsibilities around their work lives.

These young women have a strong commitment to material well-being and often to career, but they see their lives either as centered equally between career and home or as focused to a considerable extent around child rearing, home, and community while their children are young. While they recognize the importance of women working, they often see their work as more cyclical, fitting in with their parental responsibilities. Nicole DiMarco is perhaps a bridge between the New American Dreamers and the Neotraditionalists.

A twenty-one-year-old woman of Italian descent from New York City, she is the second-oldest of four children and a senior at a public four-year college. Her father was an ambulance driver but since a heart attack has been the chauffeur for the head of a local hospital; her mother is a head nurse and supervisor at another local hospital. She will be the first in her family to graduate from college.

Nicole plans to become a lawyer and, in fact, has already been accepted by several law schools. "I want to be smart. I want to be somebody. I want to make money," she says clearly and emphatically. But while she wants to be a successful lawyer, she says her "personal life comes first." She wants to be a "lovely wife," plans to "do my husband's shirts, take Chinese cooking lessons, and have two children." She sums up her hopes for her future life: "I want my children to be two angels and I want to have a great relationship with my husband. I want to be thin and gorgeous and have a spectacular Bloomingdale's wardrobe. I want to have a briefcase in my hands. I want to look good and feel good and be happy in what I'm doing. Happiness comes first." Interestingly, Nicole is equating happiness with the entire package—family life, career, "looking good and feeling good."

Nicole not only wants to have it all; she wants to *be* it all. As the Chinese say, she plans to "walk on two legs"—the "traditional" legs of the gourmet cook, perfect mother, and homemaker and the "modern" legs of the stunning, briefcase-toting career woman. Other college students reflect this same dual commitment, to work and to family. During the spring semester of 1988, an anonymous questionnaire was given to students in two undergraduate sociology courses, Sex Roles and Social Welfare, at Hunter College. The students were asked what they thought their lives would be like when they were ages twenty-five, thirty, and thirty-five. While the questionnaire was given to all students in the two classes, only the responses from females who ranged in age from eighteen to thirty-four (three-quarters of them twenty-three or younger) have been used for this analysis.

The Hunter College student body is largely lower middle class and working class, with a smaller percentage of more affluent and poorer students. In addition to a significant number of blacks,

Hispanics, and Asians, many of the students are from white ethnic families. In many instances current students are the first in their families to go to college. The overwhelming majority of those responding to the questionnaire describe themselves as "middle class"; one-quarter of the students categorize themselves as "working class," "lower class," or "upper middle class." Since this is a self-selected group of students enrolled in particular sociology courses, these responses are, in all likelihood, not representative of Hunter's female students.

Essentially, all the responses indicate a desire to work and raise a family. The careers the students anticipate are in general less "high-powered" and traditionally male than those of the New American Dreamers; they range from law and medicine to social work, teaching, nursing, community health education, psychology, and counseling. There is greater emphasis on political action ("I will be politically active, especially in the fight against racism") and greater emphasis on trying to make a difference in people's lives ("I will start a reading group in my community; I think it is important to get children reading from an early age to prevent them from falling through the cracks." "I will be working in Latin America, hopefully feeling I am doing something worthwhile." "I would like to open up a day-care center on the Lower East Side of New York and later develop a teen pregnancy counseling program").

But the responses also show an overriding belief in the American Dream. One woman states that by age thirty-five "I will have started a family and would be enjoying a rewarding career—and also enjoying a mink coat." Many women mention "buying a house"; one says she hopes to "travel to Paris, Italy, and Hawaii"; another reflects the attitudes of the majority of the respondents when she states that she hopes "to be married and have a house" by age thirty, and by thirty-five to "have children, be financially stable, and to be happy in my marriage and career."

The goals are for the most part dual—career *and* family. As one eighteen-year-old says, at age twenty-five she will be "in the middle of graduate school, probably married or preparing for a wedding"; at age thirty she will be "an active mother and wife and definitely a successful career woman"; and at age thirty-five she will be "totally devoted to my work and family, owning a house and a few cars and hopefully still looking young and beautiful." The very essence of "having it all"!

If the New American Dreamers are searching for their identity through work, planning to define themselves first and then make emotional attachments, these Neotraditionalists plan to define themselves through both work and family. Virtually all of them have serious, concrete career goals and plans for how to achieve those goals; but commitment to family ("I will be independent but also dedicated to my husband, deeply rooted in my marriage") is of at least equal importance.

Nicole DiMarco and these other college students are particularly optimistic, persistent, and goal-directed. Other young women whom I count as Neotraditionalists are not quite so sanguine about their ability to do it all.

Several students at one of the University of California campuses illustrate the various strategies young women are considering as they ponder their future. Four such women worry aloud about how they are going to put together their public and private lives. Deborah Warren, a senior majoring in animal physiology, feels that the central issue facing young women today is how to combine the roles of wife and mother with the role of career woman. She is hoping for a career in medicine but isn't sure if she has the "motivation, dedication, and grade-point average" to make it. She feels she needs a couple of years after college, perhaps in the Peace Corps, to think about what to do with her life. She hopes to go to medical school then but wonders aloud if it isn't "kind of selfish—working just for me for so long." (It is perhaps noteworthy that among the New American Dreamers not one worried aloud about whether pursuing a long period of training for a career was being "selfish.") She wants to combine her career with a family but cannot quite imagine how she will do it. "The future is so far away," she says. But, of course, for Deborah, about to graduate from college, the future is now.

While Deborah, although she does not see now how she will do it all, assumes she will have both a family and a career, Margaret Robinson is clearly ambivalent about a family. A tall, rangy, athletic-looking biology major, Margaret plans to become a clinical pharmacist. She wants to work in a hospital, have direct contact with patients, go on rounds, and be very much a part of the medical scene. Margaret talks about her own "unpleasant childhood" and is not sure she wants to have children at all, surely not "right now." On the other hand, she admits that "deep down inside I know I want them." Moreover, pharmacy, she feels, is a good profession, because you can "fall in and out of it and have flexible hours." Even when these young women profess ambivalence about having children, they are often planning their lives around family responsibilities.

Maria Mendez, a small, thoughtful, and extremely articulate young Hispanic woman, talks about her childhood and how it has influenced the way she sees her future: "My mother is divorced and raised my sisters and me herself. We all felt very close. My mother worked full-time as a Spanish interpreter, and that meant that we were much more independent and self-reliant than other kids. When we got home from school, we didn't just fool around—we had a list of things we had to do. In some ways it made me grow up faster than I should have. Those years from eight to twelve went by really fast. I didn't have the same freedom of being really young.

"I want to make sure that my children have a longer childhood than I did. I don't know how I'm going to do it, but that's what I want to do."

Maria, a psychology major, plans on a career as a medical professional. She is considering everything from doctor to nurse to physician's assistant, but what she does know is that she wants marriage and children. In fact, she knows that she wants children even if she has to be a single parent. "I have no qualms about that," she states definitely. "I want to have a child."

Perhaps examining another student's plans for the future will clarify some of the differences between the New American Dreamers and the Neotraditionalists. While Maria is clearly putting family before career, Laurie Jones, also part of the group at the University of California campus, plans to get her life together first, establish herself, and then think about a family. A sophomore biology major who speaks softly and carefully, Laurie says that her parents are also divorced and that she feels she's "afraid of marriage. I tend to let a relationship dominate me. I need to put a relationship into perspective. In so many situations women don't have anything to fall back on; I *never* want to be in that situation." Laurie, whose mother works full-time as a dental assistant, plans to go to medical school ("Let's hope!") and postpone any serious relationship until she is well into her residency years. If she has children, it will be when "I have established my reputation as a doctor. But by then," she acknowledges, "it may be too late." Laurie is clearly a New American Dreamer.

Four young women—bright, caring, thoughtful—all concerned about how to put the different parts of their future lives together. All of them want careers. Two of them know they want to make a major commitment to those careers but are not so sure about children. The other two know they want to make a major commitment to children but do not have a clear picture of their work life. And all of them assume they will have to solve this very difficult dilemma essentially by themselves. They hope they will be involved with caring, giving men who will actively participate; but underlying their planning for the future is the assumption that they will be doing most of it themselves.

Shawn Sullivan discusses the options. She is seventeen and a freshman at a formerly all-male Ivy League college. Her mother works at a bank as a customer-service representative, and her father is an athletic trainer at the college she attends. Shawn envisions marrying in her mid-twenties and working in advertising or on a magazine. She imagines that by the time she is thirty she'll have a child, maybe two. She can't imagine "how to handle work and kids." Her children will "come first," but she doesn't want to turn into "just being a housewife."

Most of her friends' mothers work; some are involved in volunteer work. But, according to Shawn, most of her friends want to be "different from their mothers," at least in their relationship to work. Many say that work will come first, but Shawn thinks their ideas about career will change. "A lot will fall in love and get married." She feels they want to work and know they must be independent. Moreover, they are very interested in money because they want to live well. She sees the conflicts clearly, but she doesn't offer any solutions.

Susan Carpenter, a seventeen-year-old high-school graduate who is about to enter college, points out yet another reason she wants to return to work once her children have entered kindergarten: "I feel better about myself if I'm doing something. I need to be busy—otherwise I get bored, depressed, kind of sad."

Mallory Stern, a sixteen-year-old high school sophomore who lives in an affluent suburb outside New York City, states flatly: "I'll make myself what I am." A serious young woman, Mallory has high hopes. Mallory's mother is a nurse who worked sporadically when the children were small; her father is a lawyer. The younger of two children, Mallory plans to become a lawyer too; she intends to work as a public prosecutor in the office of the district attorney. She hopes to have a golden retriever puppy and a "boyfriend" or "someone who is there." She wants to have a child when she's established in her field. "I want to have a stable family life and really be there for the kid. I want to always be there when the kids"—no more than two—"call me from school." How is this compatible with a job as a public prosecutor? She is not sure. Perhaps she won't have any children, after all, she says slowly. What she would really like is to have a life like that of the central couple of "Thirtysomething": "I'd love to have a husband like Michael and be like Hope." At the time I interviewed Mallory, Hope was being depicted as spending most of her time at home with a very beautiful little daughter. Clearly, Mallory is deeply ambivalent about career and mothering. It is this ambivalence, this dual fantasy of being a professional in a hard-driving profession on the one hand and of being like Hope on "Thirtysomething" ("really there for the kid") on the other that makes Mallory in my typology a Neotraditionalist rather than a New American Dreamer.

Julie Goldberg, a fifteen-year-old high-school sophomore from the same community, verbalizes the conflict so many of these young people feel: "My mother is a high-school teacher in the Bronx, and my father is a car salesman. Do I ever see him? No.

"Part of me wants to be single and really successful without a husband. I need to make lots of money so I can give the kids everything they want—camp, ballet, singing lessons—and not have to worry about the cost. The other part of me wants to stay home with the kids, to be there when they come home from school to give them warm, homemade chocolate-chip cookies and milk. But if I don't go to work, I won't have the things for the kids that I want to have."

When I ask Julie if her husband might not be able to provide some of those things, she gives me a withering look and says somewhat contemptuously, as though any fool should know, "You can't rely on a man! He could die; he could be laid off—I'm not relying on someone being there for me!"

These, then, are some of the issues that concern young women. How indeed can you be a public prosecutor and still be available if your child needs you during the school day? How do you make "lots of money" and have warm cookies for the children when they come home from school? How can you be an active participant in the world of work while providing the primary nurturing for your children? And how can you do it in a society that has provided few supports to help parents nurture their children?

These young women are reflecting an idealized image of motherhood developed during the nineteenth century and consolidated during the first half of the twentieth. As the locus of work moved from the home to the factory, the concept of the home as a sanctuary from a demanding, often hostile world emerged, and women's primary role became the preservation of the harmony of the home and the rearing of children. "As a result," according to sociologist Cynthia Fuchs Epstein,

> the idealized Victorian family of the nineteenth century became the basis for the "normal" family of the twentieth century in much of the world, especially in Western society. This ideology underscored the idea that woman's place is in the home, not in the labor force; the idea that the essence of femininity lies in ministering to the personal and psychological needs of husbands and children; and "the idea that mothers have a Pygmalion-like influence on their children. . . ."

This idealization of female domesticity culminated in the 1950s, that postwar period of high fertility, massive movement to the suburbs, and the child-centered family. Fifties mothers, encouraged by the culture to stay home, bake bread, grow herbs, and raise emotionally healthy children, often felt responsible for every aspect of family well-being. In that era of pop-Freudian thinking, everything from Johnny's stuttering to Betsy's slow progress in reading was thought to be traceable to problems in child rearing such as insufficient oral gratification or improper toilet training. If almost every aspect of the child's development is due to "nurture" rather than "nature," and if mothers are doing virtually all of the nurturing, then any glitch in the child's development is due to some error the mother must have made in the nurturing process. Maternal guilt was rampant!

While the 1950s may be long gone, for many the legacy of that era remains. Although most of the young women I interviewed were born during the decade between 1964 and 1974, their mothers grew up during the 1950s and could hardly avoid absorbing the clear messages of that period. The image many people, both men and women, have of good mothering stems from this era; and while we are clearly in another time, part of us measures mothering (or parenting) today against that standard.

Another critical problem is that this standard of child rearing was, of course, a white, upper-middle-class (or at the very least middle-class) standard and yet was—and for many still is—accepted as gospel for all: music lessons, nursery school, finger painting, homemade brownies, "play dates" with other children, reading to the child before bed, reading to the child after nap, reading, reading, reading. It all assumes that a caregiver will be in the home a great deal of the time, available to facilitate this vision of child rearing, and that she will have a virtually single-minded focus on the children. It is the legacy of this image that haunts so many young women today.

What is striking is how so many young people carry elements of their own childhood into their own conception of child rearing. Even when we do not want to repeat, when we want to develop a new way, new values, and new techniques for acting on those values, we are somehow drawn back to the old, to repeat patterns imbedded in our own childhood or in our culture. A parent swears he will not inflict music lessons on his child—and does. A parent promises herself "I'll never lay a finger on *my* child!"—and finds herself hitting the child in anger. A parent remembers her parents' restrictive attitudes toward sex and vows to be different—until her daughter reaches fourteen. And a parent thinks warm cookies and milk at three o'clock are not all that important ("quality time" at the end of a day at the law firm, that's what's important)—until her child is two and she finds, crazily, for no apparent reason, that she simply *must* spend more time with him, must read and reread *Goodnight Moon* and *Mike Mulligan and His Steam Shovel,* and is moved to take him to the zoo, *today*! Is it culture lag? Is it that we as a society have not developed new, viable, acceptable ways of child rearing that will enable the mother to work out of the home relatively guilt-free and at the same time provide the child with warm, caring, attentive, creative nurturing? Is it the fault of a culture that continues to promote an outdated vision of mothering, perhaps with the hope of forcing women back to the home, or at very least making them feel distressed and guilty? Or is it that we simply cannot change all of our patterns at once, that we need the comfort of repeating some of the patterns of our own childhood? If our childhood was not particularly happy, perhaps we need to try to "do it right" this time; if our childhood was on the whole satisfying, perhaps we want to experience all of those rituals just one more time.

We are such a mobile, rapidly changing society. We often live hundreds, if not thousands, of miles from where we grew up—either out of choice or out of necessity. We often do not really feel rooted in place; we're transients using a certain city or suburb to get to a standard or style of living we hope to achieve. Does repetition of at least some familiar patterns make us feel more comfortable, surer of who we are? Is it simply too alienating to change too many patterns at once? If our mothers had dinner on the table at six, do we feel guilty if we do not? If our mothers baked birthday cakes for all of their children, do we feel somehow remiss when we buy ours? And above all do we feel inadequate as women, as mothers, if we are not "available" to our children when they "need" us?

Have these young women been sold a false dream? Has the culture—the media, the women's movement, commercial interests—promoted an upper-middle-class ideal of combining career and mothering without making significant changes in the society to allow the dream to become a reality? Which dreams will these young women need to relinquish? Their dreams of "success"? Of mothering? Of "being there" for their children? Whom will they blame when they find they cannot "have it all"?

In describing the way they would like their lives to proceed, many of these young women use phrases such as "like my Mom did." For many of the New American Dreamers, their fathers are the role models for their work lives and their mothers the role models for their domestic lives; because these young women identify with the activities and concerns of both parents, they feel they must play both roles—be the active breadwinner, like the father, and the nurturer, like the mother. Many of the Neotraditionalists seem to identify more completely with their mothers, most of whom work part-time or started working when the children entered school. These Neotraditionalists know that life is not the same as it was when their mothers were becoming adults and having children; but "the way Mom did it," particularly the way Mom handled the nurturing role, remains a positive and powerful model for them. If the New American Dreamers are going to try to forge a very different life for themselves, some Neotraditionalists are going to try to combine the old and the new images of women, while others are going to try to hold on to what they treasure from the traditional role of women and adapt it to the present and the future.

One group of Neotraditionalists lives in a community that seems to have changed little over the past thirty years. It is like stepping back in time: suburban Westchester County, tree-lined streets, small shops in the center of town, bicyclists out on a clear, cold Sunday morning. On the corner, surrounded by old, comfortable houses, stands a handsome stone Presbyterian church with its Gothic-style steeple. After services parents and children slowly make their way to their cars—a father carrying his two-year-old, mothers with their teenage daughters, an elderly woman with a cane being helped by a middle-aged woman.

Inside, people are standing around talking over coffee. In the library four young women are sitting on worn, comfortable couches; a fifth rushes in a few minutes late. Talking to these young women is almost like reentering the fifties—almost, but not quite. They are wearing fairly nondescript clothing, three in pants, two in skirts and bobby sox. One is even wearing rhinestone earrings that might have come from the fifties. The only gesture to the eighties is a key that one young woman has hanging from one hoop earring, a faintly punk gesture of individuality and perhaps defiance.

After considerable discussion about college, alcohol, drugs, boys, and sex, I ask each of them what she thinks her future life will be like, what her priorities and goals are. Each one—from the minister's daughter to the slightly punk-looking, outspoken young woman who is playing with her arty black felt hat—responds that she will marry, will have children, plans to remain at home to raise her children at least until they are in school (one thought she would remain at home until her children were in junior high school), and then maybe work part-time or travel or become active in the PTA. They would like to live in a small town similar to the one they grew up in; two of them would especially like to live in this particular town. When I point out that this game plan is clearly dependent on the man they marry, and ask what kind of man they have in mind, the response, accompanied by much laughter and enthusiasm, is "Gorgeous! *Tall*—brown hair, blue eyes—college graduate, good occupation—smart, intelligent, and *really* funny!" One of them adds that he should be healthy and athletic; that hers won't be a "meat and potatoes" family. These young women are clearly looking toward their family lives to provide their primary identity and mission. If the New American Dreamers have clear, concrete career goals but only a hazy notion of their future private lives, this group of Neotraditionalists has a vivid picture of their roles as wives and mothers but only a faint, distant image of their work lives.

When I comment that their plans are also dependent on the couple staying together and ask if many of their friends have parents who are divorced, several acknowledge that they know lots of divorced couples, but all state that *they* do not plan to get divorced. One, a petite, quiet, serious fifteen-year-old, says, "I don't want to divorce. I would never get divorced just to live a happier life."

Of all the young women I interviewed in many parts of the United States, few said that they preferred not to work at all after marriage. The young woman who was clearest about her desire not to work is a Mexican-American college student who plans to work for a design company or an art gallery after she graduates, then marry and be an "active wife." "I don't want to have to work, but I want to be able to work if I ever need to. I want to enjoy life. I want to travel—I want to see what the world is like," she stated. Virtually every other young woman assumed she would work at some point during her married life, even if it was not until her children were nearly grown. Even among the Neotraditionalists, working is taken for granted as part of their future lives.

So often the stereotype of teenagers is that they are immersed in their own concerns, in their peer group, in their movies, their music, their clothes, with little time or inclination for family or for concerns beyond themselves. Many of the young women I interviewed, however, particularly the Neotraditionalists, were incredibly sensitive, thoughtful, and concerned about others. Their understanding of the world around them and their empathy for friends and family were often startling.

Several young women expressed deep concern about their parents and their well-being. A high-school student worries about her father, who owns a window-washing company and doesn't like his work. Another worries about both of her parents—her mother, who works two jobs, and her father, who is an accountant but is "depressed" because he doesn't earn enough to maintain the family at the level of most of the other families in the community.

The young women meeting at the suburban church are worried about their parents getting old; they "like them the way they are." They themselves are worried about getting old. They are worried about death. One has a friend whose parents recently died; another has a grandmother who recently died. They worry about what's going to happen to them when their parents die. They worry about "unnatural deaths" such as car accidents. One young woman spoke of her great-grandmother dying a year ago. "It makes you think that your grandparents are next, then your parents, then you," she said.

Allison Cramer, the young woman with the punk earring, worries about her parents being unhappy or hurt. "My mother has something wrong with her leg and is limping around; it hurts me to see her this way. And I worry about my father when he has a bad day." Jane Peters, a high-school senior, is concerned about the inevitable distancing that occurs when one "leaves home": "I'm worried about my parents after I go to college. My mother says, 'What will I do when you go away?' I'm worried about my younger brothers and sisters. I'm going to miss watching them go through high school; I'm going to miss their growing up. I don't want to come back home a stranger."

Perhaps Lucille Odom, the seventeen-year-old heroine of Josephine Humphreys's novel *Rich in Love,* describes these young women's feelings and concerns about their families best: "I doubt that parents have an inkling of how deep a child's love goes. It is more thorough than adult love. I loved not only my parents: I loved their love." After Lucille's mother walks out on her twenty-seven-year marriage, Lucille feels she must watch over her devastated father. She describes her love for him, her efforts to understand him, and her desire to save him:

I did love him, no doubt about that. From a burning houseful of friends and relations I would have dragged him out first and never given a thought to the others until he was safe. But the love itself, the work of it, was debilitating, requiring me constantly to imagine the world from his point of view. Dragging him from a burning house would have been easier. . . . Sometimes his perspective came easily to me, and I could know instantly what he was thinking, but more and more often the effort became a strain. It was like looking through someone else's eyeglasses: you can do it if you squint down to the exact right point and tighten the tiny muscles behind your eyeballs, but it hurts, and when it's over you can't see with your own vision for some time!

Selina, the young heroine of Paule Marshall's moving novel *Brown Girl, Brownstones,* also tries to save her father. In this instance, she is attempting to save him not only from emotional hurt but from nothing less than disaster. Selina understands the incredible gulf that exists between her parents' dreams for the future: her father's dream of returning one day to his two acres of land in Barbados, where he hopes to have a "house . . . just like the white people own. A house to end all house!" He dreams of a "white house with Grecian columns and stained-glass bathroom windows," of a "flamboyant tree" taking root in the yard. Her mother, on the other hand, dreams of owning her own brownstone in Brooklyn, the house that would symbolize their getting ahead, would symbolize some security in this country in which she has worked so hard, would symbolize for her a real piece of the American Dream. And when their dreams finally and irrevocably collide, when Selina's mother destroys her father's dream by secretly and fraudulently selling his land and destroys him in the process, Selina tells her father how she had "tried to warn him, [tried] to protect him: 'I tried to tell you,' she said, aching with each word. 'I tried to tell you she was gonna do something. Remember that day you were telling me about the house home? I tried then. I tried to tell everybody that day but nobody listened . . .' "And finally, when it's too late to save her father from despair and ultimately from death, she feels "it would never have happened if [I] had loved him more."

Lucille and Selina exemplify the concern of many young women for those around them. The young women sitting around talking in the church in Westchester are concerned not only about their families, friends, and immediate community but also about "other people, starving people, the imbalance in wealth, nuclear war." "I just hope I'm not one of the survivors," says Allison Cramer.

They start talking about the value of belonging to the church youth group: Jennifer Robinson, a fifteen-year-old in the tenth grade, states, "It's important—it becomes part of your life. It's addictive, doing things for other people. You get a natural high." Allison agrees: "It gives you the chance to explore your own beliefs, to learn about different issues, to get together with each other."

And then when someone says how much they owe to the young minister who leads the youth group, another adds that they worry about *him,* too—he spends so much time at the church and with them that they are concerned that he doesn't have enough time to spend with his family. "We're worried that he may burn out," Allison says.

There is a relaxed feeling about this group of young women. It is as though they have the time and the emotional energy to think about others. They seem to be on a slower track than the more intensely career-bound students. They too speak of college and SATs and PSATs, but they just don't have the same driven quality. It is as though they have the time and the space to care. But, of course, they are operating under a very different premise than that of the New American Dreamers: they are assuming that there will be another breadwinner in their lives, that they will not need to be the sole support (both financial and emotional) of themselves and their children; and so they do not feel the same sense of urgency as do the young women who feel they must be prepared to go it alone. It is perhaps significant that these young women seem to be from a slightly lower social class than many of the New American Dreamers. Many of their fathers are not working in the highest-paid professions, and their mothers (if they work at all) work part-time earning a relatively modest income. These young women want to maintain their present standard of living but do not seem as insistent on obtaining all of the currently fashionable consumer goods.

According to one researcher who has studied how women make decisions about work and family commitments, "Perhaps the most critical underpinning of women's domesticity is stable marriage. Permanent marriage makes economic dependency and full-time motherhood possible and contributes to a context in which childbearing and mothering seem natural." Despite their knowledge of the high rate of divorce in American society, these young women are fantasizing a "stable marriage" at the heart of their lives and are planning the rest of their lives accordingly.

One wonders, however, what will become of the fifteen-year-old who doesn't want to get divorced "just to have a happier life." What happens if due to divorce, death, or other circumstances she is indeed forced to fend for herself? Will she be able to? Will she have acquired the skills, the confidence, the know-how to deal with a world that is often so different from what she hopes and expects it will be? Is she perhaps paying a real price for her focus on domesticity? Have we set up impossible choices for our young women?

CHAPTER 3

The Outsiders

I have always been a circle within a square.

AMANDA CHAPMAN
college dropout, New Jersey

*I don't plan. I don't look to the future. I can't plan, 'cause my
plans never work out. They never go through.*

LINDA SMITH
high-school dropout, North Carolina

"It happened that green and crazy summer when Frankie was
twelve years old. This was the summer when for a long time she
had not been a member. She belonged to no club and was a member
of nothing in the world. Frankie had become an unjoined person
who hung around in doorways, and she was afraid."

So we meet Frankie Addams, the heroine of *The Member of the
Wedding,* Carson McCullers's moving novel about growing up. As
a young girl on the verge of adolescence, Frankie exemplifies the
Outsider in each of us. She suddenly, and inexplicably, belongs
nowhere. In that summer of 1943 she doesn't belong with the
thirteen-, fourteen-, and fifteen-year-old girls who exclude her from
their neighborhood clubhouse; she no longer quite belongs with
those closest to her, her five-year-old cousin, John Henry, and her
beloved Berenice, the black cook who was more of a mother to
Frankie than many people's biological mothers; she doesn't even

belong within herself. Frankie's ultimate wish that summer is to be "somebody else except me."

Who of us has not felt this way—that we fit in nowhere, even in our own skins? We feel this way sometimes as children when everyone else seems to have a friend, when everyone else has something to do during school vacation, or when we seem particularly out of step with our families. We feel it as adults when our personal life isn't working, when work is meaningless or nonexistent, when it seems that no one loves us. But we feel it most when we are adolescents, for during this period we really do not fit in. Adolescents are in that in-between state: they can no longer completely and wholeheartedly identify with their families, since one of the central tasks of growing up is to step back in order to examine and evaluate one's parents as human beings rather than as demigods; but neither are they, as yet, part of the larger society. They must examine also the outer world, weigh its achievements and deficits, its opportunities and false promises; they must do this in order to understand where they might fit in, what their future niche might be, what impact they might make on the world around them.

Adolescence, therefore, is a time of connecting and disconnecting, of questioning and believing, of trying out new roles and discarding others. The adolescent, at least in much of Western industrialized culture, must come to terms with the loss that results from seeing one's parents as full-fledged people with their own histories, limitations, and needs rather than as idealized examples of adulthood, and must then go on to forge an individual identity by exploring the self, the nature of the immediate environment, and the wider world.

As we know, adolescence is a perilous time, a time fraught with danger; yet it is also a time of enormous opportunity. One of the most perilous aspects of these years is the feeling on the part of the adolescent that suddenly she/he is a stranger, a foreigner, an alien in a once-familiar land. For the young person, what may be most frightening is the sense of aloneness.

And so the adolescent is an Outsider. One can perhaps go so far as to state that in much of Western culture, but particularly in American society, adolescents *must* become Outsiders to some degree if they are to come to terms with adulthood, for the characteristics we admire in adults in our society—self-reliance, independence, thinking and taking responsibility for oneself—require that the young adult "leave home." This "leaving home" may be a physical leave-taking—a seventeen-year-old going away to college—or it may be a psychological leave-taking, with the young person attempting to establish his/her own values, priorities, and goals. As Robert Bellah and the other authors of *Habits of the Heart* have put it, "For us, leaving home is the normal expectation, and childhood is in many ways a preparation for it." If one of the central tasks of growing up in America is to "leave home," as young people we must distance ourselves from our families in order to minimize the pain. We must to some extent set ourselves outside their orbit. "Leaving home" may also entail examining the milieu in which we are raised and may necessitate adolescents distancing themselves from this social environment as well. The process clearly varies for different socioeconomic, racial, and ethnic groups. It may also vary in degree and intensity among those who come to the United States from other countries. One of the serious points of conflict within recent immigrant families is caused by the clash between the parents' expectation that they will be obeyed as they would have been in their country of origin and their adolescents' desire to imitate the behavior of their American friends—behavior that will amount to rebellion against their parents' norms. Kate Simon, the daughter of Jewish immigrants from Eastern Europe, who came to the U.S. when she was four years old, describes this process of "leaving home": "We were . . . tearing away from the restraints of who we thought we were to the freedoms of who we thought we wanted to be, trying on a succession of identities." But adolescents are, of necessity, still part of their family units, still rooted in their environment, and so must be both Insider and Outsider at the same time.

This process is made all the more difficult because of the extended period of time that many adolescents in our culture float in this never-never land. What with ever-increasing years of education and professional training, young people are often not truly "on their own" until they are in their late twenties or early thirties. During this time of minimal responsibility for self and for others, the young person may find it difficult to get a firm grasp on the reality of work, of commitment to others, of day-to-day responsibility.

If many adolescents can be seen as Outsiders trying to grope their way toward adult identity, female adolescents and young adults have a particularly complex and arduous task, for as women they are doubly outside the system. As Simone de Beauvoir has stated, "Humanity is male and man defines woman not in herself but as relative to him . . . He is the Subject . . . she is the Other."

This statement is as true today as it was when de Beauvoir wrote it, forty years ago. Despite advances in the world of work, the majority of women are still segregated in female-dominated occupations with low status, low wages, and little mobility. The glamorous, lucrative professions of law, medicine, and finance are still for the most part run by males according to the traditional male model of extraordinarily long hours, hard work, and little or no thought for family life or personal obligations.

American politics at the national level is still largely a male club, with uniforms, norms, and financing to suit the male role. Perhaps the most graphic evidence of male domination of national politics was the ever-present image on our television screens in the early months of the 1988 presidential campaign of men of both parties in their dark suits, ties, and crisp shirts debating, arguing, testing, joking, using endless sports metaphors, but all the while looking as though they belonged to the same club. Even Jesse Jackson, the quintessential Outsider, came to look as though he belonged. And when Representative Patricia Schroeder put a toe in to test the waters, found them icy and unnavigable, quickly withdrew, and while doing so cried (on her husband's shoulder, no less), we saw that she was unacceptable. She was just not "one of the guys." She might know more about national security and the federal budget than most of her colleagues, but she could not raise the money for a presidential campaign, and she cried. When male candidates get teary, it's a sign of sensitivity, of compassion; when a female candidate gets teary, it means she is weak and cannot control her emotions. That's the way it is. The female is the "other." The male standard is the norm, the way it is supposed to be; the female is the Outsider.

Young women who are growing up know this, of course. They may be surrounded by women, even strong, accomplished women; but the values and expectations of the larger society are always there. The central character in *The Elizabeth Stories* by Isabel Huggan describes growing up in a small town in Canada and the sudden realization of the complexity and arbitrary nature of gender differentiation: "What did it *mean* to be a girl or a boy, and why did I feel like such a failure? It was as if I had touched with my toe a hidden switch that suddenly made visible, as far as my eye could see, limits and lines and boundaries over which one could not transgress without great danger and pain. There it was for the first time; the minefield of sex."

For some adolescents, being an Outsider is a temporary phenomenon, part of the growing-up process, and can be mitigated by different facets of an individual's life. One of the paradoxes of adolescence is that while the adolescent must stand to some extent outside of the environment in which she or he grew and developed, the individual has at the same time a yearning to belong. A close friend or group of friends, a high-school club or activity, a community group, political organization, or church may meet the adolescent's need for intimacy, for acceptance and belonging. For while we may plumb our souls in isolation, it is through interaction, particularly with those who share our values and our interests, that we often discover our own priorities and our capacity for commitment and connection.

Time and time again the young women with whom I spoke discussed their many activities: singing, dancing, tap, ballet, student council, flute, trumpet, French horn, cello, choir, band, long-distance running, soccer, softball, drama, religious youth groups, teaching Sunday school, and even a peace group. They acknowledged that part of their motivation for being such active joiners and participants was that they needed activities on their résumés in order to look interesting to the colleges to which they were applying, but they also asserted that it was through such activities that you meet and make friends. As several of them said, "The more involved you are, the happier you are." Some felt that they were too busy, that they had hardly any free time; but no one suggested cutting back.

For some, friendship groups are most important. Susan Carpenter describes a group she belonged to during her senior year in high school:

"I was part of a group of fun-loving girls; we never discussed anything serious. We were fast-moving, covered a lot of territory, always went to the right party. We were, I have to say, arrogant. We were very into ourselves. We went to visit colleges and felt very intellectual. We learned to use everything to our advantage.

"Actually, we lost our individual identity; we became one person. We had our own private language, our inside jokes. It got so we couldn't communicate with others—we didn't feel comfortable talking to other people.

"We were very intense. We were together all the time—at school, at sports, studying, partying, drinking at someone's house. After a while we were not going to high-school parties at all; we thought we were better than that. At the end of the year I went outside when everyone was sitting on the lawn in front of school and there wasn't one group that I felt comfortable talking to.

"Now I hang out with many different people and sometimes with my family. I feel more relaxed. For a while I was afraid to leave the group to go to college, but not now. Now I feel ready."

It is almost as though Susan's group was a transitional group, a bridge between high school and college, a substitute family while Susan was distancing herself from childhood. Such a group is surely a way to try out a new identity and a sense of independence while still safely part of something.

Others spoke of different groups. I asked the group of Westchester high-school students mentioned in chapter 2 why they belong to the youth group attached to their Presbyterian church. One young woman responds: "I don't believe in God or in religion. We don't worship anything. It's the community. That's why we come—not to pray. It's a channel to get to other things. We call it 'fellowship,' and that's what it is."

In the summer the group goes to work camp for a week to ten days and performs community-service work for members of the community who could not otherwise afford to have the work done. They paint houses, do cleaning as well as minor building and repairs; at the same time they explore their common concerns. They make the point that there are no cliques in this youth group. As one young woman describes it, "Everybody is together as one."

Not far from the Presbyterian church is a Jewish temple that has a similar program. This congregation was formed by Jewish professionals who grew up during the 1960s and who retain many of the values of that period. The building is a refurbished house, simple and unpretentious. The room in which services are held also serves as a gathering place for the congregation's social activities and, for one night every other week, as a sanctuary for nineteen homeless men. There was some debate within the congregation about the propriety of using the place where religious services are held to house the homeless, but the final decision was that if they are going to call it a sanctuary in the religious sense, they should really make it into a sanctuary.

The youth program is run by Billy Dreskin, a young, outgoing, extremely caring assistant rabbi. While he feels, on the one hand, that these young people are obsessed with academic achievement and future success, he also feels that they are exceptionally responsive to community projects, that they have a "natural inclination within them to be altruistic." In their youth programs the young people have an opportunity to participate in community-service projects—to provide food for the hungry, to help prepare for the homeless who stay at the temple twice a month, to go to Washington to participate in demonstrations in behalf of Soviet Jewry.

A couple of months after I talk with the rabbi, I have the opportunity to talk with several of the young women who are particularly active in the youth groups. They range in age from fifteen to seventeen and talk at length about why they belong to the group. Several indicate that they come because of friendships within the group. A young woman who goes to a high school with very few Jewish students says, "I feel more secure here, around people like me. I can share things that I can't share with someone who goes to church." And then they start to talk about the young rabbi, who is clearly a very special person in their lives: They come to talk to Billy. (Everyone calls him by his first name.) They come to be with him. He's young enough to relate to them, they say, but still has an adult point of view. As one young woman says, "He knows how our minds work, and he respects us." A very thoughtful seventeen-year-old adds, "The world is changing, and it's hard to figure out where you belong. Here we have friends; we do social action, which gives you confidence that you can do something; we have a stronger sense of identity. Coming here helps you to learn who you are."

On the other side of the country, Angela Dawson and Ariel Martin, high-school juniors from southern California, talk about their myriad activities. Ariel is on the track team, plays field hockey, is involved in school activities, particularly the honor society, and volunteers at the local children's museum. Angela acts in school plays, volunteers at an AIDS project, is involved in registering people to vote, in demonstrating against nuclear war, sexism, and racism, particularly South African apartheid. In addition, both young women point out that homework takes a great deal of their time.

Their commitment to these activities seems to reflect, particularly with these young women but with many of the others as well, a belief that one must actively participate in one's world and that one must take an active role in shaping one's own future. Angela and Ariel are not sitting around waiting for life to happen to them. Angela says it clearly: "We need to be in control of our lives."

Young people who have not found a niche for themselves, a place where they feel they belong and feel fairly comfortable, are likely to be particularly vulnerable to the fads and pressures within adolescent culture, which in turn reflect those of society in general. No matter what the topic—sex, alcohol, drugs, clothes—the young women with whom I spoke emphasized the power of peer pressure and the desire to be accepted, to be popular.

Why do high-school students in an affluent New England college town, including females, drink so much? "Because they are insecure and need to be part of the crowd," said one nondrinker. Another talked about the pressure within some groups to have sex—pressure from the guys and pressure from the girls. Even grades are subject to pressure. In one small community in the Northeast it was not "cool" to get grades over 90 in the eighth grade. If you did, you were "too smart." It was "cool to get a 70." And, of course, what you wear, how you look, where you live, how much money your family earns, your grades, which colleges accept you all determine whether you are in or out. According to one mature fifteen-year-old, "The most important thing is popularity: everybody liking you, everybody looking up to you, everybody kissing your feet—that's what everyone wants."

For many adolescents, being an Outsider is a transitional stage, one that may pass in time and in the meanwhile can be offset—as the interviews we have just discussed illustrate—by belonging to specific friendship or interest groups. But there is another group of adolescent Outsiders, those for whom being an Outsider permeates their existence and may last a lifetime. While some young women feel entitled to "have it all," others clearly have great difficulty thinking about the future. When asked what they hope for, what they plan for, how they would like their lives to be, they say with a dismissive wave of the hand, "I can't think about that" or "I just have to get through tomorrow." If the New American Dreamers and many of the Neotraditionalists dream of work, family, success, and material rewards—in short, "the good life"—many Outsiders are unable to dream at all. They are either so burdened by day-to-day living or feel so hopeless about their lives that they can barely envision a future for themselves.

There are many ways of not belonging. Amanda Chapman, a young woman from New Jersey, describes herself as "a circle within a square"; she just never quite fit in. "I might appear to be part of things," she said, "but I don't quite get along with my peers. I never really fit in. Right now I have four friends, and that's not too many." When I spoke with her, she was five months pregnant. She had dropped out of college and was living at home. She never quite fit in there, either. Her mother often told her when they got into a fight, "You're not worthy of anything." Most recently, because she is pregnant and home almost constantly, her parents are insisting that she do all the household chores—the cleaning, the shopping, the dishes. She even must drive her sixteen-year-old sister everywhere she wants to go. "I don't want to feel like the black sheep," she says, "but I've got no choice." It is almost an updated Cinderella story—but Prince Charming is not likely to come along with a glass slipper.

Dorothy Kovak is nineteen and lives in central New Jersey. Dorothy's mother, a computer programmer, and her father, a truck driver, are divorced. She talks about being an Outsider in her small town: "My crowd? We all wore makeup, tight jeans and thought we had to be cool. We hung out, we partied—there was nothing else to do. Movies weren't cool; bowling is totally impossible. So we hung out at the roller rink.

"There were basically three groups: the jocks, the brains, and the burn-outs. You had to fit in somewhere, so we were the burn-outs; we were in with the outcasts."

Dorothy thinks back and tries to explain how she got to be one of the "outcasts": "I was always an outcast in school—at least until the seventh grade. My home was all screwed up. My mother and father were either drinking or fighting, so I couldn't bring people home. I didn't talk to people, and they didn't talk to me. If you're not *in* in kindergarten, you're not in.

"And I wanted friends. I wanted someone to be my friend. The only way I found I could have friends was to be part of this group."

Dorothy described her group as being heavily into drugs and alcohol since they were eleven, twelve, and thirteen. They drank daily and used "a lot of pot, speed, and cocaine. We would party till we dropped." She says she used speed every day for two years; she didn't use downers because "I was already depressed and certainly didn't need downers." Dorothy talks about the summer when she was sixteen: "I just wanted to die. I had contemplated suicide for some time. It was a major part of my thought process during the day. I felt like shit. I hated myself.

"The train tracks in Manville [New Jersey] are famous for suicide. Trains go through at about sixty miles an hour. A kid I went to school with committed suicide on the tracks, and it hit me real hard. I just didn't want to deal with life anymore. I felt I had a choice: commit suicide or get high. I would come out of blackouts on the tracks."

Dorothy is describing an all-too-frequent phenomenon in contemporary American society. Every 1.1 seconds a teenager makes an attempt at suicide; every 80 minutes one succeeds. According to the Federal Center for Disease Control, since 1950 the suicide rate has tripled among young people ages fifteen to nineteen. In 1977 the rate peaked at 13.3 deaths per 100,000; in 1984 a total of 5,026 young people aged fifteen to twenty-four took their own lives. Females are more likely to attempt suicide; males are more likely to succeed. The suicide rate for men between the ages of fifteen and twenty-four rose 50 percent between 1970 and 1980. Comparable rates for young women rose 2 percent.

National attention focused on teen suicide in 1987 when four young people from Bergenfield, New Jersey—two boys and two girls, aged sixteen and nineteen—killed themselves in a suicide pact. Within six days four more young people were dead in the Chicago suburbs, and other "suicide clusters," as they are called, were reported in Westchester County, New York; Plano, Texas; and Omaha, Nebraska. Some estimates suggest that four hundred thousand teenagers attempt suicide each year. Why are so many of our young people contemplating suicide, attempting to kill themselves, and all too often succeeding?

Explanations of this phenomenon vary. Some experts point to the easy access of instruments of death such as drugs and guns, teenagers' favorite methods of killing themselves. Others attribute teenage suicide to a variety of contemporary social problems: "faster-paced lives, the decline of organized religion, competitiveness at school, the tightening of the job market and, in less affluent families, bleaker prospects for the future." Some mental-health professionals link teenage suicide to "the drugging of America," the availability and widespread use of both legal prescription drugs and illegal drugs. Others suggest that young people are victims of intolerable levels of anxiety and alienation. Parents and other adults are less available to give support and reassurance. According to one psychiatrist who specializes in the treatment of adolescents, "From the point of view of most adolescents there's not much that looks secure or desirable. They're faced with anxieties I was not exposed to at that age and they're able to experiment with drugs or sex before they're ready to deal with the emotional consequences of those things." Yet another theory is that the pressure for them to succeed—academically, economically, socially—is so great that they often perceive personal failure as a sign of worthlessness.

Adolescent suicide is, of course, part of a larger pattern of risk taking on the part of young people. From the enormous use and abuse of alcohol among all classes and among children as young as twelve and thirteen, the continued although somewhat diminished use of illegal drugs other than crack, which is increasingly used, dangerous driving (automobile accidents are the leading cause of death for people up to age thirty-nine), and sexual intercourse without appropriate protection against both pregnancy and sexually transmitted diseases, young people are risking their well-being and indeed their lives with astonishing frequency. Of particular concern to many experts is the rise in problem drinking among young women, particularly among single, well-educated young women. According to one expert on alcoholism, "What we are seeing is the first generation of women who drink like men." Studies indicate that women under thirty are starting to drink earlier and more heavily than did previous generations, often "consuming five or six drinks at one sitting." According to Dr. Sheila Blume, a psychiatrist who works with alcoholics, "Young women, seeking to ease some of their social pressures, are turning to alcohol at an alarming rate. But because of their greater sensitivity to alcohol, they are going to have bigger problems, and sooner, than men." A recent survey of eleven thousand teenagers found that 26 percent of the eighth graders and 38 percent of the tenth graders studied said they had had five or more drinks on one occasion in the two weeks preceding the survey; one in ten said they had smoked marijuana, and one in fifteen said they had used cocaine, in the past month. Forty-two percent of the females and 25 percent of the males said they had "seriously thought" about committing suicide; nearly one in five girls and one in ten boys said they had attempted it.

These data help to explain Dorothy's rather offhand response when I asked her what had happened to the other members of the group. She responded casually, "Oh, the usual—some are dead, some have been put away, some are out there getting worse."

Today Dorothy is seven months pregnant and about to be married. She started college at Fairleigh Dickinson but after two weeks found out she was pregnant. She seriously considered having an abortion but couldn't bring herself to do it. Her future husband is a floor waxer and carpet cleaner; she is currently working at a job doing data entry. "It's boring," she says in a flat tone of voice.

What kind of future does she envision? "It's going to be hard. There are going to be rough times. But we can make it. We've survived everything else. We'll just have to take one day at a time."

Taking one day at a time is something Linda Smith, a seventeen-year-old high-school dropout who lives in North Carolina, feels she needs to learn. After her parents divorced and her mother made it clear that she did not really want her around, Linda went to live with her grandmother. During her senior year she discovered that she was pregnant by her boyfriend. She decided to have an abortion, arranged and paid for it herself. "I wanted to get it over with," she said. "I didn't even get scared until I was on the operating table."

Linda currently works in a fast-food restaurant and plans to take courses for her high-school equivalency diploma. In thinking about the future Linda has a clearer picture of what she does not want than what she does want. "I don't want to stay in one place. I don't want to have kids until I'm thirty. I don't like to depend on a man." While she says she likes to travel, likes to communicate with different people, and might like to be an airline stewardess, when asked about plans for the future she responds, "I don't plan. I don't look to the future. I can't plan, 'cause my plans never work out. They never go through."

Norma Merino, a slight, pale, worn-looking mother of two who lives in Arizona, is two and a half months pregnant with her third child. She has been with the father of her children for seven years, since she was twelve and he was eighteen. Their first child was born when she was fourteen. "Thank God he never left me when I was younger," she says. "I know a lot of girls whose guys left when they got pregnant." Norma has thought about going back to school. She is currently receiving AFDC (Aid to Families with Dependent Children) but knows she needs to be able to take care of herself, because "I can't count on John and I don't run to Mom and Dad."

How does she see her future? "I don't even think about it. What if I die tomorrow or today? I just hope God gives me lots of days until the children are of age." What she does want is for her children to "grow up and finish school, not be out there in the streets, and to have a better life than mine."

Sex or gender is not the only minefield that females must face as they are growing up; there are also the minefields of class and race. The poor and the near-poor are surely Outsiders in this affluent, commercial society in which we are all relentlessly driven to consume. The working class is at best marginal, holding on as long as nothing goes wrong, as long as the factory has not been closed and the paycheck keeps coming in, as long as everyone remains healthy. But if any disaster strikes, a working-class family can become Outsiders in a flash—outside the workplace, outside the health-care system, outside the feel-good system of consuming, even literally outside on the streets.

Are the ultimate Outsiders nonwhite as well as poor? For while the rest of us can try to "pass" as insiders even when we know we are really living beyond the pale, nonwhites cannot. Gary Hart, like millions of Americans from immigrant families, can change his name to escape being identified as coming from ethnic stock; but blacks, Asians, Native Americans, and other nonwhites in our society have no such option. The identification is there every minute of the day. Black men are surely Outsiders within American society, but if adolescents by virtue of their developmental stage are Outsiders, if female adolescents by virtue of their gender are also outside the system, if the poor are outside the American Dream, then, if we think in terms of concentric circles, those who are poor, nonwhite, and female must be farthest from the center, farthest from our image of what is good, what is shining, what it means to be an American. Can these young women on that periphery even see the center? Can they touch it? Can they imagine it? Or is it just too far—too far even to dream?

Toni Morrison has written perhaps the most compelling description of what it is like to be the true Outsider:

> Outdoors, we know, was the real terror of life . . .
> There is a difference between being put *out* and being put outdoors. If you are put out, you go somewhere else; if you are outdoors, there is no place to go. The distinction was subtle but final. Outdoors was the end of something, an irrevocable, physical fact, defining and complementing our metaphysical condition.

Ellen Simpson, a college student in her mid-twenties, talks about what it was like growing up as a Japanese-American girl: "My mother was Japanese and my father was American. When I was growing up, I was taught to be a servant. Women were supposed to serve others. My mother would have tea parties; I never interacted, I never participated—I just served.

"We came here from Japan when I was five. When I entered school I remember speaking Japanese and the whole class laughed. There were always insults about Pearl Harbor, but I bore them and kept them inside. I had Japanese mannerisms like bowing to people, and I felt ostracized.

"I didn't even look right. Growing up in California everyone was supposed to be tall, blond, very thin. I was five-feet-two, dark, mild, soft-spoken, and I had been taught that if I seemed too intelligent it would be threatening to others. I wanted to be attractive but was scared of drawing attention to myself. Instead, I had hair down to my knees—I parted it in the middle and hid behind it."

Ellen talks about W.E.B. Dubois's theory of "double consciousness." In 1903, DuBois wrote in *The Souls of Black Folk*:

> The Negro is a sort of seventh son, born with a veil, and gifted with second-sight in this American world,—a world which yields him no true self-consciousness, but only lets him see himself through the revelation of the other world. It is a peculiar sensation, this double-consciousness, this sense of always looking at one's self through the eyes of others, of measuring one's soul by the tape of a world that looks on in amused contempt and pity. One ever feels his twoness,—an American, a Negro; two souls, two thoughts, two unreconciled strivings, two warring ideals in one dark body, whose dogged strength alone keeps it from being torn asunder.

Ellen feels DuBois is saying that the Negro in him needed to love himself while the American in him needed to hate himself. Ellen says she felt the same way. "I finally stopped bowing," she says somewhat wistfully.

Three young Chicanas discuss growing up as Mexican-Americans while trying to cope with the phenomenon of "double consciousness." Cecilia Martinez, a lively, bright, articulate twenty-one-year-old college student who hopes to become a city planner, was bused to an integrated school not far from her neighborhood. She feels that the "Anglos" were not accepting of Mexican-American kids and that she "had to learn white ways." She describes how discrimination persists in her life today, how "guys come on in a very cheap way" when she and her friends go to a club in the evening. They "assume we are there for sex." Their view is "Oh, she's a dumb Mexican bitch!" Even at school, where she is a member of the finance committee, she's always aware that she's "the Mexican member of the committee."

Tory Hostos describes growing up in an all-white area in southern California and attending nearly all-white schools: "When I was a little kid I had secondhand clothes, and while I was the prettiest, I was also the poorest. Then my family acquired some money, and the kids in school started to hate me. They used to say Mexicans were dirty, and I hated that. I hated being Mexican. I used to say 'Don't call me that,' and I tried to be white.

"Once in high school I got a perm and it came out looking like an Afro. Then they spray-painted my clothes, ruined all my stuff, and called me 'nigger.'

"I constantly switched schools and learned to play white people's games. I hated Mexicans. I dated white guys—Italians, Jewish guys—and even forgot that I was Mexican. Once I drove with this guy into Mexico (he came from a very white family), and he's saying all these terrible things about Mexicans and treating me as though I'm white. I suddenly thought, 'I must be a disgrace to Mexicans. I'll just have to start acting like I'm Mexican.' But really I felt that I'd rather be dead."

Jacqueline Gonzalez has had a somewhat different experience. She grew up in a working-class Mexican-American family in the barrio but was one of the students who were bused from her neighborhood to a very affluent neighborhood. She feels that the students at her new school always felt they were superior, always looked down on the Mexican-Americans. As a result, she says, she became "really shy, afraid to express myself; I never felt like one of them." She continues: "I didn't want to be Hispanic, but I had to be; I couldn't be Anglo. I was caught between the two groups."

Jacqueline feels that she will most likely marry someone who is Hispanic; but she hopes that later, when she's a successful lawyer, she can live in the same area to which she was bused all those years. Those "Anglos" might have treated her badly, but Jacqueline wants to live an upper-middle-class life among them. Tory feels she will almost certainly "marry someone who is white" and says that the worst part is that "every day I wake up and have to deal with it all over again."

Pamela Vincent is a dynamic, articulate, outgoing black woman in her mid-twenties. Like Tory she grew up in an affluent neighborhood in southern California; her family was the only black family in the area. Even though they were middle-class, she says, "I always felt different—like an outsider. The other girls were little, with blond hair; I always felt I wasn't any good. People talked to me using terms they thought black people use; I was always fighting against the stereotype."

A turning point in her life came during the summer between her junior and senior years in high school. Through a program run by the American Field Service she went to Brazil, lived with a family there, and fell in love with the culture. "I loved it there!" she says. "I loved the energy! I loved the jazz and the dancing! I loved their focus on the family." Pam has been trying ever since to integrate Brazilian music and dance into her life and into this culture. One of her dreams is to develop a multilingual, multicultural program for children in the schools, combining movement, music, and other aspects of culture to help Americans become more sensitive to the differences between groups in our society. Pam is trying to use her experience of feeling like an Outsider to bring people a bit closer together.

These Asian-American, Mexican-American, and African-American women feel like Outsiders primarily because of their racial and ethnic backgrounds. What does it feel like to grow up both black and poor? Four young black high school students describe the town in which they live—interrupting each other as people do when they know one another well and are involved in the topic. "It's like a circle." "No, it's like a Q—one road in, around in a circle, and the same road out." They are describing a small city in northern California, a black ghetto nestled in the lush, green hills of affluent Marin County, where chardonnay and Brie are staples of life.

This city was developed in the early 1940s to house the thousands of workers employed in the shipyards of Sausalito. During the Second World War the community was integrated and thriving. At the end of the war most of the shipyard workers left, and virtually all business within the area disappeared. Black residents remained, and by 1980, according to the U.S. Bureau of the Census, the city was 75 percent black, 23 percent white, and 2 percent "other." This composition contrasts dramatically with that of Marin County, which in 1980 was 88.6 percent white, 2.5 percent black, and 8.9 percent "other."

In addition to being a predominantly black community, Marin City is also a poor community. In 1980 its median family income was $8,676; Marin County's was $29,721. In the same year 29 percent of Marin City's residents lived below the poverty line, and in 1984 the unemployment rate was 23 percent.

What are the key issues facing young women in this black ghetto today? The answer is immediate: "Drugs. Pregnancy. Having kids." Candida Dixon, an articulate seventeen-year-old senior who quickly becomes the spokesperson for the group, says, "Ninety percent of the people here are doing drugs. And maybe 50 percent of kids our age. They're doing cocaine, some weed." And, they all agree, more girls than guys are doing drugs. And alcohol—more girls than guys are drinking. Why? They all say at once that there is nothing else to do. What are the guys doing? They are out driving around in their cars, if they have one, and selling dope—"Every guy is selling dope." Candida continues, "If you don't have a car, you hang around out on the street. You get drunk or high just to have fun. Otherwise, everyone is bored, just standing around doing nothing."

"And lots of kids are pregnant," says a quiet sixteen-year-old. "And lots of abortions," chimes in another. "And at twelve and thirteen—seventh and eight graders!" states a third, as though speaking disapprovingly about the younger generation. "And they're doing it with guys twenty and older!" "And," says another, "everyone is related—everyone has sex with everyone. Sexual diseases—chlamydia, AIDS—are a big problem."

I ask them why they think all this is going on. The theories come all at once: " 'Cause the mothers are on dope." "The parents don't care; some let their kids run wild." "The mothers don't have time to teach them." "They are trying to be grown up; the girls feel important going with dope dealers."

These young women go to an integrated regional high school in a nearby upper-middle-class community, home of California yuppies, BMWs, and kids taking swimming lessons at the nearby swim club after school. These high-school students recognize that most of the people they are describing are so outside the system that they'll never get back in. They describe a desolate scene and vow that they themselves will get out. Lerae Andrade, a seventeen-year-old high-school senior, says she hopes to go to a local community college, transfer to UCLA, and become an X-ray technician. June Bennett, also seventeen, wants a fancy car and maybe to marry "someone rich." Candida, by far the liveliest of the four, plans to go to law school, marry, have kids, be "well off," with a "nice home" and "some travel." Three of the four are New American Dreamers; the fourth cannot imagine life beyond tomorrow. When I tell a friend who has worked and taught in the area that three of the four plan to leave the ghetto, she shakes her head in disbelief and says, "No one ever gets out of there."

The next morning at the San Francisco airport the magnitude of the effort necessary to fulfill their dreams struck me with incredible force and sadness. A little girl in a pink-and-white flowered dress trimmed with eyelet and lace, with puffed sleeves and a sash that ties in the back, was waiting patiently at the American Airlines gate; she was wearing white tights, white shoes, and pink barrettes to hold back her light-brown curls—Shirley Temple, Goldilocks, a young Daisy Buchanan come to life! She was five years old and going to Mexico on a holiday with her grandmother. Her name is Alison, but people call her "Muffin." A golden girl already! Seeing her after just talking with the young women from the black ghetto spotlighted the enormous gap in life chances between those who are born Insiders and those who are born Outsiders. What a long way these women have to go! Can they possibly have sufficient strength and stamina to make it out of the ghetto, one with economic, social, and psychological walls at least as high as the stone walls that separated the Jews from mainstream Italian life in sixteenth-century Venice and that gave us the word "ghetto"?

A recurring image among nonwhite girls and young women is that "everyone else," or at least everyone who counts, has blond hair and blue eyes. The United States is, of course, made up of many people who have neither blond hair nor blue eyes; but this is the image of beauty—and, more than beauty, of goodness and perhaps power—that has been transmitted throughout the decades. Still, today, in this heterogeneous society of ours, when designers want to place the ultimate stamp of authority on their clothes, furnishings, or other artifacts, a model or group of models with an upper-class, WASP image is often used. It is no accident that Ralph Lauren uses all those generations of models from children to supposed grandparents, all looking like Boston Brahmins out for a sail in Chatham Harbor on Cape Cod. The hegemony of the upper-class WASP image is still very much a part of our symbol of success and belonging and legitimate authority in this society.

Toni Morrison describes what it meant to small black girls in the 1940s to be growing up in a culture that idolized Betty Grable, Ginger Rogers, and, above all, Shirley Temple. When Claudia, the young narrator of *The Bluest Eye,* is given a Shirley Temple doll for Christmas, she describes her reaction: "I had only one desire: to dismember it. To see of what it was made, to discover the dearness, to find the beauty, the desirability that had escaped me, but apparently only me . . . All the world had agreed that a blue-eyed, yellow-haired, pink-skinned doll was what every girl child treasured." But while Claudia readily admits that at first she "destroyed white baby dolls" and, moreover, wanted to do the same to "little white girls" in order to discover the "secret of the magic they weaved on others," in time she, too, learned to "worship" Shirley Temple ("knowing, even as I learned, that the change was adjustment without improvement"). Today, when people are haunted by being "different," they need only to go to the nearest optician, where they can purchase contact lenses that will instantly alter the color of their eyes. We should not be surprised to learn that blue eyes are by far the most popular.

Sociologist Patricia Hill Collins discusses the importance of

"Black women's insistence on self-definition, self-valuation and the necessity for a Black female-centered analysis":

> The status of being the "other" implies being "other than" or different from the assumed norm of white male behavior. In this model, powerful white males define themselves as subjects, the true actors, and classify people of color and women in terms of their position vis-a-vis this white male hub. Since Black women have been denied the authority to challenge these definitions, this model consists of images that define Black women as a negative other; the virtual antithesis of positive male images.

This analysis is, of course, equally applicable to Native Americans, perhaps the quintessential Outsiders in American society. The Papago Indians live in the Sonoran Desert in Arizona and Mexico. It is a land of dust and cactus, thorns, century plants and prickly pear. It is a land of 115-degree summer heat, of dry reservoirs, and of jackrabbits, blackbirds, desert cottontails, and gophers. And yet when ethnobiologist Gary Paul Nabhan asked a Papago child what the desert smelled like, he responded with little hesitation, "The desert smells like rain." Ironically, it is that which is rare and treasured that gives the desert its scent. Nabhan points out that the Papago are fascinated by the unpredictability of the rain and that this fascination with unpredictability has led to a society that is "a dynamic, lively world, responsive to stormy forces that may come at any time."

One group of Papago Indians lives on a reservation in Arizona. The land, flat with mountains in the distance, is covered with sandy dirt and dotted with low brush and delicate trees. Shades of beige, brown, and taupe set off the yellowish green of the trees and provide a quiet, arid background for the houses, made of brown or sand-colored cement blocks. In the distance is a mountain covered with cactus, behind which, it is said, is a secret burial ground.

According to a physician who works at the local health clinic, the main problems of the local residents are alcohol consumption, obesity, diabetes, and unemployment. While unemployment is not as severe as it is among other groups of Native Americans, primarily because the reservation is so close to the city, most people on the reservation are nevertheless unemployed. According to one health worker, "There is nothing to do here and no transportation to get to work in the city."

Girls become pregnant at fourteen or fifteen. A health worker reported that they used to be given IUDs but that these are no longer approved. Many of the women "don't use the pill successfully"; health workers give out foam and condoms "like water." Do the men use the condoms? "No. We do it to ease our consciences."

Alberta Montoya is a thirty-two-year-old licensed public nurse who looks more like forty-two. She has five children, who range from fourteen years to nineteen months. She was eighteen at the birth of her first child and gave birth to a second child two years later. Somehow she was able to overcome the enormous disadvantage of being a single mother, finished high school, then trained to be an LPN. She feels that some of the girls on the reservation don't understand the connection between sex and pregnancy and that virtually none of them understand what they are getting themselves into when they have a baby. Some young women have had such difficult and painful childhoods, she says, that it's a wonder they survive at all.

Lucy Barrow and I stand outside of the house where she lives with her two children, a two-year-old and a baby of just four weeks, and with their father, his parents, and other family members. Ten people live in what looks to be a very small house. Lucy prefers to talk standing in the sun, leaning against a car. Beer cans are everywhere, and in the next yard is a junk heap with assorted pieces of machinery.

Lucy is eighteen. Perhaps her story illustrates the need for Papago Indians to be "responsive to stormy forces that may come at any time." Lucy seems hesitant at first about talking but gets involved in her story as she goes along.

She starts by describing how the tribal council took her older daughter from her when she was three days old: "They took her from me. She was sick, and they said I wasn't taking care of her because there was no adult living with us. They gave her to another family living far from here, but finally her father helped me to get her back.

"Now everything is okay. We live with his family, and everything seems easy. He works but keeps getting laid off. He's twenty-four. No, we're not on welfare—he gathers wood and his parents help us out."

Until now Lucy has been talking slowly, hesitantly, as though she's not sure what to say. I then ask her about her childhood, and she starts to speak with no prompting from me, picking up speed until my note taking can barely keep up with her story.

"My mother died when I was just a baby. I lived with an aunt and then was switched back and forth between my aunt and my grandma until I ran away. Then I stayed with a cousin and was going to school. They [the tribal council] took me from my cousin's and placed me in a children's home, but I ran away. I ended up in juvenile court, and they sent me to a foster home far away. I was there one year, but I didn't like it. I found out who my sister was and stayed with her for a while but was picked up and sent back to the children's home.

"Then they sent me to boarding school, and then I stayed with a lady here for two years. I quit running away and stayed there. She understood everything.

"But then I started messing up. I started meeting girls, not staying home. I would stay at their houses. So I had to go back to the children's home, but I didn't like to be there so I ran away. I didn't want to do what they wanted me to do—I didn't want to stay with other people—so I ran away. I stayed with friends. Then the police picked me up and took me to detention and they sent me back to the children's home. I didn't like to be there, but I stayed until I was released.

"I then lived with another lady. One day I went to the clinic. I said I wasn't pregnant; I didn't think I was pregnant, but they told me I was. The first lady I stayed with told me she would help me out if I would stay with her. But I didn't want to give her more trouble, so I went back to juvenile detention; but I finally went back and stayed with her while I was pregnant.

"Now I'm eighteen and I'm glad, because now I don't have to worry about where they'll send me."

When I asked Lucy what she thought her life would be like in the future, she said, "I don't know. I think about that. I need to go to school; I need to get a job so I can take care of myself and the children. I know I'm not going to be with him [the father of her children]. When's he's drinking, he gets violent. But he's nice. It's only when he's drunk. He says he's going to quit drinking. I tried to get help for him, for his drinking, but he doesn't want help. He has a terrible temper. He used to hit me a lot, but now he watches himself. Now when he's drinking he goes off to be by himself and comes back when he's sober. When I want to go for help at the clinic, he says we can solve our problems ourselves.

"I don't know what to do when he's drunk—I don't know how to treat him. He gets mad and yells at us. When he's sober, he does lot of things for us. It's just when he drinks. My only problem is the drinking part."

Among the young women I interviewed, there were clearly levels of Outsider-ness. There are those young women who are transient Outsiders. Many adolescents fall into this category: after a few years, they will find their group, their goals, their dreams. Some who are more fundamentally outside the culture because of race, religion, class, or family structure will succeed in spite of their Outsider status. These are the lucky ones, the talented, the super-bright, the ones who are able to develop, in the words of W.E.B. DuBois, a "true self-consciousness" and separate their image of themselves from society's image of them. Some will succeed in some sense because of the strength and insight they have gained by coping with being outside of the system. But many young women, as American society is at present constructed, are permanent Outsiders. They have no dreams for themselves. The most they can hope for is a future for their children. They themselves may never feel part of the culture; they may never feel entitled to a future.

While Americans are often held to a middle-class or upper-middle-class standard of behavior and achievement under the prevailing myth that everyone has an equal chance at achieving success, the reality is that the opportunities are far from equal. Young people who grow up in a technologically advanced society but do not even learn to read and write know that they will always be outside the system; Americans who do not have enough to eat while the government pays farmers millions not to grow crops are being told they are expendable; and children who spend months, perhaps years, in roach-infested welfare hotels are being sent a clear message about their value to society. The ideology of the American Dream may be based on the notion that we Americans control our own destiny; but in reality, our destiny is often based on myriad factors over which we have little or no control.

Perhaps in no other area is our ideology as remote from our practice as in the area of education. We communicate to our young people every day our hopes and expectations for them by the condition of the schools they attend, the quality of the teaching, the attitude of administrators. But while we believe that democracy should "begin at the schoolhouse door" and that every child should have an equal chance in the race toward success, we know that in reality, life chances vary enormously by class, race, ethnic group, gender, and even geography, and that these differing life chances are mirrored in the educational system.

According to sociologists Peter W. Cookson, Jr., and Caroline Hodges Persall, authors of *Preparing for Power: America's Elite Boarding Schools,* certain schools train select young people for a life of power and privilege and enable elite families to maintain their social class. The young women and men in these schools learn how to exercise power over others, how to have the "habit of command," how to acquire "taste," how to use money and yet conceal it, how to be elite and yet "disguise their eliteness," and learn, above all, that they are worthy of power and privilege. Cookson and Persall describe how even the physical atmosphere creates a sense of individual worth:

Wood paneled rooms are graced with antique furniture, oil paintings, and china bowls brimming with fresh-cut flowers . . .

In one sense the beauty of prep school campuses is an exterior validation of the student's sense that "Yes, I am special," or perhaps even, "Yes, I am beautiful." A headmaster articulated his belief that architecture affects a student's psyche when he reported that a student said, "This school requires quality in what I do, because I have leaded glass windows in my bedroom."

If paneled rooms and leaded glass windows signify the expectation of quality work, what are the messages of schools with "insufficient heat," "perennially clogged toilets," and "inadequate lighting"? What are schools such as one in the South Bronx, "a 66-year-old dull, brick building down in a landscape of vacant lots, dead cars, stray dogs and troubled men," telling the students about society's commitment to their future? When suburban schools look like affluent community colleges and inner-city schools look like London after the blitz, what are we telling our young people? If some schools are preparing students for power, can we not postulate that other schools, those in our poorest neighborhoods, are all too often training many of their young people for a life of failure and despair? Many of our young people do not come out of school with the skills or the credentials to work in the regular economy. Why, then, are we surprised at the rate of teen pregnancy, crack addiction, gang membership, or at the flourishing of the underground economy?

The messages are clear—that nothing is too good for the children of the elite and that not even the bare minimum will be provided to the children of the poor and near-poor. As a 1988 report issued by the Carnegie Foundation for the Advancement of Teaching stated, urban schools are "little more than human storehouses to keep young people off the streets." The report continues, "No other crisis—a flood, a health epidemic, a garbage strike or even snow removal—would be as calmly accepted without full-scale emergency intervention."

If young people who receive an inferior education are often outside the system, what about the growing number of homeless people in the United States? Are they the ultimate outsiders? Estimates of the number of the homeless in the U.S. vary widely, from the Reagan administration estimate of 250,000 to the estimate of the National Coalition for the Homeless of as many as three million people.

According to a survey conducted in forty-seven cities by the Partnership for the Homeless, during the winter of 1987 families with children became the largest segment of the homeless population. From November 1986 to mid-March 1987 the number of homeless families rose by 25 percent; this increase meant that by

March 1987 families with children made up 35 percent of the homeless—the largest group within the homeless population. What messages are we sending these Americans? What does it mean to grow up homeless in America?

The effects of homelessness, particularly among mothers and children, can be devastating. The homeless receive grossly inadequate medical care and frequently have a far higher rate of health problems than do other comparable groups. A recent study indicated that one out of every six homeless children suffers from chronic health problems. Homeless children frequently are unable to attend school because schools are reluctant to accept students on a "temporary" basis. Conditions are incredibly crowded, often several people to a room, with a lack of cooking facilities and grossly inadequate sanitation. Often families housed in emergency shelters eat only one hot meal a day. Moreover, these shelters are often places of violence and exploitation. Drugs are sold freely, alcoholism is rampant, teenage girls are recruited into prostitution, and fights and child abuse become everyday occurrences.

Not far from the Presbyterian church in Westchester—symbolic of all that seems safe and secure in American society—nearly seventy homeless adults and children are housed in a motel. The rooms have neither hot plates nor refrigerators. The only way to keep milk is if you are lucky enough to have a cooler.

Most of the adults in this motel are young black single mothers. Lisa, twenty-one years old, is the mother of three children, ages three, two, and ten months. She and her children were evicted from their apartment; prior to that, she had worked driving a van for the disabled. She says that the worst thing about living in the motel is the stigma. Even when she crosses the street to go to the supermarket, "people follow you like you might steal something." Lisa dreams of a job and a two-bedroom apartment.

It is clear that there are many levels of Outsider-ness among young women in American society—from those who feel temporarily outside their family/community/society to those who because of a complex convergence of factors become virtual pariahs. While we must recognize that young women of any class, race, and family background may at some time feel like Outsiders, that an unhappy childhood, an unintended pregnancy, abuse of alcohol or drugs may precipitate hopelessness and alienation, we must also recognize that the structure of American society and American social policy often combine to thrust millions of young women into either temporary or permanent Outsider status. Growing up with little sense of community or connection to others, growing up poor in an affluent society with little hope of moving into the working or middle class, growing up nonwhite in a profoundly racist society, growing up illiterate in a complex technological society, growing up homeless in a society that largely ignores and disdains the homeless, and growing up female and feeling passive and powerless to determine one's future leads all too many young women to feel disconnected, irrelevant, and often despairing. While the New American Dreamers hope to take control of their lives and capture some of the power and wealth American society promises, and the Neotraditionalists hope to connect and combine their worlds of work and home, to these young women, the Outsiders, the American Dream seems not only remote and unattainable but often unimaginable as well.

PART II

Realities

In Part I, I attempted to portray young women's dreams about their lives, about their futures. They speak of their hopes and their concerns, of their anxiety and ambivalence about their future roles, and, in some cases, of their hopelessness and despair.

Part II is an examination of key aspects of the reality of women's lives in the United States today. My goals in presenting this counterpoint between the young women's visions of the future and the reality of life for women in late-twentieth-century America are twofold: first, to present the cultural context in which young women are developing and maturing, and second, to evaluate the likelihood of their living the kinds of lives to which they aspire. In chapter 4 I examine selected aspects of popular culture in the hope of deciphering some of the powerful messages women relentlessly receive about who they should be, what they should look like, and how they should play their multiple roles. Some of these forms of popular culture may have more direct impact on young women than others, but my working assumption is that any major current within popular culture both reflects societal values and contributes to their formation, and therefore has significant impact on our images of ourselves, our personal values, and on our processes of decision making. A young woman does not need to watch "Thirtysomething" or to have seen *Fatal Attraction* in order to be affected, however indirectly, by their existence. Certain elements of popular culture virtually take on a life of their own, become an integral part of cumulative American experience, and thus have impact on our lives, often despite our best intentions.

In chapter 5 I attempt to separate myth from reality around the issue of sexuality. How do young women feel about sex? How much have sexual mores really changed over the last quarter-century? Has there been a "sexual revolution" for these young women? Why does the United States have one of the highest teenage pregnancy rates in the industrialized world? How is sex connected to their search for intimacy? What are young women looking for in their sexual relationships?

In chapter 6 I examine through the experiences and words of women in their thirties and early forties the realities of seeking and finding a serious love relationship. The vast majority of younger women with whom I have spoken hope to find such a relationship. What is the likelihood they will do so? What are some of the rewards and dangers of intimacy today?

Virtually all of the young women described in Part I plan to work during their adult years. Chapter 7 explores how their hopes and dreams about work compare with the reality of women's work today and in the foreseeable future. Some view work as its own reward, but most see it as a stepping stone to upward mobility, to an affluent life-style. How realistic is this view? What work do women really do? How much status do they really have? What are they really paid? How much progress has been made over the past quarter-century, and what are the barriers to further progress?

And finally, what about the children? Most of the young women plan to have children. While many do not seem to have a clear picture of how their children would be cared for, others are very concerned about how they would combine work and mothering. What are the realities of this dilemma? What are their viable options? What do the options—and lack of options—tell us about our values and priorities as a society? Chapter 8 raises these issues.

In each of these areas I have attempted to compare young women's hopes, assumptions, and images about life in the United States with the current day-to-day reality of women's lives. I have often used the concrete experiences of somewhat "older" women in order to portray that reality. My hope is that through a clear delineation of the gap between dreams and realities we can examine and evaluate the dreams that are being transmitted to our young people. We can then, in Part III, see with greater clarity the steps we must take in order to develop a society in which all of our young people have dreams for the future and in which their dreams have a reasonable chance of being translated into reality.

CHAPTER 4

Mixed Messages

Love the mansion. But do I really want to be mayor?
Woman speaking on the telephone
in a Diane Von Furstenberg
advertisement

She comes out every evening in a different sexy dress—some with ruffles, some strapless, some with sequins or lace, some short, some long, provocative yet somehow sweet, but all ultrafeminine, the old-fashioned way. And she's always smiling, smiling and clapping. Not applauding—clapping. She's Vanna White, recognizable by millions of Americans. She walks, she pirouettes, she models jewelry and furs, and she turns letters. She is the "girl" of the fifties, the Barbie doll come alive on our television screens six times a week—in some cities twice a day, six times a week.

And then there is Bonnie Blair. Lean and determined, she skated into our consciousness in her peach-and-gray body suit, which was neither masculine nor feminine but was made to help her do the job. When she realized she had set a world-record time of 39.10 seconds and had won the gold medal in the 500-meter speed-skating race at the 1988 Winter Olympic games, she threw her arms up and her head back in a thrilling moment of accomplishment and exultation.

Two images of women: the woman who is and the woman who does; the woman who is exhibited and exhibits herself as a commodity and the woman who because of skill and hard work is valued for her accomplishments. This duality of images of woman is all around us: on the one hand, the women lawyers and M.B.A.s in their suits, carrying briefcases, the perfect wife/mother/professional of the television sitcoms, the oh-so-successful women jumping, leaping, running in action shots about the pages of fashion magazines; and on the other hand, the women featured in the *Sports Illustrated* "swimsuit issue," the socialites on the women's pages in the latest designer clothes, and the nude women provocatively displayed in the pages of *Playboy* and *Penthouse*.

What are our young women to fathom from these disparate images? What are the messages we send them in our popular culture with every advertisement, every song, every film, and every sitcom? What are we telling them about our expectations of their future roles in society?

There is no doubt that woman as success story has been a major theme of the 1980s: women in law, women in medicine, women in banking, even women on Wall Street—but also women employees who have a clever idea for the firm and are promoted to vice-president, and homemakers who have a clever idea and become successful entrepreneurs. Above all, there is the image of the professional woman who, combining hard work and commitment, "makes it" in the world of work.

In magazines, in the "style" sections of newspapers, and on television she is often portrayed—this prototype, this model of how to do it all, be it all, and have it all—as outgoing, attractive, personable, bright, and "assertive" but surely not too "aggressive." She is likely to be in her thirties; she exercises, has a snappy executive wardrobe, flies all over the country or the world with relative ease, is comfortable eating alone in upscale restaurants, and, while never pushy, certainly does not allow the maître d' to give her a table in front of the kitchen.

If she is married, her husband is comradely, egalitarian, "supportive," and "does his share" at home. If there are children, they are smiling and happy and she is involved with them, too. Despite her often hectic schedule, she makes time for their plays and recitals, and the family gets away for companionable weekends together— often skiing. Above all, she is confident, fulfilled—and she can even whip up a quick, elegant dinner for eight when necessary. She's a woman for our time.

But despite the number of women in the work force and the number who are the primary breadwinners and caretakers of their families, the role of sex object is by no means obsolete. The objectification of women is still all around us. Beauty pageants remain a booming business for the sponsors, the participants, and the media. The onlookers are in a real sense participants as well. While some of us may scoff and mock this archaic vestige of another era, an estimated 55 million Americans—75 percent of them women—tune in each year to watch the Miss America Pageant. Many yearn, sometimes against their will, to look just like the contestants, and feel any deviation must be due to personal failure. "If only I dieted enough and exercised enough," the fantasy goes, "I could [should] look like that, too." If we doubt that these women are models for how millions of Americans would like to look, we need only examine the statistics on diseases such as anorexia nervosa and bulimia ("women's diseases," virtually unknown in the male population but particularly prevalent among women in their late teens and early twenties) to realize that women are tyrannized by the desire to be thin. A recent study reported in the journal *Pediatrics* found that by the age of seven girls come to believe that thin is beautiful. By adolescence most girls think they are fatter than they really are; according to the physician who conducted the study, "One young girl broke into tears when her mother asked her to go for a swim. The girl said she'd look too fat in a swimsuit, when in fact her weight was normal for her height."

And, of course, it is not just the Miss America Pageant but the Miss Universe, Miss USA, Miss Teen USA, and all the state and local pageants that feed into the grand finales. That amounts to a lot of young women in bathing suits walking up and down a lot of runways and being judged, for the most part, on how they look. In 1987, for example, some eighty thousand women vied for the title of Miss America in local and state contests. No matter how well they juggle or sing or play "Malagüeña" on the accordion, we all know that it is their measurements and pretty faces and how well they turn that are really being judged. And the message is not lost on the young women who are watching and trying to figure out who they are, what they want to be, and how they will get there. According to clinical psychologist Dr. Susan Schenkel, the Miss America competition is "the contemporary embodiment of the traditional fairy tale: it's like magic elevating you to success. Because most of us are exposed to these images at a very young age, they remain a visceral part of us, no matter how much we may resist them intellectually." Dr. Rita Freedman, author of *Beauty Bound,* a book about images of women's beauty, states, "Physical attractiveness is still a major source of women's power and they tune into these shows to find out what an attractive female is supposed to look like. They want to know how to package themselves."

To "win," it may even be necessary to transform not only one's body but also one's ethnic image. The 1988 Miss California, Marlise Ricardos, tried three times to win the title. It was only after she changed her hair color from brunet to blond and wore blue contact lenses when she competed that she became entitled to represent California in the 1988 Miss America contest in Atlantic City. As journalist Anne Taylor Fleming has observed, "She's the ultimate self-made competitor, a chemically 'sun-streaked' miss who rid herself of both pounds and ethnic identity to please pageant judges."

Women are also told in a variety of ways that although many of them may be executives on the way up, they must also still be warm, expressive, and frivolous, perhaps more concerned about what they wear than about the next corporate merger. An excellent example of this double message is an engaging Smirnoff vodka advertisement that shows three young, upwardly mobile women having drinks (all with vodka, presumably) while laughing, gesturing in typically feminine ways, and admiring a pair of red, slingback, spike-heel shoes. The message the ad seems to be giving is, "You're working women now, you're out for a drink without a man, you're 'liberated,' but we know that underneath all that you're still into feelings and fashion."

This ad at least presumes by their clothes that these are working women out for a relaxing, good time. A far more disturbing example of advertising that seems to be urging a retreat from feminism is the Diane Von Furstenberg ad in the *New York Times* special section *Fashions of the Times* in February 1988. A woman is sitting on a chair talking on the telephone, one shoe kicked off, her fashionably short skirt halfway up her thigh. She says, "Love the mansion. But do I really want to be mayor?" The next page shows her with a tall stack of packages wrapped in a way that indicates they are from fashionable shops, and gives the answer: "No, there are better ways of having it all—and for a lot less!" What are the implications of this incredible ad? That the only reason women are interested in being mayor is to live in the mansion? That they are not really interested in power and substance and hard work? How is our woman in the advertisement going to get the "mansion" and all those consumer goods? There is certainly no indication that she plans to go into law, banking, or medicine instead of politics. Is the implication really that she is going to get them through a man, that she would rather marry the mayor than be one? In 1988? What is going on?

Recent fashion trends have surely indicated that there has been substantial backlash in reaction to the women's movement and to the changing nature of women's roles over the past twenty-five years. In 1987, just about the time that women's wages reached the all-time pinnacle of 65 percent of men's wages, fashion took an abrupt turn—many would say backwards. The stylish look moved from relatively simple clothes with shoulder pads, a modified dress-for-success look, to plunging necklines, bare shoulders, "waistlines snugly fitted, and skirts . . . rounded in an egg shape, tightly draped, or flared and poufed with myriad petticoats." Tops are "translucent if not transparent," dresses often "look like lingerie, with slip tops and lacy edges." And everywhere the short skirt. Skirts two, three, and four inches above the knee in the board room, the courtroom, and the operating room? Skirts above the knee to sell insurance and real estate or to do the taxes of a Fortune 500 company? Are women really going to get pay equity or run for the House of Representatives in a plunging neckline and a draped skirt? Why did we see "the most seductive, feminine-looking clothes since the days of Napoleon I's Empire" in the late 1980s? Did we try to go too far too fast? Is this the backlash to all those career women of the past decade? One designer said that women in his clothes will look "like little dolls"; one analyst has termed it "bimbo chic." These clothes, which hark back to the fifties but are far more provocative, are clearly not for the aspiring CEO or the nurse's aide. To their credit, millions of American women rejected these extreme styles and simply stopped buying for the period of time when that was all that was available. While the shortest skirts have all but disappeared, many clothes still end an inch or two above the knee, giving women a little-girl look hardly compatible with positions of power and respect in a society in which the dark blue suit is the ultimate badge of authority.

There is, moreover, the stereotypic look of the prostitute about some of the clothes and poses in many contemporary advertisements: black net stockings; see-through black lace; women draped over chairs, waiting to be used. The most flagrant advertisements showing woman-as-erotic-object and man-as-powerful-manipulator are those for Guess jeans. These ads, which appear in a variety of women's and general-interest magazines, are frequently several pages long, as though they are telling a story. The man is older, perhaps in his fifties, sinister looking, with dark glasses; the women are young, intense, and often partially nude. In one picture a woman, nude above the waist, her skirt pulled up to show black net stockings, sits on the man's lap. There is a table nearby indicating that they have had dinner and possibly a good deal of wine. In another picture in the series, a young woman is leaning over him as though she is about to mount him. He has a faint smile, almost a sneer, on his face. He is calling the shots; she is there to amuse him, to service him. The final picture shows a young woman, in her late teens or early twenties, dressed only in what looks to be a black leotard and a jean jacket (jean jackets can be worn anywhere!), kneeling at his feet. We know he is rich, because the door to the room is in dark-grained wood with a handsome brass handle. She looks up at him inquiringly, obediently. Is she about to perform fellatio? Is he going to beat her, whip her? There is certainly a sadomasochistic tone to this series of advertisements. At the very least, we are seeing the "ritualization of subordination," as sociologist Erving Goffman has termed it, which is often manifested by "lowering oneself physically in some form . . . of prostration." There is no doubt in these ads who is in charge.

Yet another series of advertisements for Guess jeans is centered on the toreador theme. The women are again young, in provocative clothes, and are either waiting for the great man to appear or swooning, almost literally, against a poster of the handsome bull-fighter. On the opposite page the toreador is shown in action: on a horse, the adoring multitudes all around, fighting the bull, and finally walking off in glory to resounding cheers. It is no accident that Guess jeans uses the most macho of all male images—the bull fighter—and pictures women as flimsily dressed, yearning, passive, carried away by desire. These advertisements seem targeted to the adolescent young woman. Is it the ad agencies' view that adolescents are "turned on" by pictures of submissive women and dominant men, by implied sadomasochism? There is certainly evidence that sadomasochism sells in the culture at large; much of the content in sex shops and sex magazines and the incredible amount of violence in films and on television attest to the pervasiveness of the themes of cruelty and pain. Sociologist Lynn Chancer has, in fact, suggested that sadomasochistic relationships are deeply imbedded in many aspects of American culture, particularly those that involve male-female interaction.

These are not the only ads in which women are portrayed as being "carried away," either literally or figuratively. In magazine after magazine, in image after image, women are literally being carried by men, leaning on men, being helped down from a height of two feet, or figuratively being carried away by emotion. When men and women are portrayed together, men are invariably solid citizens, responsible, dependable, in charge, busy; women are emoting, leaning, giddy, carried away—clearly not the persons you would choose to perform your neurosurgery, to handle your money, or even to care for your child.

While many designers have retreated from the extreme clothes of 1987, in part because women refused to buy what one observer called "a new boffo outrage each season," women are still often portrayed as little girls, seductive, passive, dependent, and, above all, beautiful and thin, with knock-'em-dead figures. After twenty-five years of the women's movement, is it how we look that is really important after all?

Women's magazines are key transmitters of values, attitudes, information, and the latest consensus about appropriate behavior.

They help to socialize young women into their adult roles and enable more mature women to stay *au courant* with norms, expectations, and style. In a period of rapidly changing expectations, they have played a crucial role in molding women's attitudes toward work, toward family life, and toward themselves.

In an effort to understand the messages young women are receiving, fourteen women's magazines for March 1988 were systematically examined for content, for the ways in which women were portrayed, and for the values and norms that were both subtly and directly communicated. The magazines, chosen for their appeal to a broad spectrum of women by age, class, and interest, were *Seventeen, Mademoiselle, Glamour, Cosmopolitan, Harper's Bazaar, Vogue, Ladies' Home Journal, Working Mother, New Women, Self, Working Woman, Savvy, Ms.,* and *Essence.* All of the magazines focused, in varying degrees, on beauty tips, hair, fashion, fitness, health, food (both nutrition and recipes), and work. Virtually everyone pictured is clearly middle class; several magazines (*Vogue, Savvy,* and *Harper's Bazaar*) are upper middle class in tone, with an emphasis on upper-class life-style. A few of the magazines openly disparage the lower middle and working classes: a comic strip in *Seventeen* indicates that any high-school student foolish enough to invite a guy who works in an auto muffler shop to the school prom will find that he is no better than a prehuman ape, and *Mademoiselle* cautions women who want to move up the career ladder not to "leave the ratty little sweater on the chair just like the secretary does." Among the hundreds of features, viewpoints, articles, occasional fiction, advice, and how-to columns, there was not one instance of members of the working class being depicted in a positive light.

The overall message, transmitted both explicitly and implicitly, is "You can be all you want to be." You can be fit, thin, and trim; you can have a good job, be upwardly mobile, and invest your money wisely; you can wear stunning suits in your march toward success or slinky, sexy, almost childlike clothes, if you prefer; you can have an attractive, no-fuss hairstyle and blend just the right, ever-flattering makeup; you can have great (albeit safe) sex and know just what to do when *he* cannot perform; and, above all, you really *can* have it all—a warm, close family life and lucrative, pleasurable work. You really *can* have both love and success. It may mean starting your own business at home, but there are all those success stories to serve as models: Mrs. Fields, who has made millions on her chocolate-chip cookies and looks gorgeous too; the woman from Virginia who does $1 million worth of business annually making flags and is about to license national franchises; or the woman from Scottsdale, Arizona, who delivers teddy bears as special-occasion gifts the way FTD sells flowers and currently owns two stores, twenty-three franchises, and has annual sales of $1.5 million. What could be easier? And all that is involved are skills that women already have! Women are being told that they can use traditional female skills and make a fortune without ever leaving the kitchen or the sewing machine. The implication is that the fulfillment of the American Dream can be simply one clever idea or marketing strategy away.

Different magazines appeal, of course, to different constituencies: in March 1988, *Seventeen* features prom gowns and many advertisements for sanitary products; *Working Mother* had numerous articles on parenting and homemaking; *Vogue* and *Harper's Bazaar* showed the trendiest and most expensive clothes; and *Essence* dealt, for the most part, with issues particularly relevant to black women. But the overall message is that "working women" are "on the way up," that "you're headed for the top," and that you can "be your own boss."

Not only can you remake your career but you can also remake your looks. The "makeover" (frequently called the "five-minute makeover") is ubiquitous and offers the promise of instant results. Often using "ordinary" people, neither models nor film stars, the makeover is meant to show us all how much more appealing and contemporary we can look by the ever-changing standards of beauty. Are we to have accented lips or accented eyes? Slightly unmanageable long hair or a trim, stylish short cut? Must we still diet until we are reed slim, or is it once again fashionable to look voluptuous? If you do not look like the models and celebrities smiling on every page, you are not exercising properly, eating the correct food, getting the right haircut, using the appropriate gel or mousse; or perhaps you need cosmetic surgery—liposuction, eyelid surgery, nose alteration, or breast enlargement or reduction. The

magazines often feature pro and con articles about cosmetic surgery, but the bottom line is that it is yet another legitimate weapon,
currently very much in vogue, in women's endless struggle toward
a more attractive face and body.

"Older" women are frequently exhorted by women's magazines
to be beautiful, fit, and above all, youthful. While the positive
aspects of the emphasis on mid-life beauty and fitness are that
women in their forties, fifties, sixties, and beyond often see themselves today as vibrant, sexually attractive and truly in the prime
of life, there are negative aspects as well. Columnist Ellen Goodman
points out that the women who are currently held up as paragons

> raise the threshold of self-hate faster than the age span. . . .
> Those of us who failed to look like Brooke Shields at seventeen
> can now fail to look like Victoria Principal at thirty-three and
> like Linda Evans at forty-one and like Sophia Loren at fifty.
> When Gloria Steinem turned fifty . . . she updated her famous
> line from forty. She said, "This is what fifty looks like." With
> due apologies to the cult of midlife beauty, allow me two
> words: "Not necessarily."

And what is so sad, and in some sense shameful, is that a broad
spectrum of businesses and advertisers are playing on that self-
hatred in their unending quest to sell products and services. It is
the combination of self-hatred and "willful suspension of disbelief"
that leads women, over and over, to those cosmetics counters,
health spas, and plastic surgeons. Maybe we can come just a little
closer to what they tell us we should look like. . . .

Even *Ms.* promised that "whatever it is we want, we can succeed." Despite the opening paragraph of the editor's essay, which
suggests that all women might not choose the stressful life of a
"corporate or government job," the ultimate message is that whatever we do choose, "we can succeed." The *Essence* editor's column
gave the same message: that although there are powerful forces
"arrayed against us—racism, sexism, poverty, homelessness, illit-
eracy, poor health"—black women must reach for the sky, saying
"I can!" The message is that changing our lives is fundamentally
within our control: "If you're living below your standard, get busy

devising a plan to improve your life. If your work is a bore, renew your attitude. . . . Surround yourself with positive people who encourage you. . . . Each of us must become an active participant in empowering ourselves and our people. Only the single-minded succeed."

To their credit, *Essence* and *Ms.* were the only magazines that suggested that the well-being of the individual is at all connected with the well-being of the larger group and made a point of urging their readers to work toward "empowering ourselves and our people."

Are women's magazines the Horatio Alger novels of our time? Part of their mission is to help women cope with a rapidly changing society. From the "tips" on hair, fashion, and makeup to the reviews of books, films, and drama and the longer, often thoughtful, articles on health, sexual mores, or work options, they put women in touch with current attitudes, norms, and expectations. And at the same time they reaffirm the American Dream: by telling women repeatedly that they can, if they work hard enough, exercise long enough, eat correctly, and dress fashionably, achieve their dreams, these powerful agents of socialization are reinforcing the ideology that in America the individual can indeed make of herself whatever she chooses. Since there is rarely a suggestion that opportunity is related to economic, political, or social factors beyond the control of the individual, if a woman does not succeed after all these how-tos, perhaps she has no one to blame but herself. Moreover, the constant emphasis on celebrities, on stars, on those who have succeeded beyond most people's wildest dreams serves to reinforce the message.

Some of the magazines deal explicitly with the American Dream and extend it beyond the individual to the family unit. With the March 1988 issue, *Ms.* began a new series entitled "Tracking the Dream." In the series the magazine plans to explore "how families are faring in the late 1980s." For their first family they chose a young couple with two small children who live in a small town in Pennsylvania. In this era of divorce, single-parent families, step-families, urban alienation, and the "new poor," *Ms.* chose a family straight out of Norman Rockwell's America. The husband works repairing furnaces; his wife is a full-time homemaker. They live in the same community in which they were raised, with their extended family all around, able and willing to help one another. Their two children are "blond, curly-haired, blue-eyed, and have the [family's] famous . . . dimples." They are a Shirley Temple, "Leave It to Beaver," "Father Knows Best" family come to life.

Although their 1987 income was $29,565, just the U.S. median family income, "they have acquired a home [traditional Dutch colonial] of which they are rightfully proud, they eat well, and they enjoy life." They have a swimming pool in the back and swings in the basement playroom. They don't buy on credit; nor, by the way, do they vote. The husband does not want his wife to work and expects his daughters to live the same life as their mother. *Ms.* admits that this family is representative of only 6 percent of all Americans—those who "still live in families with a working father, a homemaker mother, and dependent children." And if we factor in living in small-town America with a readily available family support system, they are typical of an even smaller percentage of the American population.

Why, then, would *Ms.* choose such an old-fashioned, atypical family for their first "documentary portrait of American families today" and then portray their life-style in such glowing terms? Do the *Ms.* editors think that we want to believe in this traditional image of the United States, where men are men and women are women and children have dimples and grandparents are there to help out? Do they think that reaffirming our image of an America straight out of the Frank Capra film *It's a Wonderful Life* will woo more traditional women to the *Ms.* readership? But of course in selling themselves they are selling an ideology; they are reinforcing a largely outdated image of America that has clear implications for the formulation of social policy. *Ms.* is clearly sending a message that self-reliance, mutual aid, the importance of the extended family and traditional family roles are alive and well in the United States in the late 1980s. With families like this, why would we need job training programs, day care, or a comprehensive family policy? Did they choose this particular family in order to reaffirm that old American Dream, to say to the faint of heart, the disbelievers, the urban cynics, "You see, it can still be done"? If it had been put onto videotape, the entire piece could have been a Ronald Reagan campaign commercial.

That same month, March 1988, *Ladies' Home Journal* also ran an article on the American Dream. The lives and finances of four families, each with two children, were described: a black family with an annual income of $28,600, and three white families, one with an income of $43,000, another with an income of $60,000, and the last with an income of $150,000. Each of the families has two parents, and in all but one both parents work. (In the remaining family, the wife plans to return to work within the year, when the younger child enters school full-time.) All of the families own their own homes and various luxury consumer goods—VCRs, stereos, a cabin cruiser, central air conditioning—and one has taken an anniversary trip to Hawaii. The family earning $28,600 says that life is a constant struggle but stresses that they have come a long way from the near-poverty days early in their marriage. The family earning $150,000 is striving for an income of $250,000; the husband states, "Success is being able to work a four-day week and still get what you want." The *Ladies' Home Journal* summarizes, "The American Dream of the good life for all is still very much with us."

In all these magazines, scattered among the hairstyles, the fashion layouts, and the endless advertisements is perhaps the central message: the American Dream is alive and well. If you work hard, believe in yourself, and consume relentlessly, you too can be a success in America.

One of the most appealing twists on the "having it all" theme was pictured on the cover and inside the December 1987 *Harper's Bazaar* in an extensive and lavish layout. Amid the holiday glitter, the "festive fantasy" of "blazing gold sequins," "paillettes," and "huge faux gems," actresses Shelley Long and Phylicia Rashad and model Christie Brinkley were pictured in sumptuous designer gowns and jewels while holding their own young children, also dressed in lavish outfits. *Bazaar*'s Christmas issue is not only celebrating gorgeous women who are performers and mothers ("The most popular mom on television, 'The Cosby Show's Phylicia Rashad does an equally good job of parenting in reality" and

"Nothing expresses the true meaning of this season more clearly than the special glow between mother and child") but is also celebrating the family ("For even in this age of high-tech and high finance, the primal bonds of family—no matter how stretched or strained—remain squarely at the heart of Christmas"). Nothing is sacred in the selling of consumerism—especially at Christmas time. The message is clear: these women truly have it all—money, beauty, fabulous careers, husbands, and beautiful babies. Should the rest of us expect anything less?

Yet another example of the having-it-all-including-baby theme is a Donna Karan advertisement in the August 1988 issue of *Vogue*. The "mother" is lying half on the bed and half on the floor, dressed in a black, scoop-backed bodysuit. She is presumably a professional woman, since she is reading papers concerning shareholders. Strewn around the bedroom are clothes, pocketbooks, shoes, and scads of jewelry. A baby is sitting on the bed, presumably a girl, also "working" with pen and paper, an open notebook nearby. The child is wearing nothing more than a diaper and a necklace— a Donna Karan necklace, one assumes. The message again is clear: it *is* possible to have it all—and, by the way, it is never too early to teach a girl to want pretty things!

If the fashion world and women's magazines are giving us contradictory messages about women's roles and goals in the late 1980s—that women should achieve in the workplace and take greater control of their lives but that they should also look great, feel great, consume ceaselessly, and play the old roles of sex object, dependent woman, and devoted mom—what is television telling us? According to a recent study conducted by the National Commission on Working Women, nearly one million adolescent girls watch prime-time network television programs every night, and many of the programs they watch contain adolescent female characters. The study found that "viewers are likely to see girls with no visible skills, no favorite subjects in school, no discussions about college majors or vocational plans. . . . These images create the impression that one can magically jump from an adolescence of dating and shopping to a well-paid professional career." The report continues by pointing out that "on TV, girls' looks count for more than their brains." Plots focus on shopping, makeup, and dating—

girls are often pictured as misfits if they do not have a date on Friday or Saturday night. Adolescent girls outnumber boys on prime time, but boys are usually the center of the action while girls play more passive, subsidiary roles. Furthermore, 94 percent of adolescent girls on TV are middle class or wealthy; very few are working class or poor. In reality, over one-third of teenage girls live in families with incomes under $20,000.

The study does find some positives—intelligent teenagers who are pictured as likable and successful—but they are relatively rare. Far more common are outmoded, insidious stereotypes that suggest that young women are shallow, vain, materialistic—and sometimes the traditional dumb, sexy blonde. On one episode of "Who's the Boss?" "a young practical nurse, depicted as a dim-witted buxom blonde, claims she entered nursing after failing beauty school, where she was undone by the pressure of remembering different shades of nail polish. Unable to wash a dish or run an appliance, she's eager to give Tony, her patient, a sponge bath. 'I'm Doreen the practical nurse,' she purrs. 'I do it all.' "

The depiction of adult women on TV tells us, on the one hand, that working women are very much part of the culture. Women are lawyers ("L.A. Law" and "The Cosby Show"); women are doctors ("Heartbeat"); women are members of the police force ("Cagney and Lacey"); women manage bars ("Cheers"); and they even run funeral homes ("Frank's Place"). Women can be on their own ("The Days and Nights of Molly Dodd," "Designing Women," "Kate and Allie," "Murphy Brown"), can kill as easily as men ("Miami Vice" and assorted other programs), and can find alternatives to the nuclear family ("Designing Women," "The Golden Girls," "Kate and Allie," and even "Beauty and the Beast"). But what we still rarely find on TV are straightforward, intelligent, admirable heroines who are working class (Mary Beth Lacey of "Cagney and Lacey" was a notable exception; and, sad to say, that excellent, human, courageous program was canceled at the end of the 1987–88 season) or poor or even a realistic depiction of what life is really like for working women today. The female lawyers on "L.A. Law" are simply too stunning, too elegant, too affluent; the one featured woman on that program who is a secretary is significantly less attractive and less savvy than the female lawyers and, moreover, was for a significant period of time in love with her womanizing lawyer/boss, who takes her devotion for granted and never quite sees her as a full-fledged person. Even Miss DiPesto, the secretary on "Moonlighting," while she is a marvelously zany and lovable character, is pictured as less than attractive (particularly compared with Cybill Shepherd!), worshiping her bosses, not quite in control of her own life, someone who barely muddles through.

"Nightingales," a program supposedly about nurses, *is* in actuality, according to the managing editor of the *American Journal of Nursing,* about sex. The program, she states, is a "mindless series" which humiliates and ridicules nurses on prime time. It is unlikely to encourage women to go into nursing the way "L.A. Law" has encouraged women to go to law school.

"Roseanne," the hit sitcom of the 1988–89 season, does portray a working-class family. Both parents work, breakfast is appropriately chaotic, the husband helps out around the house, and Roseanne keeps everyone in line with firmness, wisecracks, and a considerable dose of wisdom. While the program sometimes seems to be putting down upper-middle-class pretensions, one wonders if it isn't also an upper-middle-class putdown of the working class. Roseanne solves most daily problems with a combination of clever one-liners and a level of sensitivity unusual on TV sitcoms, but her comments are often so extreme, her delivery so abrupt, and her weight so omnipresent that the program sometimes seems like a parody of working-class life rather than a sympathetic and realistic depiction.

While the viewer at least sees Cagney and Lacey and the female lawyers on "L.A. Law" at work, one rarely sees the four characters on "Designing Women" or Bill Cosby's wife working. These women may indeed work, but it is their home life, their interpersonal life that we are shown. Even in the daytime soap operas, where most women characters today "work as lawyers, surgeons, and journalists and discuss their problems over business lunches or hurried snacks in the hospital cafeteria . . . these professional women are rarely shown doing their work. What concerns them most are the problems of their family and friends and their own romantic and sexual adventures." Yet, with all the preoccupation with appearance and sex and romance, the "media's version of feminism" is, fundamentally, that "women can have, and do, it all—without help from men."

And what about all those female social workers, teachers, and firefighters out there? Couldn't they be the heroines of gripping weekly programs? They might even have problems with child care, after-school care, getting enough money together to pay the rent, or worrying about their own elderly, ailing parents. For, while much television programming has responded to the recent changes in the roles of women, both within the workplace and in the home, few programs show the nitty-gritty of daily life. "Thirtysomething" does exactly this but focuses on the upper middle class. "Frank's Place" tried to portray real life for the black working class; but, of course, Frank was a former professor—and the show was canceled after one season.

Perhaps Hope, the central female character on "Thirtysomething," tells us something about the current messages women are receiving. It is no coincidence that several young women whom I interviewed used "Thirtysomething" as a model for the lives they hoped to lead. According to a 1988 A. C. Nielsen report, 43 percent of the eighteen-to-thirty-four-year-old women surveyed watched "Thirtysomething," ranking it eleventh out of eighty-one television shows for that age group for the season. During the first season Hope, a Princeton graduate and the mother of a toddler, was at home caring for her daughter and agonizing with her friends about their possible choices and options. At the beginning of the second season, Hope had returned to work part-time, and she and Michael were still agonizing, this time over the timing of a second child. Hope had just begun to mesh her work life with her home life, but Michael was eager for another child. After an episode in which Hope imagined the lives of those who lived in their house during World War II and which focused on the fragility of human life and love, Hope succumbed. During the Christmas/Hanukkah episode, which showed Michael realizing the importance of his religious heritage, Hope announced that she was pregnant. The reaffirmation of traditional values was complete.

If Hope, intelligent, beautiful, thoughtful, upper middle class, married to Michael, sensitive, caring, and loving, cannot effectively integrate work and home, who of us can? When the high-school student from Westchester County tells me she wants to be a lawyer *and* be home to give her children the proverbial "milk and cookies" but that what she *really* wants is to be like Hope and be married to Michael, isn't she saying that she too recognizes that she cannot have it all—at least while the children are young? But while on one level she seems to understand the limitations that are built into many women's lives, on another level she has internalized the message that she must succeed, achieve, and be able to stand alone. The media have very effectively played on both sides of women's ambivalence and presented very few models of women—or, rather, families—who have managed to work out the work/family conflict.

While TV is making a gesture at portraying working women, how are men currently being portrayed? For much of the 1970s and early 1980s, the ideal American man as rendered by television was an Alan Alda type, caring, sensitive, able to relate to others' feelings as well as to his own. Frank Furillo, the captain on "Hill Street Blues," was perhaps the prototype of the sensitive, aware hero of the past decade. But by the late 1980s the new male on American television is, according to one analysis, "spontaneous, unhesitant, sure. In action drama, his antagonists are unqualifiedly bad, and he disposes of them accordingly, shooting first and getting in touch with his feelings later, if at all. In comedy, he is a womanizer, eager for the easy score." The new heroes are the "supercool, super-detached detectives" of "Miami Vice," the "lecherous bar proprietor" Sam Malone in "Cheers," and the "unreconstructed chauvinist" David Addison in "Moonlighting." And even Bill Cosby is the authoritative, all-knowing head-of-household on "The Cosby Show."

Several analysts have seen the changes in male heroes in the mid- and late 1980s as a direct reaction to the feminist movement. Glenn Caron, the original producer of "Moonlighting," has stated, "I very much wanted to see a *man* on television." The message of many recent programs is that for a man to be a *real* man, he must try to "conquer" rather than "relate," be a relentless womanizer, and surely be aggressive, willing to kill at any opportunity. The introspective male hero who sees many sides of an issue and is torn apart by his understanding of individuals and their limitations as well as society and its limitations is being replaced by characters who see issues in starker terms and who believe in individual accountability rather than societal accountability. According to sociologist Amitai Etzioni, "There is a mild reaction to the women's movement. There is some part of the population which wishes men to reassert themselves. You see, the new world turned out to be very complicated. You don't know what relationships are proper, and the world yearns for something simpler."

A few recent TV programs (for example, "Murphy Brown" and "Anything but Love") feature gutsy, risk-taking women and "wimpy" men. As one observer has noted, these programs seem to be "delving into the 'male' side of women and the 'female' side of men." But these efforts are all too rare.

Analyzing films is considerably more difficult than analyzing television programming, in part because of the wide variety of films made for different audiences: the teen film; the action film; the intellectual, arty film; the issue film. All the same, some generalizations are possible. First, there seems to have been a significant retreat from the films of the late 1970s and early 1980s, which regularly featured strong, positive, even heroic female characters: Sally Field in *Norma Rae* (1979) and *Places in the Heart* (1984), Jane Fonda in *The China Syndrome* (1979), Jessica Lange in *Frances* (1982), Meryl Streep in *Silkwood* (1983), Jane Alexander in *Testament* (1983). Over the past few years there have been Sigourney Weaver in *Gorillas in the Mist* (1988), Meryl Streep in *Out of Africa* (1986), and, most notably, Barbara Hershey in *A World Apart* (1988)—a film that features strong, serious, substantive roles for three women, including a black and an eleven-year-old. Nevertheless, heroic roles for women have been in shorter supply.

Today we have the either/or film: *Broadcast News* (1987), the either-professional-success-or-love film in which the heroine (Holly Hunter) is so driven by professional ambition that she confides to her friend and co-worker, "I'm beginning to repel people I'm trying to seduce"; or *The Good Mother* (1988), the either-sex-or-motherhood film in which the leading character, played by Diane Keaton, is not only without rewarding work but loses both her child and her lover. One must wonder why the novel from which this film was made was so popular. It was seen almost as a fable for our time—that women had better not enjoy sex as much as men do, or they may lose everything.

As the late 1980s was a time of ascendancy of "real men" on television, so it was in films. The movie plot of the "virile lower-class male [who] subdues the haughty lady who is his social or professional superior and who 'needs' to be taken down a peg" is with us once again. In *House of Games* (1987) Lindsay Crouse plays an "uptight psychiatrist and best-selling author who is lured by a seductively sleazy con man (Joe Mantegna) into a high-stakes game that allows her to release her own inhibitions." In *Overboard* (1988) Goldie Hawn is a "brittle heiress" who is "humanized by a carpenter." In *Baby Boom* (1987) Diane Keaton, a yuppie ex-ecutive, is melted by a "woodsy veterinarian" played by Sam Shepard. As Molly Haskell has stated, "The toughness of the woman in each of these films is often a facade: she gives herself away, but only to a certain kind of man, a man who has little respect for the rules of the power world in which she was raised." These men may be the social inferiors of these women, but they are not intimidated by them, and in fact are really in control.

Female nudity, often for its own sake, is perhaps a signal that "misogyny on film may be far from dead." In the adaptation of Milan Kundera's *The Unbearable Lightness of Being* (1988), the hero, Tomas, often opens a conversation with a woman he has just met by saying, "Take off your clothes"—and many, of course, are only too willing. As Janet Maslin points out, the success of *Blue Velvet* (1986), in which "Isabella Rossellini performed much of her role stark naked, and was violently abused again and again by Dennis Hopper," gave "kinkiness in the art film . . . a new lease on life, and sexism in a serious context was respectable all over again." Today it is far more common than it would have been five to ten years ago for leading American actresses to provide flashes of nudity.

And, of course, no discussion of misogyny in films would be complete without a mention of *Fatal Attraction* (1987). The film may pretend to be concerned with the woman who is used for a weekend fling and then forgotten, but it is really a cautionary tale for both men and women. A central moral of the film is surely that women who play around with other people's husbands and enjoy it are not only driven mad by the experience but will not live to do it again.

While the overt message of much advertising and of many of the articles in women's magazines is that women today should be able to "have it all," in fact, the underlying message of many films and television programs and even advertising is that women actually cannot "have it all." It is the rare woman in films, for example, who really manages to have a satisfying job and a gratifying private life. In several recent films, the professional woman is portrayed as either obsessed with work to the exclusion of love and intimacy or obsessed with a man. When she is obsessed with a man, she not infrequently destroys him or herself as part of the resolution of the conflict.

The obvious exception to this pattern is *Working Girl* (1988), a modern fairy tale starring Melanie Griffith as a working-class secretary from Staten Island who makes it in New York's financial district and gets the man as well. While on the one hand it is a satire of the cutthroat, success-at-any-price norms of Wall Street, it is also a Horatio Alger story for women, a triumph of talent and gutsiness over privilege based on class and gender, a reaffirmation of the American Dream. That we identify with Tess McGill and cheer her on all the way is, I believe, crucial to the success of the film. Tess is played so softly, so sweetly, and so sexily that we never see her as a threat; she is never "aggressive," merely a bit nervy—and in any case, she is entitled to practice one or two deceptions, because her boss, masterfully and oh-so-nastily played by Sigourney Weaver, has tried to steal Tess's big idea. We see her as the quintessential American underdog, deserving and hard-working, proof that the American Dream can still work for all of us.

Mystery novels are yet another example of popular culture tuning in to changes in society, sometimes mirroring those changes and occasionally moving ahead of the culture in terms of the role models they portray. Recently there has been a spate of mysteries in which the sleuth is a woman—not the elderly, wise, quick-witted, all-observant sleuth like Agatha Christie's famed Miss Marple but gutsy, fast-talking, fast-moving women who far more resemble Sam Spade.

Perhaps the most conventional of the women sleuths is Kate Fansler, the central character of the Amanda Cross books. A professor by trade, married, upper middle class, Kate Fansler is in many ways the opposite of the typical loner-detective who lives from case to case on meager earnings and in somewhat dingy surroundings. She and her husband have cocktails before dinner, eat out with intellectual, entertaining friends; and in between professional meetings, semesters, and exam periods, she manages to solve the mysteries and murders that come her way. Fansler is unusual in yet another respect—she has an aura of authority around her. She has the authority of middle age, the authority of status by virtue of her profession, and the authority of class. She doesn't need to earn the respect of others; she already has it.

Maggie Ryan, heroine of P. M. Carlson's novels, is also married; and in *Rehearsal for Murder,* she carries her five-month-old daughter, Sarah, with her as she shuttles on the New York subway between her work as a consulting statistician, her actor-husband's theater, and the various New York City sites relevant to the plot. Woven in and around the plot are the pressures a new baby brings to marriage and the image of a family in which the father does a fair amount of the child care. Through it all, Maggie manages to solve the crime, protect her baby, and maintain an enviable relationship with her husband!

Jemima Shore, the central character of Antonia Fraser's series of British mysteries, is a savvy, attractive, well-known television investigator who often travels among the glamorous and the affluent. A single, independent woman who is clearly in charge of her life, Shore has relationships with men as she chooses and is pictured as being able, for the most part, to take them or leave them.

Anna Lee, also British and the heroine of mysteries by Liza Cody, is far more typical of the modern female sleuth. A private investigator by trade, she is competent, persevering, somewhat cynical, and very good at repairing cars. A loner who must struggle for minimal respect even within the agency in which she works, she typically has her own individual sense of morality. She may bend the truth and the rules to figure out what is going on, but she is loyal and caring with her friends and generally on the side of those who are hurting.

V. I. (Vic) Warshawski, a half-Jewish, part-Italian, part-Polish lawyer turned private investigator, is the central character of Sara Paretsky's Chicago-based mysteries. Typical of this new breed of women detectives, Warshawski is tough, intellectual (she reads Primo Levi in the original Italian), wisecracking, courageous, and has a solid inner sense of self-worth. She has a close circle of female friends (bright, achieving, independent women who are also role models for a new kind of woman) to whom she is extremely loyal and a circle of male characters with whom she holds her own. She provides a key to the character of many of these women when she says that action is what every detective needs. While she spends a fair amount of time mulling things over in a hot bath or drinking Johnnie Walker Black, when action is needed or she is faced with a dangerous, even life-threatening situation, she packs her Smith and Wesson into her tote bag or into the waist of her jeans and forges ahead.

But perhaps Kinsey Millhone is the epitome of this new heroine. The private investigator at the center of Sue Grafton's alphabetical mysteries (*"A" Is for Alibi, "B" Is for Burglar, "C" Is for Corpse,* etc.), she introduces herself:

> My name is Kinsey Millhone. I'm a private investigator, licensed by the state of California, operating a small office in Santa Teresa, which is where I've lived all my thirty-two years. I'm female, self-supporting, single now, having been married and divorced twice. I confess I'm sometimes testy, but for the most part I credit myself with an easygoing disposition, tempered (perhaps) by an exaggerated desire for independence.

Like most of this new breed of sleuth, Millhone lives alone and has definite, very individual habits. Whenever the weather permits, she jogs on the beach at six a.m. because

> I notice the older I get, the more my body seems to soften, like butter left out at room temp. I don't like to watch my ass

drop and my thighs spread outward like jodhpurs made of flesh. In the interest of tight-fitting jeans, my standard garb, I jog three miles a day on the bicycle path that winds along the beach front.

She is outspoken, self-reliant, and yet capable of intense empathy. In *"D" Is for Deadbeat,* she attempts to talk a fifteen-year-old out of committing suicide:

"Tony, listen," I said finally. "What you're talking about is dumb and it doesn't make any sense. Do you have any idea how crummy life seemed when I was your age? I cried all the time and I felt like shit. I was ugly. I was skinny. I was lonely. I was mad. I never thought I'd pull out of it, but I did. Life is hard. Life hurts. So what? You tough it out. You get through and then you'll feel good again, I swear to God."

These novels provide an image of women very different from most popular culture. These women are smart, independent, and somehow centered within themselves. They do not need a man in order to feel worthwhile. They have men friends and women friends, and while they are sometimes lonely, they would rather be alone than live with someone they do not respect. Several of these characters have, in fact, walked out on husbands who are pictured as affluent and successful but inferior to them in character and intellect. They are physically fit, capable, and not shy about speaking their minds, even if the language is not always pretty. They sleep with whomever they please and have no regrets in the morning. But, perhaps most important, they are women of both action and compassion.

It is noteworthy that among the various forms of popular culture, mystery novels are almost unique in portraying women who either manage to have both intimacy and professional gratification or who have forsaken traditional family involvement in favor of a more independent, androgynous life-style. Why are women pictured so differently in mysteries than they are in films or on television? First, most films and television programs are made to appeal to a wide, general audience, while mysteries have a smaller but devoted audience, most of whom are aware of and committed to the conventions of the genre. Moreover, the typical sleuth, usually male, is traditionally a loner, an outsider, with few ties to family or community. The typical detective, private investigator, or Scotland Yard superintendent stands apart, somewhat outside of society, thereby able to see individuals and groups with greater clarity, to understand complex motivation, to think in unconventional ways about behavior and the extremes to which people can be driven. It is this distance of the loner, the stranger that enables him or her to think more creatively than the person who is tightly connected to one segment of society. Being "unconnected," in a sense, gives the sleuth the freedom to go, literally, where the action is, to keep irregular hours, talk to unusual people in unlikely places, to connect facts and human responses in ways the more conventional among us would never consider. If women are to play the role as effectively as men, they must be willing to take on a similar life-style; if we are to believe in them, they must be willing and able to play the role in ways we have come to know so well. It is a ready-made part; what is new is that women are now playing it using their own particular style, strengths, and values, and in doing so they are breaking new ground.

What, then, is popular culture telling young women? The messages are clearly conflicting. The fundamental message seems to be that while women's lives have changed dramatically because so many of them are in the work force, supporting or at the very least helping to support themselves and their families, many other aspects of their lives have changed very little. The message is that women can be successful in the workplace and look the part as well but had better not forget how to be provocative, sexy, dependent; that women are to be in charge of their own lives yet "carried away" either by their own feelings or by men; that women can be it all, have it all, and do it all, but while ability and hard work are important, looks are still crucial. With the right clothes and the right look—in other words, the right packaging—women can market themselves the way any other commodity is marketed and achieve their dreams in both the public and the private sphere.

The messages of television and films are more complex. On the one hand, women can be anything they wish, but on the other, their personal lives, not their work lives, are nearly always predominant. You may be a lawyer, but your private life is what is really important. In much of popular culture the women may wear suits and carry briefcases, but their new roles often seem grafted onto the traditional ones of the past—the sex object, the "caring" person more involved with private than with public concerns, or the individual in search of fulfillment through love. Because American society has not truly accepted the implications of women's new roles and therefore not adapted to those profound changes, most popular culture has not really integrated these changes, either. It is often as though a veneer of pseudofeminism is lightly brushed over the story line but underneath that veneer is the same old message. Issues such as dominance and subservience, autonomy and dependence, and how to truly, realistically mesh career and caring are rarely explored seriously. When they are, conflicts are often resolved through traditional solutions.

Moreover, television's need for a wrap-up of the problem each week (or occasionally after two or more episodes) requires simplistic solutions that are invariably within the control of the individual. Seldom are problems depicted as larger than the individual's or the family unit's capacity for coping; rarely are problems depicted as systemic, originating in the very structure of society. The individual generally finds a solution, a formula for working out the problem or conflict, thereby further strengthening the ideology of individualism, an ideology that states, week after week, that we are indeed in charge of our lives and can make of them what we wish. Women may find it harder to regulate their lives because of their presumed greater need for love and approval or because of their again presumed greater conflicts around doing and caring, but in the long run the illusion of self-determination is generally preserved.

But the message of popular culture is above all that everyone is middle and upper middle class. Women are portrayed as doctors, lawyers, and television stars, rarely as salespeople, secretaries, nurse's aides. And when they are playing working-class roles, they are nearly always objects of derision, of sympathy, or of humor. For young women growing up today, the options as reflected by much of popular culture are upper-middle-class options. You need to have a job with status, dress stunningly, and live well if not magnificently. Other measures of success are rarely portrayed. While little in popular culture tells you how to get there, the implication is that the American Dream is there for those who want to make it a reality.

This narrow definition of success and the media's emphasis on individualism have clearly had an impact on all three groups of young women whom I interviewed. The New American Dreamers have most clearly accepted the upper-middle-class model and adopted it as their own. They sometimes see conflicts down the road but assume, as though they were in a thirty-minute sitcom, that they will work out the problems. The Neotraditionalists have more problems with the "having it all" model. While they too hope for a comfortable life-style, they more clearly reflect the conflicts portrayed by the characters in "Thirtysomething." They want to do and to be, but they also want to care and to nurture; and while they accept the ideology that these issues are individual problems to be worked out on an individual basis, they can't quite figure out how to put it all together. The Outsiders are perhaps most poignantly affected by much of popular culture, because they do not see themselves anywhere (except in the occasional film and in much contemporary popular music). Where are the teenagers who have had a baby and now must go it alone? Where are the "burnouts" who feel they fit in nowhere—not at home, not at school, not in their communities? Where are the poor, the near-poor, and the working class struggling to pay the rent and feed their children? "The Cosby Show" may be an advance in a medium that often ignores or denigrates people of color, but what can this quintessentially "Father Knows Best" upper-middle-class family mean to a single woman with two children living in a welfare hotel? By excluding so many Americans from the images and content of popular culture, the society is clearly reinforcing their feelings of being outside the society while simultaneously holding out the promise of the American Dream. Are working-class blacks supposed to feel that "if Bill Cosby can live like that, so can I"? Does identification with the Huxtable family show the way to millions of low-income black Americans, or does it, rather, deflect the anger they might otherwise feel at being largely outside the system? Does it, in other words, promote an unrealistic identification with an improbable, if not impossible, dream?

By defining success almost solely in terms of status, wealth, and power, we are presenting few realistic options for the vast majority of American women and men. Popular culture, by focusing almost entirely on the lives of the top fifth of the population, reinforces the ideology of the American Dream but implicitly devalues all those who will never achieve it. And when young women describe their dreams for the future—their hopes of affluence, their images of themselves as successful professionals, their conflicts around doing and caring, their belief that they must be able to take care of themselves and solve their problems on an individual basis, or, in some cases, when they speak flatly of their inability to imagine a future at all—we know they have been listening to the mixed messages of much of American popular culture.

CHAPTER 5

Sex: The More Things Change . . .

Sex is everywhere, but it is sex without repercussions. People have great sex on TV and they don't get pregnant. People have great sex in books, in movies; friends talk about great sex. But no one talks about reality issues such as birth control and pregnancy.
LIBBY ATWOOD
single mother of two, southern California

That night when he came to claim her, he stood on the short lawn before her house, his knees bent, his fists driven into his thighs, and bellowed her name with such passion that even the friends who surrounded him, who had come to support him, to drag her from the house, to murder her family if they had to, let the chains they carried go limp in their hands. Even the men from our neighborhood, in Bermuda shorts or chinos, white T-shirts and gray suit pants, with baseball bats and snow shovels held before them like rifles, even they paused in their rush to protect her: the good and the bad—the black-jacketed boys and the fathers in their light summer clothes—startled for that one moment before the fighting began by the terrible, piercing sound of his call.

In her novel *That Night,* Alice McDermott captures some of the torment of young love. It was another time, the early 1960s, a time before the legalization of abortion, before teen pregnancy was on everyone's lips, a time when a pregnant "girl" who had "gotten into trouble" was spirited away—in this case from Long Island to Ohio—to have her baby, immediately give it up for adoption, and resume life as though nothing had changed. In reality, of course, everything had changed. It was a time of shame, of confusion about sex and reproduction, of "good girls" and "bad girls." It was a time when young women like Sheryl, the fifteen-year-old protagonist of *That Night,* had little control over their lives, when they simply had to live with decisions made by others.

That time seems light-years ago, and in some sense it was another world. The pill and *Roe* v. *Wade* have supposedly transformed that world forever. But how much has really changed for young women over the past twenty-five years?

"And what about sex?" It was a question I asked about halfway through every interview, and it was invariably acknowledged seriously and forthrightly, with little or no hint of embarrassment, discomfort, or surprise. Sometimes we discussed the interviewee's own experiences, feelings, and decisions; sometimes we discussed the norms within her particular group or community; and in many instances we discussed both. Oddly, while sex was surely an important and absorbing topic, it never took on the intensity of either the need to get good grades in order to get into college or the almost desperate desire to be part of some group. And sometimes, even when it led to life-changing consequences such as unplanned pregnancy, it was seen as almost incidental.

Although one of the dominant themes of the New American Dreamers and the Neotraditionalists is the importance of taking control of one's life, most young women spoke of how difficult this is in their relationships with men. Many of the young women with whom I spoke are still buffeted, as so many women were twenty, thirty years ago, by the need to please a man or the desire to keep a man. Person after person told me, in the words of one student, "There's a real emphasis on guys. Girls focus too much on them; they are the center of their lives." Margaret Robinson, a senior biology major at the University of California, puts it this way: "Women spend too much time thinking and talking about guys—'I don't know if he really likes me,' 'Why doesn't he call?' " She continues, speaking slowly, deliberately, "Women feel like they're not whole without a guy—they're not good if they don't have a guy. They spend so much time trying to look good so they can attract a guy. It's really a big deal!"

These young women are describing a familiar theme—that a woman does not feel whole, like a full-fledged person, without a man. She doesn't feel special, lovable, complete if a man has not singled her out, put his stamp of approval on her. Perhaps a young black woman from a ghetto outside of San Francisco says it best. When I asked if girls think about guys a lot, the response—almost an aside, hurried and muffled—was unclear. I asked what she had said and she repeated the phrase, but I still could not understand. Finally, another young woman deciphered it for me, to great laughter all around. She was saying, "Twenty-four, seven, thirty-one." Young women think about men "twenty-four hours a day, seven days a week, thirty-one days a month!" Of course: twenty-four, seven, thirty-one. That says it all!

Terri Bartlett, executive director of Planned Parenthood in New Orleans, suggests that young men and young women are in a sense trapped in their roles—in what society tells them they must be. "Guys think, 'If I don't make a move on her, it will be all over school that I'm not macho or, worst of all, that I'm gay.' And," she continues, "young women are looking for validation. They set it up because if he comes on to her, it indicates to her that she's attractive. The media tell her that she must be sexy and beautiful, and his coming on to her validates that image of herself." In order to validate her sense of worth, a young woman will ask, implicitly or explicitly, "Don't you think I look pretty? Don't you like me? Don't you *really* like me?" And the guys, according to Bartlett, will say anything to get her quiet, to go on to the next topic or the next stage in the moves toward sex. She suggests that women, either through a fear of rejection or through a fear of "not looking cool," are really functioning as passive objects, "keeping their feelings out of it." There is a vast difference, she points out, between being truly "intimate" and "keeping their real selves separate. There's a big difference between having sex and making love. You don't even have to like somebody to have sex with them."

Kathy Cherwinski, a nurse practitioner at the Somerset Family Planning Service in Somerville, New Jersey, agrees that many women are still extremely passive. "Very few women are truly assertive," she says with feeling. "I see women stepped on all the time, women from all classes. The pediatrician says to the professional woman, 'You have your child in day care? No wonder she's sick all the time.' He's telling that woman that she's a bad mother. I'd tell him, 'Take a hike, buddy!' Young women coming in here have a very hard time making decisions for themselves; they are always saying 'My boyfriend says this,' 'My parents say that.' They can't even decide what birth-control method to use without invoking all those other authorities!"

Today's women as passive objects? Keeping their real selves out of it? Trying to gain approval and "validation" through age-old techniques? Is this where we are after decades of feminism and a supposed "sexual revolution"? Or is this a return to earlier, more traditional ways that reflect the attitudes and norms of the conservative Reagan era? Many women with whom I spoke seemed to indicate that relationships between men and women have not changed all that much after all. Maria Mendez, the bright, lively San Diego college student, firmly states, "I will not call a guy to ask him out. I cannot do that. And I like it better when he pays. Guys don't like women to pay—it hinders their manhood."

Several young women talked about the first time they had sex and indicated that "one-night stands" or relationships that did not mean anything were common patterns. One young woman from an affluent New England college town declared, "Kids *are* having sex. Most girls are sexually active by the time they graduate from high school, or else they are teases. And usually you lose your virginity out of the blue—with a random person, a one-night stand." She added, almost as an afterthought, "And I've never heard of a bad experience." A young woman from a small southern city, who had recently had an abortion, recalls that she first had sex because she was curious, "not 'cause I liked it." She was sixteen and does not now regret "doing it with someone I didn't care about. My *real* first time was with someone I care about, someone I have a real relationship with; *he's* my first love." She is describing the young man she is currently seeing. "He was *really* my first," she states firmly.

They might have intercourse with someone they barely know in order to be initiated into the world of sex, or into adulthood, but the "first time" that has any meaning is the time with someone they care for. It is almost as though it has to resemble a movie version of "first love" or it doesn't count. These young women are, I believe, reflecting a wider social phenomenon, one that separates sex, or at least sexual initiation, from emotional intimacy and that often views sex as an end in itself, not necessarily as an element of romantic love. Sex as it is often portrayed by popular culture is a rather mechanistic activity, performed for its own sake and often devoid of any deeper meaning. "First love" is clearly viewed by many young women as quite different from first sex. First sex is essentially a technical term; first love is a description of feelings within a relationship.

Libby Atwood, a divorced twenty-five-year-old mother of two, feels that she first had sex because she wanted to experience the next stage of life. "I felt I was ready," she said. "A lot of kids are too young to have sex—too young. You're really making love to yourself, getting off on head trips. It would be wonderful if you were masturbating, but what you're doing is not a game anymore. It is changing your life." She points out that "sex is everywhere, but it is sex without repercussions. People have great sex on TV and they don't get pregnant. People have great sex in books, in movies; friends talk about great sex. But no one talks about reality issues such as birth control and pregnancy." She feels that people are really searching for intimacy and that sex may be seen as a fast way of achieving that intimacy. She wonders if young people view contraception as some kind of barrier to the intimacy they are searching for. Is it only through the risk-taking behavior of sex without contraception that young people can really indicate their connection with one another?

Interestingly, it was often the New American Dreamers, the young women who feel they must achieve and be independent, who feel they must be able to go it alone, who spoke most openly and most casually about sex. At a time in their lives when they are breaking away from dependence on family and yet not involved in a love relationship, is sex seen as a way to compensate for some of the psychological isolation they may feel? Is sex indeed seen as a temporary substitute for intimacy?

Have women moved toward greater sexual equality, or has our

sexually "liberated" society simply made it easier and more convenient for women to be exploited? Judy Donato, a fifteen-year-old from New York who is part of a Greenwich Village group who identify themselves as "punk," feels that some girls are "insecure" and "do it with anybody" because they "need somebody to love them." Most girls she knows start having sex at around age fourteen, and it is largely because the guys are pressuring them. "At sixteen or seventeen," she states flatly, "that's all the guys want from the girls. Then the girls have sex; the guys dump them and never talk to them again." It is worth noting that virtually no one with whom I spoke, young women or professionals, described situations in which the young women were the aggressors sexually. This is not to say that there aren't such situations; but the frequency with which women were portrayed as having sex to get or hold a man or because it was expected indicates that some patterns have changed surprisingly little.

Several people, both the young women and the professionals with whom I spoke, connected excessive drinking and sex. A social worker and a school counselor in an affluent college town call drinking the "rite of passage" and say that it is particularly serious within the local Ivy League college. High-school girls are "used and abused" by the college guys, particularly those in fraternities. "It's not good to be beautiful in this town," the school counselor declares. The girls, sometimes called "frat rats," start by "hanging out" on Fraternity Row while they are still in junior high school; by the time they are in high school, they dress up and serve as "hostesses" during the fraternity "rush" week. "Many girls get into trouble sexually because of liquor," the counselor continues. "They have sex; they don't enjoy it—they do it to please the man. They want to marry men from this college; they think the men are going to make a lot of money." But she sees the young women the next morning when they are having serious thoughts about the night before. She sees the "girls who go from male to male." She sees the victims of gang rapes when the rapists are all upper-middle-class sons of professional fathers.

Penelope Brazile, the director of human resources in the office of the mayor of New Orleans, says emphatically, "Today it's cool to screw! We used to hug and kiss—they are renting hotel rooms or screwing in the back of a car." While poor kids may turn to sex because they see so few real options in their lives, middle-class kids, children of baby boomers, are also in trouble, she feels. "We left them alone. Baby boomers are into work; they give their kids love in terms of money and consumer goods, so the kids who are looking for love are acting out sexually."

Many young women, of course, are having intercourse within the context of long-term relationships. One college freshman indicated that if two people have been seeing one another for a year or two, she assumes they are having sex. But other young women are not. In 1985, 47 percent of teenage women in the United States aged fifteen to nineteen were sexually active. Many with whom I spoke indicated that they were too committed to school, to their various activities, and to their futures to be involved sexually. Among the young women I interviewed, those who could best be described as Neotraditionalists seemed to be the ones most likely to be postponing sexual activity. Several indicated that they had other priorities and did not want to be sidetracked. Many of the New American Dreamers indicated that they were sexually active, while others were devoting their energies to academic pursuits, a wide range of extracurricular interests, and friendship groups. Among the Outsiders, however, most were sexually active.

One young woman stated that when she does get involved with someone, she tries to control the intensity of the relationship. She does not want it to "take her over," nor does she want to become alienated from her friends. Long-term relationships often seem to devour those involved, particularly the women. They lose touch with friends in school, with family, even with activities that do not involve both partners.

Despite the young women who speak so eloquently about career, material success, and independence, a curious strain of passivity, of not quite being in control, runs through many of the interviews. A young woman, bright, articulate, born and raised in a middle-class family and currently a student at the University of California, illustrates this passivity, this functioning almost as an object, to be manipulated as circumstance or another person wills.

Libby Atwood is currently a full-time student majoring in linguistics; she has studied intensively Korean, Latin, Spanish, and

French. Libby's parents were solidly middle-class, and she spent much of her childhood in Arizona. During her senior year in high school she became pregnant, went to live for several months in a home for unwed mothers, and after the baby's birth gave the infant up for adoption. She went on to college in Colorado, but says, "I didn't know what I wanted in life," so she enlisted in the Air Force. Around the same time, she met her future husband. After she finished basic training, they were married. She describes him as "jealous and insecure" and feels they married at this time because he desired to do so.

Soon after they married, they began having serious problems, and she considered having the marriage annulled. She found out almost immediately, however, that she was pregnant. She wasn't using birth control at the time, because "I didn't think I was going to get pregnant—and anyway, we didn't have sex that often. I thought I knew my cycle." They didn't use condoms, because "I always felt too awkward having men wear condoms." In any case, she really "didn't think about becoming pregnant."

What about an abortion, since the pregnancy occurred at the time she was considering breaking up the marriage? "No, I couldn't have an abortion. I believe in abortion, but I don't think I could ever have one. I couldn't hold that memory. You know how sometimes you know you're going to regret something? That's how I felt. It would have haunted me."

After she knew she was pregnant, her husband told her that she had to leave the Air Force and come to live with him in Florida or that was the end of the marriage. In 1982 she left the Air Force and went to live with him. After the baby was born, they continued to have severe marital problems. She had been using a diaphragm, but during one particularly difficult time she put a pin through it right in front of him, so they had "no sex for a long time." Just when "everything was going wrong, neither one of us was happy," and they had finally decided to separate, they had sex "one more time, for the good times."

Three days later she left him. A few weeks later she discovered she was pregnant once again. She says, "I wanted to go back to him, but I knew it would be a rotten existence. Instead, I went on welfare, and they sent me for job training to become a secretary—

something I never wanted to do and never will do." Her ex-husband has seen the children only once since they separated and has never paid any child support.

After the second baby was born, she went back to Arizona and cared for her father, who was dying of cancer. "It was an incredibly difficult ordeal. He was in terrible pain and needed care twenty-four hours a day. At first I was the only one there, but then my mother and sister came to help. It was horrible."

Libby feels that this experience changed her life. She became more serious. She says, "I plan now. Even though I do not necessarily expect my plans to go through, I plan—just in case. Now I know I'm going to die. Now I don't think I'm invincible; I never thought about that before. Now I know I'm not going to have another chance. Now I know it's not so bad to take responsibility. If you screw up, it's okay. I used to be able to say 'It's really not my fault.' Now I know if you leave the responsibility to the air or to men, things might really get screwed up."

For a significant period of time during her late teens and early twenties, Libby was clearly not in charge of her life. She is highly intelligent; she had options. And yet she could not take hold and direct her life as she might have wished. She was involved with a man who was wrong for her; she became pregnant at inopportune times; and though very able, she found it virtually impossible to harness her ability and develop a satisfying vocational plan. After considerable pain and suffering, she seems to have finally found a direction and a way of using her talents, but one wishes she had not had to suffer quite so much in the process.

Why are so many young women today so curiously passive about the direction of their lives? While this passivity, or willingness to be used and directed almost as an object, cuts across the three groups I have described, the consequences are most severe for the young women who see themselves as Outsiders and for those who verge on Outsider-ness. Nonetheless, this phenomenon was discussed by young women in all three groups. Many New American Dreamers described heavy drinking, casual sex, and women's absorption with men but made the point that many young women like them minimize the long-term risks, either because they have a future agenda from which they are not going to be deterred or because severe, long-lasting implications would not be tolerated by their families or their social group. As one high-school student put it, "They can't get pregnant—they have too much to lose." Many Neotraditionalists also described an almost 1950s mentality on the part of women toward men—the desire to please, to be loved, the waiting around for him to call, and the yearning for the status that "having a guy" bestows. But Neotraditionalists are often more conservative in their behavior and therefore also minimize the risks. They too are restrained by family and social pressure and to some extent by their hopes for the future. Not unexpectedly, it is the Outsiders and those who verge on Outsider-ness who are most likely to be swept into a series of circumstances over which they seem to have little control.

It is clear, as one listens to these young women, that they are composites of the old and the new—the woman who must charm and cajole and hope for the telephone to ring, whose status and sense of self is in significant measure dependent upon her connection with a man, and the woman who hopes to function as an equal, hopes to achieve her own place in the world and to take responsibility for herself. As analysis of popular culture indicates, young women still grow up absorbing both messages; should we be surprised when they act them out?

Furthermore, while the messages for many women contain at least elements of the new as well as the old, how much have the messages for the majority of men really changed? If a seventeen-year-old young woman wants to be "popular," she must somehow accommodate to male images of femaleness; and although many young men have vastly different views about the role of women than were prevalent twenty or thirty years ago, Americans are bombarded by macho views of men—Rambo and Rocky, Superman and Arnold Schwarzenegger, Bruce Willis and Don Johnson. Tough-guy John Wayne/Clint Eastwood personas have become so accepted and ingrained in American culture that George Bush's line during the 1988 presidential campaign "Read my lips: *no new taxes*" was an instant communication to millions of Americans that he was, in reality, a macho, take-charge, Clint Eastwood kind of guy. That Bush and his advisors chose this way of symbolizing firmness and strength and that he was elected at least in part because of this new persona certainly tell us something about the characteristics at least some late-twentieth-century American voters want from men. And if men identify with the often brutal tough-guy images all around them, how are women to respond?

Whenever we feel that we as a culture have solved some of the issues of power and dominance between men and women, we have only to glance at the statistics on battered women. They range from Surgeon General C. Everett Koop's estimate of approximately 15 million physically abused women in the U.S. to other experts whose estimates indicate that as many as one-third to one-half of all American women are battering victims at some time in their lives. The legitimization of male authority and aggression and of female subordination and passivity is still very much a part of our culture, and in a variety of subtle and not-so-subtle ways it has been passed on to the next generation.

One of the most critical consequences of the mixed messages young American women receive—mixed messages about their roles, about sexuality, about relationships with men, about birth control, about controlling their own lives, and about their life options—is a rate of teenage pregnancy in the United States that is higher than in twenty-seven out of thirty industrialized countries. Among younger teenagers, those seventeen and under, the U.S. rate is higher than that of any industrialized country except Hungary. A study sponsored by the Alan Guttmacher Institute compared data on teenage reproductive behavior in the U.S. and thirty-five other industrialized countries. The study then examined in detail five countries thought to be reasonably similar to the U.S. and found that in 1981 the birthrate of all U.S. women ages fifteen to nineteen was nearly double that of England and Wales, twice the Canadian rate, more than double the French rate, nearly four times the Swedish rate, and almost six times the rate of the Netherlands. If we look only at white teenagers in the U.S., we see that their rate of teenage pregnancy is still double that of France, over one and a half times that of Canada and England and Wales, three times that of Sweden, and over five times that of the Netherlands.

In the United States approximately one million teenagers become pregnant each year. Over four hundred thousand of them obtain induced abortions; nearly one-half million give birth; the remainder have spontaneous abortions. Between 1984 and 1985 the birthrate among teenage women rose by one percent; this was the first time since 1979 that the birthrate increased among all teenagers aged fifteen to nineteen. Who are the young women having babies? First, it must be noted that, despite popular misconceptions and stereotypes, the majority of teen births occur to white teens. In 1985 white teenage women were responsible for 67.6 percent of all teenage births. White married women aged eighteen and nineteen made up the single largest group, approximately 27.6 percent; white unmarried women aged eighteen and nineteen made up the second largest group, 16.9 percent. Black and Hispanic teens accounted for 42.2 percent of all teenage births; but since they make up only 23.7 percent of all women under twenty, a disproportionate number are giving birth.

Second, the vast majority of teen mothers are between the ages of fifteen and nineteen. One out of every twenty teenage women between the ages of fifteen and nineteen gave birth in 1985. Nevertheless, out of the 477,705 births in 1985 to women under the age of twenty, 10,220 were to teens under fifteen.

Third, 58.7 percent of all teens giving birth in 1985 were unmarried. While teen births have decreased sharply from 1970 to 1985, more births are occurring to unmarried teens. In 1970, three out of ten babies born to teens were born to single mothers; in 1980, almost five out of ten; and by 1985, the number was almost six out of ten. In 1985 there were 178,000 fewer births to teens but 80,000 more births to unmarried teen mothers. That same year, 45.1 percent of all white births to teens, 51.9 percent of all Hispanic births to teens, and an incredible 90 percent of all black births to teens were to unmarried women. This rate is, in all likelihood, due to several factors: marriage rates among all teens, including those who get pregnant, have been declining rapidly in recent years; it is more and more acceptable for unmarried women to have and keep their babies; and the antiabortion efforts of both government officials and private groups may be turning some young women away from terminating their pregnancies.

Studies have shown, furthermore, that the U.S. rate of unplanned pregnancies and abortions, among both teenagers and older women, particularly women in their twenties, is considerably higher than those of comparable industrialized countries. Women in the U.S., for example, have an average of 2.56 pregnancies during their reproductive years. In comparison, Canadian women have lifetime averages of 2.04 pregnancies and an abortion rate half that of the U.S. Why do American women, particularly teenage women, have such a high rate of unplanned pregnancies?

A serious problem with much of the discussion of teenage pregnancy is the isolation of the topic from the social context in which young women live. We tend to separate out the pregnant teen or the teen mother from other young women with similar characteristics, with the resulting implication that she is somehow deviant. It is part of our tendency to blame the victim, a tendency that places the blame on the individual for indulging in "self-destructive behavior" rather than on a complex social environment that determines much of human behavior. Discussions with dozens of young women make it clear that they are often caught in a web not of their own making. Many young women today are victims of biological changes, rapidly shifting norms, conflicting messages, an irrational social policy, inadequate life options, and, above all, societal ambivalence about women's roles, women's sexuality, and mothering. Not only must teen pregnancy be seen within this larger societal framework and within the framework of class, gender, and race, but if we look closely we will find that many young people are doing *exactly* what our culture expects and, implicitly or explicitly, tells them to do.

First, it must be stressed that in addition to the social, psychological, economic, and cultural factors that influence the behavior of young people, the biological fact of early maturation is an element in the increase in teenage sexual activity and teen pregnancy. Over the last 150 years the age of onset of menstruation has dropped significantly due to improved nutrition and health. The median age of menarche in the U.S. today is 12.5 to 13 years. Not only are American girls biologically able to have children at an earlier age, but they must also cope with accompanying hormonal changes, newfound interest in sexual activity, and the development of secondary sex characteristics that may send off signals of readiness for sex before young women really are socially and psychologically ready.

Robb Forman Dew, in her poignant coming-of-age novel *The Time of Her Life,* describes this onset of sexual desire:

> Claudia and her friends had become ill with desire about age twelve. They were, most of them, obsessed with the need to be kissed and caressed and touched and fondled, and by necessity they spent a great deal of their time consumed with interest in all the games and contests of the compellingly awkward teenaged boys. But not one of these girls cared much one way or another about the contests; they simply longed for proximity to those male bodies hot and damp from football practice or a baseball game.

While girls with higher hormonal levels show increased interest in sex, the relationship between age of menarche and the increase in hormonal levels on the one hand and sexual activity on the other is unclear. Most researchers seem to feel that other factors, such as the social environment, are more influential in determining sexual behavior. But, of course, the social environment is presenting girls as sex objects at younger and younger ages. The theme of *Lolita,* which was seen as shocking when it was published in 1955, is today virtually commonplace. With films about child prostitution, such as *Pretty Baby* (1978), lurid stories about the sexual abuse of children on our television screens with depressing regularity, and jean advertisements featuring "nymphets" who look no more than twelve or thirteen, the sexualizing of children is a fact of life in late-twentieth-century America.

Moreover, not only does adolescence begin at an earlier age but, because of prolonged periods of education and delayed economic independence, it extends later and later, often through the mid-to-late twenties. During this extended period, not only is the onset of sexual maturation earlier but marriage is being postponed. In 1960 the median age for first marriage among women was 20.3 years; by 1984 that had risen to 23.0. For men, the median age rose from 22.8 years in 1960 to 25.4 years in 1984. Reasons for postponing marriage, of course, differ widely from group to group, person to person. Some young people are at best ambivalent about marriage because they have witnessed the disintegration and dissolution of their own parents' marriages. Others, particularly black women, look at the high unemployment rates of young black men and feel the prospects for "establishing economically viable and stable marriages are slim."

According to William Julius Wilson, "the number of black children growing up in fatherless families increased by 41 percent between 1970 and 1980, and most of this growth has occurred in families in which the *mother has never been married*" (italics in original). Never-married mothers are likely to be younger and to be living at home than are divorced, separated, or widowed mothers, and they tend to have less education, less work experience, and fewer financial resources. While studies indicate that many white women (and some black women) delay marriage and parenthood because of educational and/or career aspirations, many black women's late marriages are due to what has been termed a poor "marriage market." As Wilson forcefully points out, "the extraordinary rise in black male joblessness" is "perhaps the most important factor in the rise of black female-headed families." He goes on to point out that "the decline in the incidence of intact marriages among blacks is associated with the declining economic status of black men" and that "black women nationally, especially young black women, are facing a shrinking pool of 'marriageable' (i.e., employed) black men."

If more young people are sexually active, then the use of birth control clearly becomes critical. The percentage of sexually active teenage women rose sharply during the 1970s from 31.7 percent in 1971 to 43.4 percent in 1979 and rose more modestly during the 1980s to 47 percent in 1985. Black and Hispanic teens, particularly black teens, were more likely than whites to be sexually active. Among 1,000 white, black, and Hispanic women aged fifteen to nineteen in 1985, 447 white, 585 black, and 471 Hispanic women were sexually active.

One of the most difficult issues facing young women is the use of birth control. The percent of teenagers using some form of birth control rose steadily during the 1970s and leveled off in the early 1980s. In 1982 approximately 85 percent of sexually active teenagers ages fifteen to nineteen reported that they had *at some time* used a method of contraception. The key problem, of course, is the irregular use of contraception.

Most experts agree that few unmarried teenagers become pregnant intentionally. If most young women do not wish to become pregnant, why don't they or their partners use contraception? One answer is that many young people, particularly younger teenagers, do not really understand reproduction. Innumerable myths such as "You can't get pregnant the first time," "You can't get pregnant if you don't enjoy it," "You can't get pregnant standing up," "You can't get pregnant if you drink ice water, because your reproductive system will be frozen," and "Contraception, particularly the condom, significantly diminishes the man's pleasure" are still in the late 1980s passed from teen to teen, effectively sabotaging the regular use of birth control.

In addition to the young women who do not really understand the need for contraception are those who understand the issue but think, "It will never happen to me." Whether this is part of adolescent risk-taking behavior or whether it is a result of what some experts have called "magical thinking," many young women just do not believe that anything terrible will happen to them. They are invincible, indestructible, immune from disaster. They think that they can drive dangerously and arrive in one piece, that they can drink and drive and still survive, that they can experiment with drugs and not become addicted, and that they can have sex without protection and not become pregnant. According to one professional who works with teen mothers on a daily basis, "Ninety percent never thought it would happen to them. They never, ever, ever thought they would get pregnant!"

Kathy Cherwinski, the nurse practitioner who works with young women in Somerville, New Jersey, feels that this lacuna, this gap in their understanding, is "developmental." She feels that many adolescents do not yet have the conceptual ability to put the facts together and understand, in a way that will motivate them to action, that sex without contraception equals pregnancy. She reports that some young women with strong career goals are getting pregnant and having abortions without telling anyone; after the abortion they start using contraception. So it is not necessarily that affluent young women with goals for the future use birth control any more effectively but that they are choosing not to have the baby once they are pregnant. The middle- and upper-middle-class young women I interviewed corroborated this view: they and their friends may not use birth control when they first start having sex, but once they are having sex more regularly, they often go to the family-planning clinic in a nearby town to obtain contraception. For many of them, having a baby is virtually unthinkable. If they were to become pregnant, they would have an abortion immediately.

Cherwinski feels that we do not really understand the way adolescents think. "They are getting too many messages and cannot deal with all of them and put them into action," she states. "Sex is everywhere in the society—in the media, on TV, the movies, twenty-four hours a day. We can't tell them all the time that sex is good, that it is a normal part of life but not for you."

A recent study by Louis Harris corroborates Cherwinski's observation. It found that the three major television networks broadcast 65,000 references to sexual behavior in the 1987–88 television season, an average of twenty-seven sexual references an hour. They found, in addition, that daytime programming had 50 percent more sexual content than prime time. Many young women are addicted to soap operas, scheduling college classes so that they have time to watch their favorite "soap," taping the program when they cannot be home so that they do not miss a single episode. "Love and passion," daily soap topics, take place largely outside of marriage. Individuals are constantly "threatened by temptation" and must on a daily basis cope with "bigamy, adultery, betrayal, illegitimacy, love triangles, deception, and sexual rivalry." As Faye Wattleton, president of the Planned Parenthood Federation of America, has stated, TV viewers are subjected to a "constant barrage of fictional characters engaging in sex without discussing it, without considering the risks and certainly without using birth control."

Cherwinski continues: "Adults who deal with adolescents think of them as younger adults, but they are not. We know quite a lot about two-year-olds but not that much about fourteen-to-nineteen-year-olds. We're dealing with delayed adolescence, with risk-taking behavior, and women are getting more and more into risk-taking behavior. Adulthood is when you reach that point in life when you know that certain actions have consequences and that you can intervene to encourage or prevent those consequences. That is the hallmark of adulthood, and most teenagers are not there yet." Sociologist Mary Curry echoes some of these thoughts: "Our assumptions about how people behave depend on who we are; we tend to think everyone is like us. Kids don't have the experience that adults do; they don't understand the consequences as we do; they may not know the consequences as we do."

Terri Bartlett of Planned Parenthood has a slightly different point of view. According to her, many young women do not think about pregnancy and its consequences because they don't see themselves as sexually active. She says, "If you ask them 'Do you have sex?' the answer is yes. If you ask them 'Are you sexually active?' the answer often is no." Indeed, they may well see themselves as passive participants in occasional sex rather than as active participants who need to plan for the consequences.

There are other barriers to adolescents using birth control. Amanda Chapman, a young woman from New Jersey, explains that it is not the "in" thing among young women she knows to take the pill. Her parents arranged for her younger sister, age sixteen, to obtain oral contraceptives, and although the pills are in the top drawer of her bureau she has never used one. According to Amanda, her sister is a cheerleader and has "something of a reputation with the boys." But there is considerable peer pressure on her *not* to use the pill. If a girl uses the pill, particularly if she already has "a reputation," it confirms what others are saying or thinking about her.

College students at the University of California who volunteer as health advocates confirm that this is a common attitude. Some women do not fill their prescriptions for the pill; others forget to take it or take it at different times every day and often miss days. They feel that many young women are ambivalent about taking control of their lives and that they are taught subtly, unconsciously that they should be passive. They recognize that they are sexually active, but nonetheless the notion that "only bad girls plan for sex" is widespread. Young women who plan for sex are, as many said, "sluts."

According to Ethel Levine, a school psychologist in a junior high school in Westchester County, the boys are expected to have a "macho image," to be sexually experienced, and to brag about "getting to first base, second base, and so forth," but girls who are thought to be sexually active are called "sluts." Ms. Levine made a point of emphasizing that the girls are the first to use the term.

An eighteen-year-old unmarried pregnant woman from New Jersey confided to one friend that she was pregnant; subsequently, she received abusive telephone calls, the news spread through the community, and at a local basketball game, three girls (including a friend of hers) hissed at her as they walked by, "You're such a slut!" As much as attitudes and sexual mores may have changed over the past twenty-five years, for many young women the same old double standard is still operating. A sensitive, thoughtful seventeen-year-old high-school junior indicates the way many young people feel about sex when she said, "A friend of mine mentioned that she had a uterine infection. I was so shocked because I thought she was innocent." "Innocent"? "Slut"? These seem like words out of another era—possibly the 1950s, when teenage girls took "purity tests" to show that they had engaged in enough sex play to prove they were desirable but not so much that they were considered "loose," a word then very much in vogue. These same words, the same concepts are used today, and used with feeling, by many of today's young people.

What in the late 1980s is a "slut"? High-school juniors and seniors define the term: If you "go out with more than one guy," you're a slut; if you're "constantly all over them [boys]," you're a slut; if you "dress to accent your figure" and "hang on some guy," you're a slut. You don't need to be sleeping with someone; that's just the "worst case." And if you talk about your sexual life, that's dangerous and likely to get all over school.

Young women are clearly trapped. The movies say "Do it!" TV says "Do it!" Songs, advertisements, and surely young men say "Do it!" But we are also giving the message "Don't plan for it or you're a slut!" An incredible catch-22—if having sex is a rite of passage into adulthood but taking appropriate precautions is considered unacceptable, what choice does a young woman have?

Furthermore, the young women with whom I spoke were very

concerned about using all of the major methods of contraception. Many stressed that they do not have sexual relations that often or that regularly and therefore have little incentive to use contraception regularly. They were concerned about the pill because they don't like to put something "foreign" in their bodies and were worried about its side effects. A study of repeat abortions within one year in New Jersey showed that most of the repeaters discontinued the pill because of side effects such as spotting or moderate weight gain. One professional who participated in the study feels that the women used these relatively "minor" side effects as an excuse to stop using the pill. Their attitude is, she said, "If I don't think about it, maybe it will go away."

A group of young unmarried mothers from Arizona confirms this reluctance to use the pill. They agreed that few young women they know take the pill regularly. They feel that the pill "makes you sick, it makes you fat," and the women they know "won't use it." Recent studies indicate that the pill may indeed increase the risk of breast cancer. While such a link may or may not be proven in the future, the mere possibility fuels "the anxiety of women about the safety of this contraceptive technique." And what about the guys? I asked. According to one young woman, the guys feel "it's up to us. To them it's just a one-night thing. They get up and shake the sheets and walk away."

In addition to misgivings about the pill, many young women are extremely reluctant to use the diaphragm. It does not suit their lifestyle, particularly the unplanned nature of their sexual activity; and many young women are uncomfortable inserting it. The condom, of course, brings other problems. Virtually everyone expressed anxiety about insisting that their partners use condoms, whether for birth control or because of the AIDS epidemic.

American culture is clearly giving mixed messages to its young women about taking control of their bodies and indeed their lives. These mixed messages include both the use of birth control and abortion. What with the short-lived "squeal rule" (the attempt of the Reagan administration to insist that parents of women under age eighteen be informed if their daughters request contraception), the conflict around school-based gynecological services, the debates about educating people about the threat of AIDS through condom advertising on television, and the ever-present effort of "right to life" groups to repeal the legalization of abortion, or at least to make it as difficult as possible for women, particularly poor women, to choose abortion, our society has made it abundantly clear that while images invoking sex and sexuality may be acceptable and omnipresent, particularly if they sell products, for many groups within American society it is still not acceptable for women to take control of their sexual lives.

These mixed messages are having a clear impact on young women, particularly around the issue of abortion. The rate of abortion rose steeply during the 1970s and then leveled off during the 1980s. Young women's attitudes toward contraception and abortion are central to the rate of teenage pregnancy. These attitudes vary, furthermore, among different groups in the culture. Significant differences exist between black and white teens in sexual activity, contraceptive use, pregnancy rate, abortion rate, and birthrate. In 1985, for example, black teenagers were more likely to be sexually active than white teenagers and more likely to have used contraceptives. Blacks are also more likely to delay the use of contraception after initiating intercourse and to use contraception inconsistently. Moreover, they are less likely to have abortions. Thus, black teenage women in 1985 were 2.3 times as likely as white women to give birth.

Many of the young women whom I interviewed, both black and white, spoke of their negative feelings toward abortion. One black teenage mother in Arizona said, "Abortion? My mother would kill me!" Another, a seventeen-year-old mother of two, said, "In our family we don't believe in abortion. My grandmother would disown anyone who had an abortion." She would not consider abortion, because she "might regret it later." She feels that among women who have abortions it "sometimes haunts them that they killed their baby." She is echoing Libby Atwood's words: "I couldn't have an abortion. . . . I couldn't hold that memory. . . . It would have haunted me."

Yet another young woman, who thought her boyfriend was sterile and was "shocked" when she found she was pregnant, feels that "abortion is killing." (It is unclear whether he purposely deceived her or truly thought he was sterile.) She continues, "My mind was set against abortion. If a girl goes out and gets pregnant, her responsibility is to go through with it." Is "going through with it" possibly seen as punishment for having had sex? A family-planning worker feels that many young women who have abortions are very guilty afterward and bent upon punishing themselves. "It is a very traumatic experience for them. Some of them get pregnant again out of guilt and then have another abortion. Some are simply not emotionally capable of assimilating the experience."

The image of young women blithely having sex, understanding the consequences and refusing to use contraception, becoming pregnant and having abortions without a qualm, and then, perhaps, repeating the whole process simply does not ring true. The women with whom I spoke either see sex as a rite of passage to adulthood or feel they must have sex to get or hold on to their boyfriends. Sex, in their minds as in much of the culture at large, is not connected to reproduction; it is what all those glamorous people do on TV, in movies, and in novels. Yet once they find they are pregnant, many agonize over whether or not to abort; and whatever they decide, they must then live with the consequences for the rest of their lives.

The threat of AIDS is, of course, making a very difficult and volatile issue even more complex. The young women I interviewed, from Massachusetts to Ohio to Arizona to California, differ about how much the schools are educating high-school students about the nature and prevention of the disease. In an affluent school district in New Hampshire a recent high-school graduate described the attitude of her peers toward AIDS: "They think it's a joke. They blame homosexuals and say 'It could never happen to me'— just like they say 'I could never get pregnant' and 'I could never get hurt drinking and driving.' " A recent study of New Jersey high-school students indicates profound ignorance about ways of contracting AIDS. Fifty-nine percent of the students questioned either believed they could get AIDS from mosquito bites or were not sure, and 40 percent had the same fears about toilet seats. Fewer than half of the students were willing to attend school with an AIDS victim, and 44 percent said they did not know where to be tested for AIDS.

Other studies, however, yield very different results. A much larger, government-funded study of eleven thousand eighth and tenth graders nationwide found that more than 90 percent of the teens surveyed knew that sexual intercourse and sharing needles with someone who has AIDS increase the risk of being infected. More than eight out of ten also knew that having multiple partners increases the risks and that using condoms reduces it. They found, on the other hand, an "appallingly low" level of knowledge about other sexually transmitted diseases.

Investigators at the Johns Hopkins School of Public Health found that 90 percent of teenage girls know that unprotected sex places them at risk for AIDS but that less than 40 percent used condoms the last time they had intercourse. According to one of the researchers, "The girls have a high level of AIDS knowledge, yet they engage in high-risk sexual behavior."

A group of young women in Akron say that AIDS is "not a real big issue" and that school programs stress birth control but not condoms. On the other hand, a professional involved in family planning in New Jersey says that she is "amazed" at the number of "kids" she sees who are using condoms; she thinks it's the threat of AIDS. She believes the use of condoms has "skyrocketed." A recent study on contraception by the Alan Guttmacher Institute indicates, however, that despite the fear of AIDS and other sexually transmitted diseases, sexual activity among unmarried women has increased from 1982 to 1987. In 1982, 68 percent of women ages fifteen to forty-four had engaged in sexual intercourse. By 1987, that percentage had risen to 76 percent. In the same year, moreover, only 16 percent of sexually active unmarried women aged fifteen to forty-four were using condoms. Clearly, knowledge about AIDS does not necessarily lead to altered behavior, particularly in a risk-taking population like adolescents. The sense of invulnerability, of indestructibility, that permeates much teenage thinking, along with the difficulty of discussing sexual matters, often leads teens to close their eyes and hope for the best.

Teen pregnancy poses numerous risks—health risks, economic

risks, social risks—to both the mother and her baby. Infants born to teens are significantly more likely to be born with a low birth weight (5.5 pounds or less), which is strongly associated with both infant mortality and health problems later in life. In 1985, infants born to teens accounted for 12.7 percent of all births but accounted for 17.6 percent of all low-birth-weight births. In 1985, 6.9 percent of all babies born to mothers ages twenty to twenty-four were of low birth weight, while 9.3 percent of babies born to mothers fifteen to nineteen and 12.9 percent of those born to mothers under fifteen were of low birth weight.

If we consider prenatal care, the discrepancies become even wider. Women aged fifteen to nineteen are far less likely to receive early prenatal care than women aged twenty to twenty-four, and the youngest women (under fifteen) are the least likely to receive adequate care. If we look at mothers who receive late or no prenatal care, the youngest group, the most vulnerable, is most likely to receive late or no prenatal care, while the oldest group is the least likely.

If we examine prenatal care by race, we again see enormous discrepancies. Three-quarters (72.3 percent) of all white women in 1985 received "adequate" prenatal care, while only half of all black women (50.1 percent) received such care. It should come as no surprise, therefore, that the black maternal-mortality rate (20.4 deaths per 100,000 live births) is four times greater than the white rate (5.2 per 100,000), or that the black infant-mortality rate (infant deaths in the first year of life per 1,000 live births) is double (18.2) that of white infants (9.3). Moreover, miscarriages and still-births are more frequent among teenagers than among adult women, and children born to teenage mothers are more likely to be injured and hospitalized by the age of five.

It is clear, therefore, that teen pregnancy poses serious health problems for young mothers and for their babies but particularly for poor, black, and other nonwhite young women and children. Teen childbearing, moreover, poses severe social, psychological, and economic problems as well. Studies indicate, for example, that young women who give birth while they are in junior high school or high school complete fewer years of school on the average than those who delay childbearing into their twenties. They are less likely to earn a high-school diploma, to go to college or to graduate school. Teenage mothers are more likely to drop out of school, either when they give birth or prior to giving birth.

It is often difficult to determine cause and effect between teenage pregnancy and educational attainment. Certainly, the older the woman at the time she first gives birth, the more years of schooling she is likely to have; similarly, the more years of education, the more likely she is to delay childbearing. Moreover, while most evidence indicates that many women who bear a child in their teenage years do continue their education, studies indicate that most will never catch up educationally with those who have not borne a child during their early years.

Conditions for pregnant students have certainly improved in recent years. Until the mid-1970s many pregnant students were forced to leave school. Since 1975 many school systems have made arrangements for pregnant teens to stay in school, either in regular classes or in alternative programs. But, of course, it is not easy for a pregnant sixteen- or seventeen-year-old to stay in school either before or after the baby is born.

In part because of their educational deficits, women who bear their first child during their teenage years are less likely to have appropriate training and marketable skills, and therefore are less likely to find stable and well-paying work, than women who delay their childbearing. It is worth noting that the effects of early child-bearing on work status and income are significantly greater for whites than for blacks. This is at least partially because black women earn significantly less than white women and so have less to lose.

Teenagers who become mothers are "disproportionately poor and dependent on public assistance for their economic support." While public assistance is frequently not their preferred means of support, and teenage mothers do not use welfare continuously, the cost to society of teenage childbearing is considerable. A 1985 estimate indicates that in the past ten years the cost for AFDC (Aid to Families with Dependent Children) ($8.3 billion), food stamps ($3.4 billion), and Medicaid ($4.9 billion) has nearly doubled, to a total of $16.6 billion.

Even if they are married, teen mothers are at high risk for poverty, in part because they are at high risk for divorce. Teen marriages are far more likely to end in divorce than marriages of couples who are older; and if and when they divorce, young mothers are then faced with all of the problems of single parenthood. Because of early childbearing, they are unlikely to have completed their education, to have acquired significant job skills or experience, and have the problem of finding accessible and acceptable child care.

While early childbearers are clearly disadvantaged compared with women who have children later in life, significant variation exists in the patterns of their future lives. A recent seventeen-year follow-up study of young Baltimore women who gave birth to their first child as teenagers indicates that while "most women were disadvantaged by teenage parenthood," nevertheless "a substantial majority of the young mothers in our study completed high school, found regular employment, and even when they had been on welfare, eventually managed to escape from public assistance." The authors state that their findings "lend some credibility to the belief that the life course remains to some degree fluid and flexible" but that the findings also suggest that there are "definite limits as to how much room early childbearers have in which to manipulate their circumstances in later life."

Why are U.S. pregnancy rates, birthrates, and abortion rates so much higher than those of comparable Western industrialized countries? The six-country case study published in 1986 and sponsored by the Guttmacher Institute indicates that one key factor is that contraceptive use, particularly the pill, is much more widespread in the five other countries than in the United States. In several of the countries condoms have been made widely available through sale not only in family-planning clinics and pharmacies but also in "supermarkets, kiosks, and ubiquitous vending machines." The study found, in addition, that in at least three countries (Sweden, the Netherlands, and France), confidentiality was assured to teenagers obtaining contraceptives.

Access to abortion seems to be another factor. Abortions are available at no cost in France and in England and Wales. The cost to the woman is low in Canada and Sweden and quite low in the Netherlands. In the U.S. more than two-thirds of the states require that the woman pay the full cost of the abortion, whether or not she can afford it.

Sex and contraceptive education differ markedly in the five other countries; but in Sweden there has been an emphasis on school-based education, and in the Netherlands there has been widespread public education through the media. In short, according to the Guttmacher study, "teenagers living in countries where contraceptive services, sex education in and out of the schools, and abortion services are widely available have lower rates of adolescent pregnancy and do not have appreciable higher levels of sexual experience than do teenagers in the United States."

What of the economic prospects for teenagers in these countries? What about the theory that young women who have little hope for the future, women who have limited life options, are the ones who get pregnant and, even more important, are the ones who decide to have their babies and keep them? The Guttmacher study found that

teenagers' prospects for economic improvement do not appear to be appreciably greater in the five case-study countries than in the United States; nor is the educational achievement of young people greater. However, more extensive health, welfare, and unemployment benefits in other countries keep poverty from being as deep or as widespread as it is in the United States.

Moreover, the study points out that income is more evenly distributed in the five European countries than in the United States. Perhaps the Guttmacher study summarizes most clearly the conflicts American society places on its young women:

In general, American teenagers seem to have inherited the worst of all possible worlds insofar as their exposure to messages about sex are concerned: movies, music, radio, and television tell them that nonmarital sex is romantic, exciting, and titillating; premarital sex and cohabitation are visible ways of life among the adults they see and hear about; their own par-

ents or their parents' friends are likely to be divorced or separated but involved in sexual relationships. Yet at the same
time, young people get the message (now subsidized by the
federal government) that good girls say no. Little that teenagers
see or hear about sex informs them about contraception or
the consequences of sexual activity. . . . Such mixed messages
lead to the kind of ambivalence about sex that stifles communication between partners and exposes young people to
increased risk of pregnancy, out-of-wedlock births, and abortions.

Finally, while adolescent pregnancy is by no means limited to
the poor, poverty and hopelessness are closely associated with
teenage childbearing. As the report of the Panel on Adolescent
Pregnancy and Childbearing of the National Research Council has
stated: "Research has shown the deleterious effects of poverty on
those caught in its cycle: attitudes of fatalism, powerlessness, alienation and helplessness that are perpetuated from one generation
to the next." To young women who have inferior education, inadequate skills, and few opportunities for jobs with a future, having
a baby at a relatively young age may not seem to be such an
undesirable option. While these young people may not actively
choose to become pregnant, once they are, being a mother is at
least a role they can envision, one with adult status and with the
promise of some emotional gratification. In any case, once they are
pregnant, these young people must sort through their own feelings
about abortion, the attitudes and values of their friends, family,
community, and possibly those of a boyfriend, and make a decision
that is likely to affect the rest of their lives.

As we have seen, young people, particularly young women, must
decode the many messages they receive from a wide variety of
sources and somehow make some sense of them. These disparate
and often conflicting messages from parents, teachers, peers, popular culture, celebrities, political leaders, and other significant opinion makers make it extraordinarily difficult and confusing for young
women to take charge of their lives. Decisions on issues such as
having or postponing sex, using or not using birth control, ter-

minating or not terminating a pregnancy (not to speak of the use of drugs and liquor or the many other options readily available to young people today) are rooted in a complex web of social, psychological, economic, political, and religious factors and have a profound impact on the individual's life, both in the immediate future and in the long term. The sorting-through of these issues and the active establishing of priorities that will maximize their life chances in the future certainly seem easier for the New American Dreamers and the Neotraditionalists than for the Outsiders. Although these decisions are difficult for many of the young women with whom I spoke, the New American Dreamers' fundamental sense of entitlement, clear, concrete goals for the future, and belief that they will achieve at least some of these goals help them to get through this difficult period with minimum damage to their future lives. The Neotraditionalists may not have such concrete individual goals and may be more conflicted by their desire to play a more traditional female role; but many of them, along with many New American Dreamers, live within a social structure that so exalts the future and denigrates any derailing of it that they too are often able somehow to handle current pressures and preserve future options.

The New American Dreamers and the Neotraditionalists might decide to have sex, but then they might well get themselves some birth control. If they don't obtain contraception in time, they are likely to have an abortion. They believe in their future; they need to preserve their chances for that future. Some New American Dreamers and Neotraditionalists indeed become pregnant. Some have abortions; some have their babies. Some, because of the experience, are shunned by family and friends and become Outsiders. But often they remain women who still believe in themselves and what they can do with their lives.

The Outsiders, on the other hand, have little faith in the future. They see few choices, few options. They don't really see where they fit in. If they have dreams, they seem to be just that, dreams, rather than plans or blueprints for the next ten to fifteen years. They are, consequently, far more vulnerable to pressures, demands, and short-term solutions than the women in the other groups.

Managing the pressures of sex and reproduction in a society so ambivalent about a woman's right to manage her own sexuality and reproduction is a formidable task. It is clear that until young women have meaningful life options, a real understanding of sex and reproduction, widespread access to contraception and abortion, and a strong sense of their own self-worth, we are unlikely to see any significant reduction in teenage pregnancy or to see young women really take control of their sexual and reproductive lives.

CHAPTER 6

The Search for Intimacy

I want that intimacy . . . that sense of continuity, of having a world together. I want a best friend.

ADRIENNE WERNER
health planner, New York

An ever-present theme in many of my interviews with young women was that they would one day find someone with whom they could share their lives. While the New American Dreamers presented work and the rewards of work as a central theme in their vision of their lives, for many of them a long-lasting, intimate relationship constituted a strong secondary theme. They recognized that marriage and work might sometimes be in conflict or operate independently of each other, almost in counterpoint; but they clearly hoped to weave the two together so that they might complement each other.

If the primary theme among New American Dreamers was work and achievement and the secondary theme relationship, among many of the Neotraditionalists the two were either presented equally or, in some instances, an intimate relationship and raising children was clearly the central agenda, with work or individual achievement the subsidiary desire. However the young women envisioned their futures, most of them considered work and a commitment to family essential. Even many of the women who were

147

not sure they would find that intimate relationship, even those who felt they had to make it on their own and be able to take care of themselves, often fantasized about a life with husband and children. In many cases, it almost seemed as though this new image of woman—competent, achieving, successful—had been superimposed on the old image—caring, loving, available to meet the needs of others. Some were concerned about how to weave these roles together; others simply assumed it would all work out.

Many of the Outsiders, however, shared neither the dream of achievement nor that of the romantic, enduring intimate relationship. Some were already at a young age saddled with the enormous responsibility of raising children and were simply trying to wend their way from day to day. Many were already in serious relationships but spoke of their foreboding that the relationships would not last. In many instances it seemed that these women viewed their children as their intimate connection with others. Men may come and go, but the relationship with their children was an unbreakable bond.

Many researchers have recently explored the psychology of women and found that women indeed speak "in a different voice." According to one group of researchers, "Women typically approach adulthood with the understanding that the care and empowerment of others is central to their life's work." According to Carol Gilligan, "Attachment and separation anchor the cycle of human life. . . . [These] concepts . . . that depict the nature and sequence of infant development appear in adolescence as identity and intimacy and then in adulthood as love and work." Gilligan maintains that "women perceive and construe social reality differently from men and . . . these differences center around experiences of attachment and separation." She goes on to state that "women's sense of integrity appears to be entwined with an ethic of care, so that to see themselves as women is to see themselves in a relationship of connection."

Jean Baker Miller phrases it a bit differently. She points out:

Male society, by depriving women of the right to its major "bounty"—that is, development according to the male model—overlooks the fact that women's development *is* proceeding, but on another basis. One central feature is that women stay with, build on, and develop in a context of attachment and affiliation with others. Indeed, women's sense of self becomes very much organized around being able to make and then to maintain affiliations and relationships.

But Miller also points out that women's "greater sense of the emotional components of all human activities . . . is, in part, a result of their training as subordinates; for anyone in a subordinate position must learn to be attuned to the vicissitudes of mood, pleasure, and displeasure of the dominant group."

Political scientist Joan Tronto expands on this theme by suggesting that caring

> may be a reflection of a survival mechanism for women or others who are dealing with oppressive conditions. . . . Another way to understand caring is to see it as an ethic that is most appropriate for those who are in a subordinate social position. Just as women and others who are not in the central corridors of power in this society adopt a variety of deferential mannerisms . . . so too it may have served their purposes of survival to . . . anticipate the wishes of one's superior.

If indeed "interpersonal competence is more important to adolescent girls than is autonomy" and women's concerns center around "connectedness," then for women a "dominant fear is of being stranded, far out on the edge and isolated from others." Major studies of male development indicate that growing up for men is moving from dependence to autonomy, that identity is based on "being and becoming," on "career achievement and independence." If, on the other hand, relatedness and attachment are central to women's identity, the search for intimacy becomes a crucial component of women's sense of self. Perhaps a professional woman in her thirties put it best when she said in our interview that a long-lasting, intimate relationship gives one "the confidence of being loved." Is it perhaps true that for many women no external, societal acknowledgment of worth and no internal sense of self-worth can provide the same sense of well-being as an intimate, loving relationship? If this is the case, finding such a relationship indeed becomes central to women's lives. This certainly seems to be the case with the Neotraditionalists I interviewed and with some of the women in the two other groups as well. But for many of the New American Dreamers, "being and becoming" and "career achievement and independence" seem to be priorities, at least at this point in their lives. Is this group reflecting a fundamental change in the way some women see their future? Are some women indeed putting achievement and autonomy above affiliation? Will these values last as they move into their thirties? Are women who feel they must choose between achievement and affiliation in an impossible bind?

Many women do, of course, find that special relationship. Headlines and stories in the popular press, soap operas, sitcoms, and films may focus on male/female incompatibility, on divorce, adultery, wife battering and other forms of domestic violence, but, as we all know, millions of couples do live at least reasonably happily ever after. Some are particularly fortunate and find, in addition to mutual love and support, a true meeting of the minds, a philosophical compatibility that serves to place the vicissitudes of life in broader perspective. And many indeed find the intimacy they seek, that component of marriage, according to Francine Klagsbrun, author of *Married People: Staying Together in the Age of Divorce,* "most longed for, and often the most elusive." Klagsbrun continues by defining intimacy as

an expression of self, an ability to feel what someone else feels, know what someone else needs and put oneself out, when necessary, to satisfy the other person's feelings and needs. Stretching oneself in this way doesn't mean losing oneself or, to use psychological jargon, fusing oneself with the other person. It does mean maintaining a constant awareness of the other person and that person's desires, even as the other maintains an awareness of you and your wishes.

This exchange of knowledge, and with it, the ability to give to another without resentment and in turn receive from that other without embarrassment is what intimacy is all about.

In the hope of trying to understand what makes relationships work today, I interviewed a number of women in their thirties who feel they have extraordinarily good marriages. These women are essentially the in-between generation, the generation between the young women who are the central focus of this book and their mothers, who are likely to be in their forties or possibly in their early fifties. They have all felt the impact of the women's movement and are attempting to work out their day-to-day lives more or less within a feminist context. Perhaps three examples will give the flavor of some of the relationships that seem to be working and the underlying principles that guide them.

The women, who are at different stages of family life, all stress the importance of common values and common interests to the health of their marriages. Janet Stein, a social worker in her late thirties who has been married for nearly twenty years, expressed this theme when she said, "We like each other so much! There's not another person I respect more, and I think he feels the same way."

Janet and her husband, Peter, also a social worker, met in the late 1960s when they were both in college. After knowing each other less than three weeks, Peter told her, "I want to spend the rest of my life with you." One month after they married Janet found she was pregnant. After their son was born, she became depressed, and Peter "knew he needed to spend more time at home." He became involved in caring for their baby and has remained extraordinarily involved in child rearing throughout their son's childhood and adolescence. She and Peter have not lived according to traditional gender roles in other ways as well. He doesn't have a "wife" in the usual sense, she states. He does his own shirts; he loves to cook. He is "not afraid of a woman who is an equal." Janet, who was and continues to be active in the feminist movement, feels that Peter's actions have often been a "crystallization" of the concepts she and the other women in her consciousness-raising group used to discuss.

Since the early years of their marriage, Janet and Peter have taken turns returning to school, she to obtain her undergraduate and graduate degrees, he to obtain a graduate degree. They have alternated earning the primary family income and have over the years supported one another both financially and emotionally. They are both also deeply committed to political and community organizing and support one another in these activities as well.

Janet points out that the last twenty years have not been easy ones for long-term relationships—many women went through a period of separatism, and there was substantial pressure to give up on marriage and become involved in lesbian relationships—but that she and Peter discussed these issues and "went through changes at the same pace." She says, "We grew up together. We took the relationship very seriously. It has matured and ripened. Neither one of us has been involved with anyone else. It never crossed my mind to have an affair with another man or with a woman, even though there have been opportunities. We have a deep commitment to each other as fellow human beings."

Recently their son went off to college, and Janet says that a "new rhythm is setting in; we're playing new music together."

Janet and Peter's relationship may be a model of an egalitarian marriage, but far more traditional arrangements can also lead to close, caring, long-lasting relationships. Diane and Bob Miller, a couple in their early thirties, have been married eleven years. They met and married when she was in college and he in graduate school. They were married seven years before their first child was born, and during this time she worked in marketing for a major utilities firm. When they decided to have children, she felt she wanted to be home with them. She has two daughters, one year apart, and is pregnant with a third.

Before the children were born, Diane and Bob shared all the housework. Now, although she does most of the food shopping and laundry and Bob is the primary breadwinner (she has done some part-time work on a consulting basis since she left her job), they do not divide up the work at home in a completely traditional way—she mows the lawn and does the budgeting, he helps cook dinner and bathes the children. She thinks a key element in their family life is that they have a relaxed relationship. When one of them sees work that needs to be done, she or he does it.

What has changed, however, is her attitude toward financial decisions. Now that she is bringing home little, if any, money and does not have her own bank account, she feels she has a "whole different mind set." She feels uncomfortable about making any major purchase, including clothing for herself, without discussing it with her husband. "If I had my own full-time income," she states definitively, "I wouldn't hesitate to go out and treat myself to a fabulous suit. My generation did go to college in order to earn our own income and to be independent. It's important to have that back."

Diane would like to work part-time after the baby is born. She used to work with computers and says somewhat ruefully, "In the computer world, I'm ancient history"—but, she muses, she could be retrained. In college everyone was looking toward business, law, medicine, or accounting; now that she and her friends are involved in caring for their children, they are looking for jobs near home with flexible hours, maybe nursing or teaching. She feels she will work it out.

Diane describes her relationship with her husband as "best friends." Being lovers is, she feels, "overrated." What's important is being best friends: "That's what's held us together all these years. We married young and grew up together. It's almost frightening how close we are. We're totally happily married. I love him to death and he loves me to death."

She stresses that they are very much alike, with the same interests and the same priorities, but states that they have real personality differences. Bob is more "structured in his outlook, more conservative, more rigid" but has the "capability to change his mind." She is, she feels, more patient, can hear what people are saying. But what is important is that if one has a stronger feeling, the other will give way. She cannot think of an issue in which that has not worked.

What about all these women like her who started out in careers and are now home having their third child? Diane feels it was her parents' generation that "opened up feminism," that she and her friends were "blessed with the opportunity to become career women" and do not feel the pressure to prove what they can do. "Bob and I were never dying for kids, but once we had them there was that maternal instinct to be home raising them." They have purposely had their children close together because she feels the option for work is "out there for the future," that soon she will be "ready to start life again." At the end of the interview she points out that while she started out marriage with a hyphenated last name, somewhere along the way her own name was dropped, and now she is known only by her husband's. She doesn't quite know when it happened, but she just thought she would mention it. . . .

Virtually all the women I interviewed who felt they had unusually close marriages used the same phrases: "He is my best friend," "We have mutual interests and common values," "The relationship has deepened over time." Lisa Richardson and Tom Marks, also in their early thirties, have been married for three years. She is in academia and he is an urban planner. They have no children as yet. Lisa points out yet another aspect of enduring relationships: that their mutual support enables each of them to be involved in many activities outside of the relationship. They are, she feels, simultaneously dependent upon and independent of each other. The relationship is both nurturing and enabling. Lisa feels that this kind of support is especially necessary "for women who are venturing into new waters. He assumes I can do whatever I want, and his confidence gives me confidence."

She also points out that while they agree on most issues, they nevertheless have very different personalities. She is, she feels, "more emotive, more introspective, more social" ("I like having and developing connections with people"), and he is "stronger, more pragmatic." These differences are, she believes, complementary and exist within a context of similarities—similarities in values, in political outlook, in their notions of how to have a good time. These relationships, often characterized by respect and care, should not be forgotten as we explore the difficulties faced by many women in their search for stable, long-lasting partnerships.

Many of the young women I interviewed, while they hope for egalitarian, companionable relationships, are only too aware of the dangers inherent in some intimate relationships. Melissa Ward, a college freshman, feels that some women her age allow men to become the "center of their lives." The couple are "around each other twenty-four hours a day," and almost all other relationships become peripheral. She, on the other hand, tries not to let a single relationship dominate her life. "I'm careful. I try to be careful when

I'm dating someone so that things don't get too intense. I have to keep my feet planted firmly on the ground. I don't want to lose contact with other people, with my friends."

Another college student, Jessica Grant, a twenty-one-year-old black woman from North Carolina, talks about her loss of identity during an intense relationship with her baby's father. "I met him here at school and fell head over heels in love. No one ever made me feel the way he made me feel. He made me lose all sense of my identity. I depended on him for everything. I let him think for me. He determined what I felt, what I did, the decisions I made. And he was a major con artist. The stuff he put me through! I would never depend on anyone like that again!"

Pamela Vincent, age twenty-five, describes her relationships with two men. In both instances this talented, dynamic, intelligent woman played a starkly subordinate role that seems strangely incompatible with her personality and abilities. Pam, a black woman who grew up in a middle-class family in Southern California, was engaged to a man while she was attending college in Los Angeles. They had already set the wedding date when, at age twenty-one, she became pregnant. She describes how she felt at the time: "I was so happy. It was something I had wanted for so long—to be a mama." She knew she was pregnant but waited before going to a doctor, because she didn't have any health insurance. "I was waiting for the insurance to kick in." But at eight weeks she knew something was wrong; she went to the hospital, found that she had a tubal pregnancy and was bleeding internally. Eventually, the tube burst. "It took me four months to recover physically," she recalls, "but two years to recover emotionally. I was really angry. I felt my baby had been taken from me. Now I have one tube, and the doctors tell me I can have children, but I don't really believe them."

After Pam lost the baby, her fiancé left her. She learned that he had been seeing someone else all along and that the other woman was also pregnant. He told her he was leaving her because the other woman "kept her baby and you didn't" and he walked out. She says, "I felt like I was on a skateboard and went *bam!* into a wall." She was in debt because of her medical expenses; she was poor and she was alone. She says, "I worked and struggled and struggled and struggled. I wanted to go back to school, but there were too many external forces."

After more than a year trying to get back on her feet, she joined forces with a Brazilian man with whom she had been friendly. "I needed help and he needed help. He needed a green card; he said he would take care of me. We got married. We got an apartment. I wanted to go on with my life; I assumed he would be able to comprehend that. He thought I was somebody's wife, somebody's property. He threw out all my clothes; he thought my underwear wasn't sexy enough and my outer clothes were too sexy. He threw out my makeup and took off the earrings I wore up the side of my ears. He said, 'You don't need these now.'

"He wanted me to stay in the house and locked me in. He started hitting me. I called the police three times, but they wouldn't do anything. Finally, I left. I called my mother and asked her to come get me."

Several aspects of Pam's experience are striking. First, she twice chose men who, in one way or another, abused her. Second, she needed to be taken care of so desperately that she entered into what was essentially an arranged marriage. She arranged it herself, but it was nonetheless based on an exchange of goods and services rather than on mutual love and respect. And finally, this intelligent, able woman with real options found herself repeatedly in a subordinate position, playing the role of victim.

The plethora of best-selling books that deal with unhappy, unequal, unsatisfying male/female relationships (e.g., *Smart Women, Foolish Choices; The Pleasers: Women Who Can't Say NO—and the Men Who Control Them; Women Who Love Too Much; Men Who Hate Women—and the Women Who Love Them*) indicates how widespread this problem is perceived to be. Women, particularly bright, assertive, successful women, are portrayed as all-too-willing victims, repeatedly choosing the "wrong" man, the one who will hurt them, the one who will give them pain instead of happiness. After analyzing the problem and presenting case histories, these self-help books provide alternative ways of behaving and relating. Their underlying assumption is that these problems are individual problems, brought on largely if not entirely by the women themselves, or possibly by their unfortunate childhood experiences, and that with enough will and positive thinking (and of course with the aid of a good book) women can alter their attitudes, their behavior, and therefore their lives. The part the larger culture plays in encouraging men and women to take on specific roles which seem to be repeated endlessly is rarely discussed.

The final chapters of many of these books are pop psychology's version of the five-minute makeover. The final chapter of *Smart Women, Foolish Choices,* for example, presents sixteen "Rules for Finding the Right Man," including "Rule Number Four—Growing up means giving up Daddy. Men want an adult lover, a friend and a partner—not a surrogate daughter. Childlike or manipulative women drive most men away." Men are presented as healthy, mature, egalitarian; women are neurotic, childlike, yearning to be victimized. The last chapter of *Women Who Love Too Much* gives the ten characteristics of "a woman who has recovered from loving too much" and the phases one must go through (almost like the Kübler-Ross phases of mourning) in the recovery process. The assumption is that it is all within the individual's control—that the "good" men are out there if only women have the right mixture of "self-esteem," "serenity," and "self-validation." That gender roles and relationships are far more complex, are deeply rooted in culture, in religion, in the economic and political system, and in day-to-day interaction, is virtually ignored. The underlying assumption, often stated explicitly, is that the individual can take control of her life and make of it what she wishes.

This domination of women by men must, however, be seen not simply as an individual, interpersonal phenomenon but as one which is built into the very structure of society. The patterns and organization of both public and private life, women's continuing economic dependence on men, particularly when children are involved, their continuing psychological dependence on an intimate relationship, and their continuing social dependence lead to a situation in which, according to one analyst, "male domination, like class domination, is no longer a function of personal power relationships (though these do exist), but something inherent in the social and cultural structures, independent of what individual men and women will."

Cecilia Martinez, a twenty-one-year-old Mexican-American woman, talks about her future and her long-term relationship with her "boyfriend." A junior majoring in urban development, Cecilia intends to go on for her master's degree and work in city planning, and would like to run for political office one day. She also plans to marry and have "as many children as we can afford."

Her boyfriend of five years, also Mexican-American, is a carpenter. According to Cecilia, he is "jealous," "macho," and believes "women should stay home and raise the children." But, she says, "we have chemistry; he knows where I'm coming from. He respects me. He protects me." It is clear while talking with Cecilia that she plans to marry this young man even though their views on many issues, particularly on the role of women, are very different. It is as though she sees the relationship as a trade-off—chemistry and protection in exchange for some loss of autonomy. But she cheerfully assumes she will work it all out.

Some women find that resisting subordination means they may well not find the intimate relationship they seek. A professional woman in her mid-thirties tells of how she always felt that she first needed to figure out who she was and then, once she knew herself, she wouldn't be subjugated and lose herself in a relationship. She has, however, not found it to be so easy. She feels that it is very difficult in serious relationships not to subordinate one's own interests and needs to another's. She suggests that while some women may be wary of undermining their own needs and desires and may be seeking more egalitarian relationships, many men—and, indeed, the larger society itself—automatically assume that the man's needs, wishes, and professional obligations take precedence. She describes, in some sense, an example of culture lag: the gulf between feminist attitudes of self-worth, self-determination, and self-preservation and the attitudes and expectations of much of the rest of society.

Carole Davis, a Connecticut-based reporter in her early thirties, who speaks quietly and thoughtfully, with an unusually self-possessed, self-assured manner, discusses this gulf between what many men want and the way some women see themselves. "My boyfriend wants someone to take care of him—to play the role of wife, plan outings, give dinner parties, do the mother thing. He wants a decorator, entertainer, caterer, and someone who will make sure his shirts are clean.

"And I'm just not domestic. I don't like shopping for furniture. I don't care what drapes are hanging by the windows. I think it is more important who is sitting on the couch than what couch they are sitting on.

"A lot of men say they like independent women, but when it comes right down to it they don't. They like a certain amount of dependence, but one person's dependence is another person's power and control."

Several months after we talked, this woman called to tell me that she and her friend were getting married. I asked how they had worked out their differences, and she indicated that he had come to see that she had other important qualities; perhaps the domestic issues were not quite so important. She indicated that the intervening months had not been easy and that she too would be doing some compromising.

It is ironic that both ends of the spectrum—having too little sense of self-worth and having a greater sense of self-worth than the rest of society is comfortable with—can impede a woman's achieving the kind of intimate relationship she desires. Some women feel there are fewer struggles over power and dominance in intimate relationships with other women than in those with men. A married woman in her late thirties speaks of her one sexual relationship with a woman: "She was the first person with whom I was friends before we were lovers. It was the most intense, meaningful relationship in my life. No one has ever loved me as much without my having to be what she wanted. She just loved me for myself. With men I had always tried to second-guess what they wanted and be the kind of person they wanted. With her I could be myself." Despite their exceedingly close relationship, this woman decided to marry in order to have a child.

When asked what women are looking for in an intimate relationship, with either a man or a woman, she says, "Acceptance." She goes on: "What's important is that the relationship will be okay even if you mess up, even if you're not perfect. What's important is getting and giving, having someone who will allow us to give to them in the way we want to give."

A gay woman in her forties from the Washington, D.C., metropolitan area who has been in a relationship with another woman for over twelve years feels that lesbian relationships are often far more egalitarian than many heterosexual relationships: "The old stereotype of a 'butch/fem' dichotomy does not exist today. Most gay couples do not assume male and female roles. They are both women. Each person does what she can do. And each one switches off caring and being cared for. I like to give and I like to receive. Occasionally we're both needy at the same time and then we have battles, but it gets resolved."

What does being in such a relationship mean to this woman, who dated men when she was young and then was, in her words, "asexual" until her mid-thirties?

"Not to have a relationship like this is really to be alone. By yourself. Empty. It hurts my heart, physically, to think about her not being here. I know she really loves me, and that says I'm worthwhile, that I can do anything. It reaffirms the goodness in me. I have had very close, intimate friends who made me feel good, but this is an entirely different order. The interrelatedness of two souls is different than the connections of very good friends. I didn't even know what I was missing until I got it. Now it would be the end of the world if I lost it."

In conversations with women, both younger women and those in their thirties and forties, the most frequent response to the question "What are women looking for in a relationship?" was, in the words of one woman, "To know that someone loves you unconditionally, like your mom. No matter what you do, he [or sometimes she] will still be there and say it's okay." Unconditional love? Like your mom's? Psychiatrist Willard Gaylin in his book *Rediscovering Love* suggests that this quest for unconditional love is characteristic of many in "narcissistic America in the late twentieth century":

What does craving to be loved for ourselves—as distinguished from our traits, our attributes, our behavior, and yes, even our possessions and our position—what does that mean? There is no inner self independent of our behavior, our character, and our form. There is only one time . . . when one is loved for oneself, independent of one's behavior. That of course is in the first stage of early infancy.

While many of these 1980s women are seeking identity through affiliation with a man, many are seeking personal validation through such a relationship. Instead of "I'm okay, you're okay," the slogan might be "We're okay, I'm okay." As Rachel Brownstein has stated, describing the "marriage plot most novels depend on": "The man's love is proof of the girl's value. . . . Her search for perfect love through an incoherent, hostile wilderness of days is the plot that endows the aimless [life] with aim. Her quest is to be recognized in all her significance, to have her worth made real by being approved."

And what if one doesn't find such love? The response then often is "What's wrong with me? If someone cannot love me unconditionally, maybe I am simply unlovable, fundamentally flawed." In a world of couples, it is once again to be the Outsider.

That theme of being loved and accepted for oneself is elaborated by Adrienne Werner, a professional woman in her mid-thirties. The daughter of German refugees, she grew up in New York City. From the time she was a young girl, she says, she wanted to be Albert Schweitzer, she wanted to "change the world." But she also wanted to have a family. "I wanted to be pregnant, have four children and adopt more. I wanted to live in a big farmhouse with something always on the stove, a place where people could drop in."

As a child, Adrienne feels, she was "shy," she "didn't fit in." She didn't date a lot in high school. It wasn't until college and graduate school that she began having serious relationships with men. She imagined marrying someone who was very well educated, an academic or an artist, but says that her mother "always told me I was 'too mature' for guys. I was too serious; I didn't know how to play." She has had several serious relationships, "a lot of almosts," but nothing has quite worked out.

At the age of thirty, she decided she "wasn't going to wait for Godot" and started thinking about what she wanted for her life. She entered a Ph.D. program and today is close to receiving her doctorate. She says a bit ruefully, "I didn't get an MRS., but at least I'm getting a Ph.D." She goes on, "It's very scary. I really would like to have a relationship and a family, but at this age you feel like you've missed your chance. And there are lots of other women like me."

Adrienne talks about what it is like to be single: "I have a fairly good network of friends, but it's not enough. I want that intimacy, that different level of intimacy, that sense of continuity, of having a world together. I want a best friend. I want that unconditional regard—someone who loves me not for my performance, not as a student or as a worker, but for myself.

"I have a tendency to take care of people. Sometimes *I* need to be taken care of—to be loved for who I am, not just for taking care of others. I've always been in leadership positions, and I know I seem confident, poised, self-sufficient; but I'm crying inside. I'm really feeling, 'Someone come over here and take care of me.' "

Adrienne feels that she's "missed the boat"—it's just too late. She points out that most professional women who are married with children did it all at once—found their mates while they were studying or as young professionals. She feels you have to work it out when you're twenty-six or twenty-seven. By the time a woman is into her thirties, it's too late. "[Men have] already chosen someone else."

Adrienne's anxiety that she has "missed the boat" has been fueled by studies during the mid-1980s indicating that college-educated women in their mid-thirties were unlikely to find a partner. One study in particular, an unpublished paper by two sociologists from Yale and an economist from Harvard, stated that for an unmarried woman of thirty, the probability of eventual marriage was only 20 percent; for a woman of thirty-five, only 5 percent; and for an unmarried woman of forty, the probability of marriage had dropped to one percent. The media—print, television, and radio— all featured the story, sending waves of fear into the hearts of many women over the age of thirty. *Newsweek* warned, "For those who wait to get married, 'not now' probably means 'never.' "

Other researchers have since calculated the probability of marriage for women at various ages and have made predictions far less dire. For example, Jeanne E. Moorman, a demographer at the U.S.

Bureau of the Census, has calculated that "a 15-year-old female who goes on to complete college before she marries has a 94 to 96 percent probability of eventually marrying. The probability of marriage for a college graduate not married by 30 is between 58 and 66 percent. At age 35, it drops to 32 to 41 percent and age 40, it is between 17 and 23 percent." As one observer has noted, however, neither the Harvard/Yale study nor the Moorman analysis "differentiated between women who want to get married, those who don't, those who favor living together without marriage, those who have plenty of opportunities to marry, those who haven't, and those who haven't given it a thought."

Nonetheless, among the young women I interviewed the vast majority expected to marry. How realistic is this expectation? In 1983, for example, 95 percent of white women and 91 percent of black women under the age of 35 had been married at least once. But what about the divorce rate? Between 1960 and the early 1980s the divorce rate rose steeply, and since then it has remained relatively stable. Over the past fifteen years almost half of all marriages have ended in divorce. For black women the divorce rate has soared over the past twenty-five years; black women, moreover, are more likely to be separated than divorced. In the 1980s over 20 percent of all married black women were separated from their husbands. In addition, among black women the percentage of never-married women is increasing significantly.

Once they have separated, remarriage becomes increasingly problematic for all women as they age. While 72 percent of separated women will eventually remarry, approximately 40 percent of women who separated while in their thirties and about 70 percent of women who separated when they were over 40 will never remarry. In addition, among those who do remarry, half will divorce seven years after their separations. These projections indicate that separation can mean long periods of single life and hardship for many women and their children, particularly for black women, only 46 percent of whom will remarry compared to 76 percent of non-Hispanic white women.

The impact of divorce on the lives of women has been studied extensively over the past decade. Virtually all studies indicate that after divorce women experience sharp declines in their economic status. One study of 60 divorced women, each of whom was middle class during marriage, indicated that 90 percent of the women reported that after their divorces their incomes had dropped near or below the poverty line. They had, in effect, become the "new poor," and this status was in most cases not temporary. The women, not unexpectedly, continued to think of themselves as middle class; while their standard of living dropped dramatically, their expectations of themselves and their children remained the same; and consequently, many of the women found themselves struggling with depression and despair. The same study indicates that these women had trouble obtaining work, had to deal with sex, age, and wage discrimination, and had to resolve the daily—and often agonizing—conflicts between work and child rearing.

While many of the young women with whom I talked recognized the high rate of divorce in American society and felt they had to be prepared to take care of themselves and their children, few were willing to acknowledge that they might become divorced. Occasionally a young woman whose parents had undergone a particularly difficult marriage and divorce stated that marriage was not for her because she did not want to go through all that pain; but the young women generally assumed they would live their lives in a traditional nuclear family. They did not anticipate that they might live in one of the 9 million U.S. households in which at least one of the spouses was remarried after a divorce or that they might be the adult in one of the 10 million female-headed households.

Black women are faced with special problems in their search for intimacy. William Julius Wilson and his associates have pointed out that when black male joblessness is combined with "relatively high rates of incarceration and premature mortality," their ability to function as true partners and to help provide economic support is far less than the ability of white men. Wilson et al. claim there has been "a long-term decline in the proportion of black men, and particularly young black men, who are in a position to support a family." They go on to point out that the relationship between joblessness and marital instability has been well documented. The result is that "black single women are less likely to marry than are white women; black women who are separated are less likely to divorce; and black women who are divorced are less likely to remarry." Over the past two decades among black families the percentage of black married-couple families has declined significantly and the percentage of female-headed families has risen dramatically. There is such a shortage of black men who can really function in a relationship and in society that, according to one black social worker, many black women are being more submissive, more compliant and willing to compromise in their search for long-term relationships. Some, she says, are knowingly sharing men in their effort to keep them around at all.

The economic consequences of this rapid rise in female-headed households is readily apparent. In 1987 the median income for black married-couple families was $27,182, nearly triple that of black female-headed households, $9,710. For Hispanic families the discrepancy in median income was nearly as great—$24,677 for married couples and $9,805 for female-headed families. The comparable data for white families are $35,295 for married-couple families and only half of that, $17,018, for female-headed families.

In 1987 12.3 percent of black married-couple families lived below the poverty line ($11,611 for a family of four) compared with 51.8 percent of black female-headed families. Among Hispanic families a shockingly high 18.1 percent of married-couple families and 51.8 percent of female-headed families lived below the poverty line in 1987. If we compare these statistics with those of white families, we find that 5.2 percent of married-couple families live in poverty while five times as many, 26.7 percent, of female-headed families are living in poverty. Young women may think they can "go it alone," but the likelihood of their doing so in poverty is very great.

The stress of raising a family alone, of poverty or near-poverty, and of loneliness and social isolation—problems common to many women who must manage on their own—takes its toll on all women but particularly on many black women. The experience of Hazel Reynolds, a black family-planning counselor in New Jersey, illustrates some of the problems that many black women face on a day-to-day basis. The mother of four daughters, who range in age from twelve to twenty-three, this intelligent, articulate, handsome forty-two-year-old woman has been married twice. Neither marriage worked out well. Her parents separated and divorced when she was in her early teens; she feels she was "in need of nurturing" and was trying to find that nurturing in her relationships with men. She had promised herself she would "marry and never, ever divorce" but had to take that promise back after her first husband abused her. He had been in several foster homes as a child and had witnessed his mother's many relationships with men. Hazel feels she was the target of his anger and frustration. His beatings often left her black and blue, and she was particularly concerned not only that her oldest daughter had witnessed many of the beatings but that he beat the children as well.

Her second husband "had everything I needed—he understood me, was compassionate, and met all my needs for nurturing." But he was a drug addict. She knew this when she married him. In fact, he would tell her, "I'm not good enough for you," but she believed he would never use drugs again. "I was naive," she says. "There has never been a problem I couldn't work through. I thought that was true for everyone else."

After thirteen years of his being in and out of drug clinics and hospitals and being brought up on theft charges, they separated. He is now "into the wet one," alcohol, and is "dual-addicted." He pays no child support. According to Hazel, "He can't even take care of himself."

Hazel talks about the experience that she feels turned her life around:

"I have always had severe asthma. Two years ago I had an upper respiratory infection and was having problems breathing. I went to the store to get some medicine. Three of the children were with me in the car. When we got there, I was having more trouble breathing. My daughter called the rescue squad, and when I tried to get out of the car I passed out. I woke up in the hospital, and two days later I nearly died from cardiac arrest. They put me on a respirator in intensive care, and I just cried out to the Lord, 'This is it. This is it for me.'

"My oldest daughter took over at home, and I said to myself, 'Who's here for me? Where are these men? Where is my husband?' And I realized my husband couldn't take care of me. My parents couldn't take care of me. I had to take care of myself. Those thirteen days in the hospital I evaluated where I was and where I should have been, and I realized I had to take care of Hazel.

"That's when everything started rolling. I started to look younger, like I became a new person. I decided no more caretaking. All my life I took care of others. Now only my children. I also realized I could not be bitter or angry. I couldn't hold resentment. I chose these men. No one twisted my arm and made me marry them."

Hazel now feels that what she's been searching for can be found only within herself. "I am the only one who can make my own happiness." She feels she has a new awareness of her own "growth and commitment," her "purpose in life." "We are all put here for a reason," she says. "We all come with talent, and sometimes we find out what it is through hardship." Her purpose, she feels, is to "help others who have been hurt to come through their painful periods in life, to help them to know that these times won't last always, that there will be better times, and that you can't drink or drug away the bad times."

What about her relationships with men now? Hazel says, "Now I am able to meet men and know exactly what I'm looking for. I don't need men. I'm going to be who I am regardless. It's nice to have dinner with someone, to go to a movie—but it's not necessary." She says that while she has not ruled out marriage, what she wants is commitment, and she will not have a sexual relationship unless the relationship is moving toward commitment and marriage. "I was tested for AIDS and the test was negative—and that's a blessing, considering I had been married to a drug addict. I'm not taking any chances. No more peer pressure; no more pressure to perform. Now I know that Hazel is okay. When you realize you're okay, that the man doesn't make you who you are—when you realize that, you've made it."

Many women hope—indeed yearn—for an intimate relationship, one in which they can love and be loved, and share values, goals, and dreams. Many indeed find such relationships. But an increasing number of women recognize that they may never find a long-lasting intimate connection with a lover or that such a connection may be fleeting. Because of the uncertain nature of relationships and women's increasing awareness of their own intrinsic value, Hazel's words may to many be particularly poignant and persuasive. Moreover, the uncertainty of relationships and women's greater sense of self, of independence have given work greater importance, greater significance. Many look with optimism toward a life of meaningful, well-paid employment. Almost all of the young women with whom I spoke plan occupations that will enable them to support themselves and define their own identity. Most also hope to combine work with a strong commitment to family. Let us now examine how realistic these goals are for the majority of women today.

CHAPTER 7

The Real World of Women's Work

The male model of work is the working model. It never lets up. If you take time off, you'll get behind—in technical expertise, in publications, in climbing the academic ladder.

SARAH STARK, M.D.
physician/researcher, New York City

It's horrifying. You have to make a strategy to divide your time between the infant with pneumonia, the screaming baby in a wet diaper, and trying to find a compassionate way to tell another set of parents that their child has just died.

LYNDA LEVY, R.N.
pediatric nurse, the Bronx

Perhaps the most startling aspect of my interviews with young women was their vision of their future work lives. The young women had basically four scenarios for the future: they would enter high-status, high-income professions, such as law, medicine, and business; they would enter more traditional women's occupations, such as art, design, modeling, or the health professions; they would be home with children for the first few years and then find part-time work that was compatible with a primary commitment to child rearing and homemaking; or they could not imagine the future at all. But, with the exception of the last group, the theme that transcends the vast majority of the responses is the desire—indeed, the intention—to be affluent. Perhaps one of the most poignant

169

examples is a seventeen-year-old black high-school senior from California whose mother is on welfare, whose father is "on dope," and whose stepfather "sits around." By the time she is twenty-five, she plans she will be working, have her "own place," and consider having her first child. She doesn't think she will be married—perhaps when she's "older." She would like to have a "BMW convertible" and "a house on a hill" by the time she is thirty. It is not clear whether she plans on acquiring the "house on a hill" on her own or by "marrying someone rich." However they plan to achieve it, the image of "the good life," the affluent life, is the common thread in nearly all the interviews.

The other common thread in the beliefs of these young women is that they cannot count on a man—that they are going to have to be able to provide for themselves. If one combines these two dominant expectations, it becomes clear that young women are going to have to earn a very good income indeed in order to provide themselves and their children (if they have any) with the life-styles they desire.

If these are the dreams, what is the economic reality for women as we enter the last decade of the twentieth century? Recent headlines tell much of the story: "Making a Living Is NOW a Family Enterprise"; "Top Labor Issue: Jobs for Single Mothers"; "For Women Lawyers, an Uphill Struggle"; "Jobs Go Begging in Human Services"; "Are Women Better Doctors?"; "New York Is Fighting Spread of Sweatshops"; "More Women in Top State Posts"; "Women Gain Little in Academic Jobs"; "Despite Job Gains, Sexual Segregation Remains, U.S. Says."

Over the past twenty years, women have entered the labor force in astonishing numbers. During the 1960s the number of women in the labor force grew by 39 percent; during the 1970s, by 41 percent. By March 1986, 64 percent of all women under the age of 65 were in the labor force.

Women's entrance into paid employment during this period was not the only dramatic change taking place; women's move into previously male-dominated professions was also dramatic. The number of women entering medicine, for example, has increased significantly in recent years. In 1970 there were 22,000 active women physicians, comprising 7.1 percent of the profession; by 1986, 79,600 female doctors comprised 15.3 percent of all physicians. According to William Marder, director of the American Medical Association's department of manpower and demographic studies, by 1996 40 percent of new medical-school graduates will be women. If we examine the percentage of female medical students, the numbers are even more startling: in 1949–50 5.7 percent of the applicants and 10.7 percent of the graduates of U.S. medical schools were women; by 1987–88 37 percent of the applicants and 36.5 percent of the first-year students were women.

While women are entering medicine in ever-increasing numbers, the professional life of women as a group differs markedly from that of male physicians. They choose different specialities, work fewer hours per week, and see fewer patients. Women are far more likely to choose specialities with regular hours, such as dermatology and pathology, or specialities focusing on doctor-patient relationships, such as family practice, obstetrics and gynecology, pediatrics, and psychiatry. They are far less likely to choose surgery, which is often thought of as the most rigid and hierarchical of the medical specialties and which is known for its years of "infamously arduous training." Perri Klass, a physician who often writes about medicine, particularly as it relates to women, suggests that the reluctance of women to become surgeons may relate to the likelihood of postponing childbearing for the five to seven years of residency.

Two of the most pressing questions about women in medicine involve the impact women are having on the profession and the impact the profession is having on women's lives. Klass suggests that the "traditional techniques used by male doctors don't work as well for women"—that women have "more trouble assuming the mantle of all-knowing, paternal medical authority" and therefore rely more on one-to-one relationships, on teaching and empowering their patients and on treating other health workers in a more egalitarian way. If women can influence the practice of medicine in these ways, the profession will indeed benefit from their presence.

On the other hand, women are not moving as rapidly as many would like into positions of leadership in the profession or in medical schools. In 1987 only two out of 187 American medical schools had female deans, and out of 2,000 academic departments, only 73 had female chairs.

If women are nonetheless having some impact on the medical profession, what of the impact on the lives of women? Many women clearly find great pleasure and fulfillment in their roles as physicians, whether they are treating patients, teaching medical students, doing research, or combining all three. But many find combining medicine with family responsibilities extremely difficult and occasionally impossible. The long hours, the demanding pace, and the often relentlessly competitive nature of medicine, particularly academic medicine, requires serious inroads in time that some female physicians would rather spend in private and familial pursuits.

Sarah Stark, a physician in her mid-thirties, talks about the pressures of working in academic medicine. A specialist in a highly technical, extremely competitive branch of academic medicine, she notes that in her department "the guys" work from seven a.m. until nine p.m. every day. "The male model *is* the working model. It never lets up. If you take time off, you'll get behind—in technical expertise, in publications, in climbing the academic ladder. Competition is encouraged. They think the more scared you are, the more productive you will be. They want you to be scared."

She and her husband, also a physician, have decided not to have children at all. She can neither imagine paying someone to raise her children ("And who would be raising the nanny's kids?") nor imagine taking time off from her career for childbearing or child rearing. She describes the options open to female physicians with children: "For women the best scenario is to have no children. Next best is to 'hatch' and go right back to work. If you actually spend some time with your children, you lose respect. When a physician who is a mother is late for a conference, the men *always* comment!"

Sarah goes on to talk about the disapproval she receives from the larger society for her decision not to have children: the fellow guests at dinner parties who tell her she will be a "lonely old lady," the taxi drivers who tell her she'll regret the decision "later in life," the "you're unnatural" looks she gets whenever the subject arises.

She points out, moreover, that no one reacts the same way when her husband says he isn't planning to have children.

She states with considerable feeling that she refuses to be labeled "nonnurturing": "People just do not recognize other ways of nurturing. Anyone who sees me with my patients wouldn't say I'm not nurturing. Anyone who sees me with people whose lives are threatened, with people who are dying, wouldn't say I'm not nurturing. We must begin to have respect for women who choose not to mother and to make their contributions in other ways."

Despite the same long periods of training and demanding work, the median income for female physicians in 1986 was just over half that of male physicians, and their net worth only one-third. This discrepancy is in part due to women's relatively recent entrance into medicine and to the fact that they are choosing less lucrative specialties, but it is nonetheless a fact of life. And, of course, females face the same astronomic tuition costs of medical school that males do, the same student loans to repay.

While women entering medicine are entering a profession that seems to be, at least temporarily, in decline (there are fewer applicants to medical school each year, and more criticism of the profession from consumers and practitioners alike), women entering law are entering a profession that continues to have great appeal for young people just out of college, for older students, and for some who have already been trained in other professions. In 1988, for example, the nation's 175 accredited law schools were "flooded" with more than 300,000 applications from 75,000 students, an increase of 19 percent over the previous year. In analyzing the reasons for the continued popularity of law as a career, experts point to the visibility of lawyers in the Iran-contra hearings, the popularity and glamour of the television program "L.A Law," and, of course, the high status and even higher income of many lawyers. In 1987, for example, the median salary of an experienced staff nurse was approximately $24,000, while that of an experienced lawyer was more than $50,000. Moreover, in cities such as New York, lawyers just entering the profession often earn salaries of $70,000 or more. Add in issues of prestige and status and it is not difficult to understand why someone would opt for law rather than for nursing or social work!

And indeed, women are becoming lawyers in ever-increasing numbers. In 1979 28 percent of the graduates of law schools were women; by 1988 that figure had risen to 40 percent. But despite high salaries, high status, and high hopes, many women are struggling to find their niche within the profession.

A recent article analyzing one of the nation's largest law firms points out that "the partners who actually govern large firms . . . are still overwhelmingly male," that "power comes from time and experience—and the ability to attract major clients on Wall Street . . . still almost exclusively male preserves," and that women are starting to be concerned about personal problems that stem, at least in part, from the "wildly unpredictable hours" and demands of working for a private law firm.

In an extraordinary demanding career such as law, it is "no coincidence that so many women lawyers are unmarried and so few have children." According to one woman, "The basic rule seems to be that either you are married when you start, or you marry the man you were already engaged to or living with, or you stay single." Working most evenings and weekends simply is not conducive to developing new relationships, a process that is time-consuming and often emotionally draining. All too often women working in law firms must choose between a successful professional career and a satisfying personal life. According to Alice Richmond, a recent president of the Massachusetts Bar Association, "We're beginning to see talented, experienced women dropping out of the profession in their thirties. It takes an enormous amount from your soul."

Several major firms have recently instituted the option of part-time work, but often such arrangements preclude becoming a partner. In any case, women partners are still a distinct minority. A recent survey by the *National Law Journal* indicates that 90 percent of the partners in the 247 largest firms are white males.

According to one woman who is a partner in a major law firm, "I have no doubt that had I had the wonderful husband and two adorable children I thought I wanted years ago, I would not be a partner today." A recent detailed study by the Boston Bar Association of two thousand lawyers in the Boston area found that women were significantly more likely than men to be single, divorced, and without children. Moreover, women lawyers, especially new ones, are more likely to be dissatisfied with their jobs. Yet another lawyer at the same firm sums up the dilemma: "There is no such thing as a superwoman. You live with a constant sense of guilt and divided loyalty. You make accommodations. You can't have it all."

There are, of course, other jobs within law—jobs in the public sector, in city, state, or federal government, jobs with voluntary organizations, jobs with a particular perspective, such as civil rights or civil liberties—and while many of them may have more manageable working conditions and lower levels of stress, they usually pay considerably less, too. For the young lawyer with tuition loans to repay, a high rent to meet each month, and perhaps a yen for a comfortable life-style, earning $33,000 a year at age thirty after three years of law school and a couple of years of clerking does not sound nearly as appealing as earning over twice as much. Even in the public sector, where nine-to-five jobs are more common and part-time jobs are possible, there is often a heavy penalty for choosing to work part-time. According to one lawyer, "There is no question there is a big penalty for working part-time. As it is, the deck [in a New York City agency] is stacked against women, particularly in terms of advancement. Unless somebody acts like a man, she is not perceived as management material."

The experience of women in major accounting firms has also been disappointing. Among the prestigious "big eight" firms, the percentage of women partners ranges from a low of 2.1 to a high of 5.6. According to the editor of an industry newsletter, "The accounting firms are only now coming to the conclusion that women are as capable as men. They simply have not looked at women with the same open eye that they view men. This is, after all, a very conservative profession." In recent years several large accounting firms have in fact been sued on charges of discriminating against minorities and women; in one particular instance a female former Price Waterhouse manager sued after being denied a partnership. The manager was criticized for "being abrasive and a lack of 'interpersonal skills.' " She was told that her chances for promotion would improve if she would talk, walk, and dress "more femininely" and wear jewelry and makeup. After two federal courts found that sex discrimination played a role in the Price Waterhouse decision, the Supreme Court found that the burden of proof must be shared and has given the company another opportunity to prove that the same decision would have been made even if there had been no discrimination.

Part of the problem is that women have only recently entered the field of accounting and are still in the pipeline, slowly making their way toward partnership. But that is not the entire problem. Industry executives acknowledge the difficulty of trying to balance the seventy-hour work week that is expected of those on the partnership track with the demands and responsibilities of mothering. Recently, some of the major accounting and law firms have begun to offer "flex time" and arrangements for extended maternity leaves; but change is clearly slow in coming.

What about women in business, in politics, in academia? The same findings apply to these fields—that women have entered these areas in large numbers but are not moving to the top rungs in any degree comparable to their presence, that there is what has been called a "glass ceiling." In business, for example, it is clear that women own and operate small businesses in much larger numbers than ever before and that they are indeed moving into corporations in significant numbers; but virtually all reports indicate that they are still not reaching the higher levels. According to Rosabeth Moss Kanter, author of the landmark book *Men and Women of the Corporation*, the rules have changed within the corporation. The emphasis today is on risk taking, on the star system among managers. Working steadily and effectively is no longer the way to the top, the road to almost certain promotion. Just as women have gotten a foot on the corporate ladder, the ladder is being snatched away, and instead, "star" performances are being rewarded at all levels. Moreover, according to Kanter, "Flex-time isn't going to help. We're talking about voluntary overtime, about people who think that anyone who just gets through his work isn't doing enough. Day care won't help. These people work at night." Sounds strangely like law and medicine, doesn't it?

A study done by the Council on Economic Priorities for *Ms.* magazine in 1987 indicated that there are indeed some corporations that are trying "to meet women halfway." The study stated:

Although there have been significant improvements for women in the corporate workplace over the last two decades (395 women directors at companies in the two Fortune 500 listings in 1986, compared to only 46 women in 1969), women are seldom found on the top rungs of the corporate ladder. Too much of women's time and energy is still spent not on career development or advancement, but on pursuing equal opportunity, dealing with work-and-family conflicts, and combating sexual harassment.

The study further found that nineteen of the twenty companies surveyed had at least one woman on their boards of directors and that fourteen had at least one female corporate vice-president. The percentage of "women officials and managers" ranged from a low of 4 percent at Ford to a high of 81.3 percent at Avon Products; most of the companies are in the 8-to-25-percent range. While several companies offered flex time and/or job sharing, the majority still treated maternity as a short-term disability, allowing only six to eight weeks of paid leave after delivery plus additional unpaid leave; roughly half of the companies offered unpaid paternal leave. Only four of the twenty companies studied provided either on- or off-site child care. There is no question that conditions are improving for women workers and for families, but these companies seem a long way from "meeting women halfway."

But what of the position of women in academia? One would think that academic institutions would be considerably more sensitive to the needs and aspirations of women than, say, corporations, whose bottom line ultimately must reflect a healthy profit. But as in the other fields, in the words of one professor, there has been "progress but no parity."

Since 1975 the number of women college presidents has doubled, with women now heading over three hundred of the nation's three thousand colleges. Today women constitute a majority of American college students and receive over one-third of all doctorates, but female professors still have a significantly lower tenure rate than do men and continue to receive significantly lower salaries.

In their stimulating and perceptive study *Women of Academe:*

Outsiders in the Sacred Grove, Nadya Aisenberg and Mona Harrington explore the reaons "why so many credentialed women . . . [have] ended up—sometimes by choice, usually not—outside the academy." In analyzing the forces that lead to "professional marginality and . . . exclusion from the centers of professional authority," they point out that the quest for professional acceptance and success requires a life of action rather than reaction, an emphasis on one's public role rather than on one's private role, an ability to see oneself and be seen as authoritative rather than submissive, and the opportunity to learn the rules of the game rather than being the quintessential Outsider. In short, female academics, and other professionals as well, must take on those characteristics directly antithetical to the ways in which they were socialized from birth to behave. They must somehow shake off those techniques of "winning a place by ingratiation and self-abnegation" which the authors term the "psychology of the dispossessed" (they might have termed it the "psychology of the oppressed") and instead transform themselves "from a passive to an active persona, from a supportive role player to a central character, a person prepared for autonomy." They must do nothing less than build "a new identity."

Aisenberg and Harrington point out how rigid hierarchy, extreme competitiveness among workers for a handful of top positions, and a narrow definition of ability and acceptability foster exclusionary policies that are bound to keep traditional Outsiders—nonwhites, women, people from lower socioeconomic groups—outside the system. This is surely one of the primary functions of such policies. It is important to note, moreover, that while Aisenberg and Harrington are describing academia, they could as well be describing medicine, law, accounting, or any of the elite male-dominated professions.

In recent years women have moved into politics in significant numbers, particularly at the state level. The percentage of women in state legislatures across the country has risen from 4 percent in 1969 to 15.5 percent in 1988. Following the 1988 election, forty-two women hold statewide office, twenty-five women were elected to the House of Representatives, and there are still only two female senators, Barbara Mikulski of Maryland and Nancy Kassebaum of

Kansas. Despite the fact that women constitute 53 percent of all registered voters, they have not moved into major offices on the national scene in significant numbers.

During the 1988 presidential campaign women were more visible than usual in key roles. Harvard Law School professor Susan Estrich was the campaign manager for Michael Dukakis; his primary foreign policy advisor was Professor Madeleine Albright of Georgetown University. Ann Lewis was a key advisor to the Jesse Jackson campaign, and Sheila Tate was George Bush's press spokesperson during the presidential campaign.

But as great as the gains have been for women in law, medicine, business, and politics at the local level, the vast majority of women still work in service, sales, and clerical jobs; and, for the most part, salaries for these jobs have remained extremely low. Young women may dream of being a district attorney, a pediatrician, or a highly paid, glamorous model, but the reality is that women workers are far more likely to be salespeople, computer programmers, and lower-level hospital workers.

According to the Women's Bureau, more than 53 million women age sixteen and over comprised 45 percent of the total labor force in January 1988. U.S. Department of Labor projections from 1986 to the year 2000 indicate that the labor force will increase by 21 million workers and that women, minorities, and immigrants will account for 90 percent of that increase. The department further estimates that almost all of the increase will be in the service sector, an area in which women are dominant. In 1986 40.5 million women, more than four out of five working women, were employed in the service sector. In health services and social services, women held more than three-fourths of all the jobs.

There is both good news and bad news in these data. The good news is that there will be more and more opportunities for women in the labor force during the coming decade. The bad news is that the occupations that will have the greatest increase in job opportunities are those that pay the least: jobs as salespersons; waiters and waitresses; registered nurses; janitors and cleaners; cashiers; general office clerks; food-counter, fountain, and related workers; nurses' aides, orderlies, and attendants; and secretaries. The number of general managers and top executives and truck drivers will also be increasing substantially, but the percentage of women workers in these fields is considerably smaller.

Furthermore, if we examine the 1987 median income for full-time, year-round male and female workers in specific occupational groups, we see that substantial income differentials persist even in the highest-paid professions: male executives, adminstrators, and managerial workers earned $36,155 while females earned $21,874; male professional specialty workers earned $36,098 while females earned $24,565; and male technical and related support workers earned $29,170 while females earned $19,559. Among workers in sales, men earned $27,880 while females earned $14,277, and even among service workers, a female-dominated occupation, men earned $17,320 while women earned only $11,000.

It is worth underlining that while the media—TV programs and advertising, news and women's magazines, the "style" sections of the daily newspapers—feature women in upper-middle-class occupations, as the latest achievers of the American Dream, the reality is that most women currently work and will continue to work in the near future in low-status, low-income, often dead-end jobs. This emphasis on the life-styles of the "rich and famous," the upper class and, more recently, the upper middle class, is of course nothing new. The belief that any individual or family can eventually live a life that resembles the lives of those far wealthier or those with high status has fueled the American Dream for over two hundred years and has fueled the consumer society since the Industrial Revolution.

These issues are particularly poignant today as both opportunity and standard of living decline for millions of Americans. Intergenerational downward mobility has become a real prospect for millions of young people. But what is it like when one's income and class status drop precipitously during one's own lifetime? What is it like for all those divorced women who must cope not only with work and child rearing but also with severely diminished economic resources? What is it like for men who assumed their white-collar jobs or their union-protected manufacturing jobs were secure only to find in their late forties or early fifties that they are unemployed and perhaps even unemployable?

As Katherine S. Newman points out in her book *Falling From*

Grace: The Experience of Downward Mobility in the American Middle Class: "Downward mobility can be conceived of as a matter of income loss alone, but it can also be defined as losing one's place in society. For most people in modern America, occupation is a crucial determinant of social status, because in addition to money, a job confers prestige and a sense of purpose." As Newman states, women are especially vulnerable to downward mobility. The economic repercussions of divorce, the relatively low level of women's salaries, the financial irresponsibility of many men, the lack of support services and support networks, and women's child-rearing responsibilities combine to make women's economic status particularly precarious.

An analysis of census data on family income prepared for the Children's Defense Fund indicates that the median income (in 1986 dollars) of American families dropped significantly between 1973 and 1986. The drop was sharpest for families headed by high-school dropouts younger than thirty (34.7 percent) and non-Hispanic black families headed by individuals under thirty (29.3 percent) but was also precipitous for families headed by females under thirty (26.0 percent). Young black families, particularly hard hit, saw their median annual income drop to the poverty line, $11,250; and among the youngest black families (headed by persons under twenty-five), the median income dropped to an incredible low of $1,092.

Young Americans earn less today for several reasons: they work fewer hours because of higher levels of unemployment for young people and because of part-time work and they receive lower wages. One of the central causes of this systematic underemployment is the changeover from a manufacturing economy to a service economy with its reliance on temporary and part-time work.

The result is a greater and greater gap between the promises of the American Dream and the reality. The one-time central component of that dream—owning one's own home—has become more elusive than at any other time in recent memory. Home ownership has fallen significantly for married couples with children: for couples in which the head of household is under twenty-five, the percentage who own their own home has fallen 26 percent from 1973 to 1987. For a household headed by a single person under twenty-five, the fall is even more precipitous, 57 percent. Even for families in which the head of household is somewhat older (ages twenty-five to thirty-four), many fewer can afford to purchase their own homes. The only groups in these age ranges who are *more* likely to own their own homes in 1987 than they were in 1973 are married couples and single people *without children*. The burden of rent has also increased dramatically for young families. Among families headed by an individual younger than twenty-five, the rent burden increased by 47 percent for two-parent families and a shocking 76 percent for single-parent families. Even among families headed by an individual between the ages of twenty-five and thirty-four, the rent increase was significant—29 percent among two-parent families and 66 percent among single-parent families. Single-parent families headed by an individual under twenty-five were paying an unbelievable 81 percent of their total income for rent. These statistics make clear the vulnerability of young families to homelessness. It is clearly impossible to meet a family's minimum requirements for food, clothing, and other essentials while paying 81 percent of one's income for rent!

Among the women I interviewed, many in each of the three groups felt that they had to be able to care for themselves and their children without the help of a man. How realistic is this attitude? Among families headed by an individual under thirty in 1986, the median income of married couples was $26,200, over double the poverty line, while the income of families headed by a single female was only $6,392, approximately one-half of the poverty line. In 1987 62.6 percent of all female-headed families lived in poverty, compared with 9.2 percent of all married-couple families. In other words, only one in every three families headed by a young female now manages to escape poverty. If we look at children in female-headed families, we see that in 1987, 89.4 percent of children in families headed by high-school dropouts, 68.6 percent of children in families headed by high-school graduates, and 15.9 percent of children in families headed by college graduates lived in poverty. Even a college degree does not protect a female head of household from falling into poverty.

Not only are elite high-powered jobs improbable dreams for most young women—and for most young men, for that matter—but while high-income, high-status jobs are touted by the media, by parents, and by peers, jobs in traditional female professions go begging. The United States is today in the midst of a severe nursing shortage. In 1988, an estimated three hundred thousand nursing jobs were unfilled, and enrollment in schools of nursing was declining. Several factors are responsible for this extraordinarily serious situation: fewer students of high-school age, increased opportunities for young women in other fields, and a general disenchantment with nursing as a career. According to the American Hospital Association, enrollment in nursing schools has declined 10 percent each year since 1974, and in recent years 40 percent of all registered nurses have left the profession to pursue other careers.

Salary levels are at least part of that disenchantment. The starting salary for registered nurses averages $20,340 nationally and with experience is likely to rise only to approximately $27,000 a year. As Pam Maraldo, chief executive officer of the National League for Nursing, put it, "Little girls don't want to grow up and be nurses anymore. It's ridiculous that a supervisor at K-Mart makes more than a nurse." While low salaries for nurses have always been a problem (women were supposed to go into nursing to "do good" and not be concerned about crass matters such as recompense!), budget cuts for the public sector during the Reagan years exacerbated the problem of recruitment and salaries in many of the helping professions. During the materialistic 1980s additional money and concern about the well-being of caregivers, particularly those in the public sector, simply was not a priority.

But low salaries are not the only reason for nurses' disaffection with the profession. Working conditions often range from difficult to horrendous. Lincoln Hospital, a city hospital in the South Bronx, had ninety nursing vacancies during the winter of 1988. During a recent protest to dramatize conditions at New York City hospitals, Carmen Fascio, head nurse in the emergency room at Lincoln, described a typical day. First she tries to help the twenty to thirty patients who are left over from the previous night, but she is constantly interrupted by ambulance sirens and a steady stream of stabbing and shooting victims and people with heart attacks. "And there I am in the middle of what looks like a war zone in the South Bronx, running around like a chicken without a head, not knowing which way to turn or who to help first. Before you know it, it's lunch time, and there's no way I can be hungry, because how can I eat when there are patients crying near me and families cursing at me?"

Lynda Levy is a pediatric nurse at the Bronx Municipal Hospital Center, a teaching hospital located in the northeast Bronx. Each day the pediatric emergency room, staffed with no more than two nurses, sees more than two hundred children. Ms. Levy describes the scene: "It's horrifying. You have to make a strategy to divide your time between the infant with pneumonia, the screaming baby in a wet diaper, and trying to find a compassionate way to tell another set of parents that their child has just died." Is it any wonder we have a nursing shortage?

Filling the gap in patient care over the past several years have been nurses from foreign countries—an estimated ten thousand across the nation, four thousand in New York City alone. Foreign nurses are often willing to work for low-level wages and may be more willing than American nurses to put up with the long hours, harsh working conditions, and a doctor-nurse relationship that often gives the doctor most of the authority and autonomy and leaves the nurse exhausted and burned out.

Other health-care professionals are also in increasingly short supply. While the nursing shortage has been developing over the past two decades, the shortage of laboratory technicians, physical therapists, occupational therapists, pharmacists, health aides, and X-ray technicians has emerged only recently. With the advent of new technology, an aging population that requires additional health resources, and the AIDS epidemic, the need for such workers has increased; but because of relatively low salaries and low prestige, women—who continue to comprise the majority of workers in the health-care field—choose to go into other fields. The problem is clearly visible in urban areas, but it is worst in rural areas, where, according to the president of the American Hospital Association, "patients have to queue up to get the care they need, or be transported far from their homes."

Chronic-care workers, who work both as aides in nursing homes and as home health workers, and are so crucial to the care and well-being of older people as well as the sick and the disabled, are also in short supply. According to a report released jointly by the American Federation of State, County, and Municipal Employees (AFSCME) and the Older Women's League (OWL), the one-and-a-half million chronic-care workers, nearly all women and a disproportionate number members of minority groups, are paid an average of $4.50 an hour, receive inadequate fringe benefits, little or no job training, and few opportunities for promotion. As Lou Glasse, president of OWL, stated, "Something is wrong when we entrust the care of our patients, our spouses and our siblings at the end of their lives to underpaid, undertrained, exploited workers. Something is wrong when we consign middle-aged older women to low-wage dead end jobs at a time in their lives when they should be saving for their own old age."

As nursing has lost prestige and professionals over the past twenty years, so has teaching. In 1968, 23.5 percent of all college freshmen were interested in becoming elementary or secondary school teachers; by 1982, only 4.7 percent of students entering college wanted to become teachers. On the other hand, by 1987 the percentage had risen to 8.1. Is this the beginning of a new interest in teaching? What is responsible for this upturn? According to one observer, "The overall climate is good for future teachers: the public is once again interested in education, salaries are up, the jobs are there, and the demographics point to continuing strong demand." Salaries are indeed up—that is, compared with previous years—but they are hardly *up*. The average beginning salary of teachers across the country in 1987–88 was $18,600 to $19,000; the average salary of teachers in primary and secondary schools is $28,300. Because of the current teacher shortage, many school districts are looking to other countries in order to educate their children. Unlike nursing, which often takes trained nurses from developing countries that can ill afford to lose them, teaching has been recruiting from both developed and developing countries. In both instances, it is striking that one of the richest countries in the world is in the position of depleting the human resources of other societies. Do we really not have enough talent and resources to train our own citizens to provide health care and education to our own population?

And, of course, preschool teachers, many with bachelor's degrees, a substantial percentage with master's degrees, earn the lowest salaries among all teachers. Many of those valiant professionals who care for our youngest, most vulnerable children for most of their waking days earn no more than poverty wages. *Working Women* magazine certainly provided an apt commentary on American values when it named nursing and teaching as among the "ten worst careers" in 1988!

Low salaries and little room for advancement characterize millions of jobs for women in the United States. But what of the women at the bottom of the wage scale? What of the women who earn $3.35 per hour, the minimum wage since 1981—which, because of inflation, was worth a mere $2.68 in 1987? It must be noted that in 1988 "in real terms, the minimum wage [was] at its lowest level since 1955 and earning it no longer [kept] a family of three above the poverty line." Among all workers earning the minimum wage in 1987, over half of whom worked in retail trade, mostly as sales clerks, 65 percent were women.

What of part-time jobs, which have grown so much faster than full-time jobs during the 1980s? Nearly 20 million Americans, a large percentage of whom are women, work part-time, and over 5 million would prefer full-time work. Two-thirds of all part-time workers receive no health-insurance benefits; four-fifths are not covered by pension plans at work; and three million part-time workers and their families live in poverty. How does the American Dream look to these workers?

What of the millions of temporary jobs that have been created over the last few years? What of these clerical workers, low-level health workers, government workers, and workers in the computer field who earn low wages, have no job security, and often have few benefits? How do they survive when they are laid off?

What about the shortage of jobs for single mothers, many of whom have inadequate education and skills? In New York City alone, two-thirds of the single mothers of working age—more than 210,000 women—live in poverty. In a city that has been "booming" with new hotels, office buildings, and luxury apartments, these women, the majority of whom are black and Hispanic, "struggle to survive on welfare or in jobs that do not pay enough to pull them above the Federal poverty level." In an economy increasingly dominated by banking and financial services, where the work is increasingly complex and sophisticated, these women are rapidly becoming extraneous.

What about the increasing number of sweatshops? At the same time that more and more women move into law and medicine, more and more women are moving into abysmal working conditions. In Manhattan's garment district, in New York's Chinatown, in Corona, Queens, women and children work in "squalid or illegal conditions." A supervising investigator with the New York State Department of Labor compared conditions in one small factory to those that set off the disastrous Triangle Shirtwaist fire of 1911. Another Labor Department official described "factories with malfunctioning toilets and others where workers were preparing food next to their machines and were eating from plates on the floor." In these shops and factories workers are paid by the piece produced and are often encouraged to bring additional work home, where they usually must supply their own thread, machines, power, and light. It has been estimated that there are over three thousand sweatshops and thirty thousand home workers in New York City alone, and of course the problem exists in other parts of the country as well.

And what about wages and working conditions of nonwhite women? If the work lives of most women in the United States bear little resemblance to young women's fantasies about their future occupational goals, what is the reality for black and Hispanic women? As women as a whole make up over 80 percent of all clerical workers, nearly 25 percent of all working black women are concentrated in just six of forty-eight clerical occupations: file clerks, typists, keypunch operators, teaching assistants, calculating-machine operators, and social-welfare clerks. Among service workers, black women are concentrated in jobs as chambermaids, welfare aides, cleaners, and nurses' aides. While black women are crowded into a few sex-segregated occupations, they are, to a significant extent, working in the least desirable, lowest-paying jobs within these occupations. According to economist Rhonda M. Williams, "Occupational segregation by gender is a longstanding and by now well-known feature of the U.S. economy . . . It is less well-known that the lion's share of the aggregate gender wage gap is

attributable to *intra-occupational* [italics in original] wage disparities," that "within occupations men work in high wage firms,
women in low wage firms." Even within the same firm, moreover,
women tend to work at lower-level jobs, and black women at the
lowest-level jobs of all. As Williams states:

> The growing service economy bodes extremely ill for black
> women, who are consistently the (proportionately) dominant
> low wage group in each industry: 81.8% of black women are
> low earners in wholesale, 65.7% in health, 87.9% in retail,
> and 67.3% in FIRE [finance, insurance, and real estate]. The
> service economy seems well suited to swell the ranks of low-
> wage black women.

This analysis is corroborated by an examination of the median
yearly income of American workers. In 1987, for example, among
full-time, year-round workers, white men earned a median yearly
wage of $27,468; black men earned $19,385; white women,
$17,775; and black women, $16,211. Hispanic workers earned the
lowest salaries within each category; Hispanic men earned $17,872
and Hispanic women, $14,893.

If we examine the earnings of all persons, including part-time
and part-year workers, the pattern remains essentially the same
while the income levels are shockingly low: the median yearly
income of white males in 1987 was $18,854; of black males,
$11,101; of Hispanic males, $12,019; of white females, $8,279;
of black females, $6,796; and of Hispanic females, $6,611. During
the same year the poverty line for a family of four was $11,611;
the only workers whose median incomes were above that level were
white and Hispanic males, and the latter were only barely above
the line. The median income of all black and Hispanic female
workers was less than 60 percent of the poverty line!

These numbers take on added significance when we recognize
that "since the early 1960s, the part-time workforce has grown
nearly three times as fast as the full-time workforce." Approximately one-third of all employed married women, one-fifth of employed divorced, separated, and widowed women, and over one-
third of single (never married) women work part-time.

The low income of black and Hispanic women is particularly disturbing because of the enormous rise in the number of female-headed families. According to William Julius Wilson:

> Whereas the total number of families grew by 20 percent from 1970 to 1984, the number of female-headed families increased by 51 percent. Moreover, the number of families headed by women with one or more of their children present in the home increased by 77 percent. If the change in family structure was notable for all families in the 1970s, it was close to phenomenal for blacks and Hispanics. Whereas families headed by white women increased by 63 percent, the number of families headed by black and Hispanic women grew by 108 and 164 percent, respectively.

Thus, the vast majority of black and Hispanic women in the work force are not working for the proverbial "pin money"; many of them are working as the sole support of their families; and that is essentially impossible on an income of $6,500 a year for part-time workers and extremely difficult on $15,000 a year, the median income of full-time black and Hispanic female workers.

Not only are women's wages problematic, but the stress of being both the primary breadwinner and the primary nurturer is considerable. Most the young women I interviewed recognized that they would be combining work and family roles. Some of them expressed considerable anxiety about how they would mesh the two sets of reponsibilities; many seem to take for granted that they would work it all out. Recent studies indicate that managing several complex and often mutually exclusive roles is not as easy as some of them might think and, in fact, can lead to considerable stress. Much of the recent research on stress has focused on males and therefore on the workplace. Findings about men, however, cannot automatically be assumed to be equally true of women. Many researchers feel that research on women and stress must focus on both family and workplace issues.

According to a recent study on women and stress, "the tendency to focus on women's reproductive role has led to the incorrect belief that menopause and the empty nest are central concerns, a belief not supported by empirical research." They go on to suggest that "midlife is not the predominant high-stress period for women," that the "peak 'age of stress' " may be the twenties, when "many young women today face difficult and unfamiliar choices and others struggle to care for young children in isolation and poverty."

While women who work outside of the home have often been characterized as having better mental health, being less depressed, and having fewer physical complaints than full-time homemakers, "role overload (having too much to do)" and "role conflict (feeling pulled apart by conflicting demands)" are sources of considerable stress for women. Furthermore, recent research indicates that a work role that combines a low level of control with highly psychologically demanding tasks leads to high levels of stress. Perhaps the prototype of such work is that of the New York City taxi driver, caught in Manhattan's semipermanent traffic jam over which she or he has little or no control while having to deal simultaneously with irate passengers. The nurses described earlier in this chapter are surely examples of workers performing psychologically demanding tasks with little control over the work situation. Often teachers, social workers, and other caregivers fit into this category as well. While high-powered executives, typically thought of as "type A" personalities, have been traditionally considered prime candidates for stress and for heart disease, they have considerably more control over their work environment than do workers whose tasks are frequently monitored for both speed and accuracy—assembly-line workers, word processors, telephone operators, and fast-food workers, many of whom are women. Often it is workers at the lower end of the hierarchy who experience the most harmful stress—stress over which they have little or no control.

Female workers must also return home each night and engage in family roles in which they once again face high demands and little control. It can be argued that women's preoccupation with the well-being of others—husband or partner, children, older family members—frequently makes them vulnerable to frustration and a sense of failure. If low income, inadequate housing, having the sole responsibility for children, and job insecurity are concerns of many women, it becomes clear that stress and all of its physical and mental consequences become additional problems with which millions of women must cope.

Many questions remain: why are so many of our young women encouraged to dream the improbable, if not impossible, dream of high-salary, high-status positions while so many urgent, essential jobs remain unfilled? Why do we send the message that success can be found in doing the high-pressure jobs that men have traditionally done when we know that once women take up the challenge and indeed "play the game," they still do not reap the full rewards of their labors? Why do we reward workers in elite male-dominated professions with extraordinarily high salaries and perquisites while others barely scrape by or live in poverty? Why do we make a full commitment to work virtually imcompatible with the kind of parenting we feel children need? And why do we make it so very difficult for women and men to both "do" and "care"?

If most women still work in relatively low-paid, low-status jobs, why do newspapers, women's magazines, television programs, and most advertising focus on "upscale" women? Why do they promote a dream that will never come true for most of us? One answer, of course, is that "upscale" sells. What woman does not want to be beautiful, glamorous, with a lovely home and family, going off to an exciting job dressed in a Donna Karan outfit? It is the new American Dream, and it sells every time. It sells clothes, cars, homes, microwave ovens, VCRs, briefcases—it will even sell vodka. Moreover, if the image is accepted as the norm, if being "successful" and "having it all" are perceived as being available to everyone if only one thinks, plans, and works hard enough, then whom do we blame when we wind up in temporary, part-time work earning only slightly more than the minimum wage? If the American Dream is alive and well, if the system is functioning as advertised, do we not have only ourselves to blame if we do not "make it"?

The new American Dream not only sells products and faith in the "American way of life" but it defuses criticism of the current system. How bad can things be when we see all around us images of happy, affluent women? We can't work out child care and after-school care? We must have overlooked something. Most of our income goes to rent? Perhaps we should move farther away from our job. The father of our children walked out and hasn't paid a cent in child support? Why did we marry him in the first place? What is wrong with us that we can't make it like everyone else? Is that the real function of the ideology of the American Dream— the preservation of the current economic system, and when it doesn't work for all of us, particularly for women, for nonwhites, and for the poor, the shifting of blame from those in power to the victims?

CHAPTER 8

Who Will Care for the Children?

The reality is that we're creating a new generation and that many of them are not being supervised, cared for, loved and nurtured. Society has to change. There must be ways of working and caring for children so that we will raise secure, emotionally complete individuals.

LINDA JEFFERSON
teacher and mother of two, northern California

Among the young women I interviewed, few issues were of greater concern than the question of how to combine work and child rearing. Women from junior high school through college spoke of their intention to work, often to embark on demanding careers, but also to have families, to be "available" to their children, to provide them with material goods but to be there for milk and cookies at the end of the school day. "Milk and cookies"—I heard it everywhere from women of all ages. It has somehow become the American ritual of good mothering. It symbolizes so much of what mothering is supposed to be about: nourishment, caring, attentiveness, putting the child's rhythms and needs before one's own.

Some of the young women assumed they would work it all out with the help of baby-sitters and husbands who would participate in household activities; others find it difficult to resolve the apparent contradictions between the kind of mothering they envision and the demands of a busy work life.

Several young women who already have children speak of how

they have tried to mesh the many facets of their lives. A group of teen mothers in Arizona cannot imagine what they would do without the special program they attend in the public-school system that provides them with emotional support, care for their babies, and a high-school education for themselves. Jessica Grant talks about growing up in North Carolina, and her life as a student and as a mother of an eighteen-month-old son: "I came from a very religious family and a community without a stop light. I am the youngest of seven; my father died when I was eight. My mother raised the last three or four with the help of her brother. We were never on welfare because we had some assets—land, a house, a car." During her freshman year Jessica found she was pregnant. Her pregnancy was completely unplanned ("I didn't think I could have children; I didn't think I knew how"). At the time she really cared about the baby's father, and abortion "was not an option." She took time out of school to have the baby and to care for him, but since his first birthday her mother has been caring for him. She plans to take the baby to live with her after she graduates and says that she will probably have to fight her mother to take him. She feels she has been away from him too long already. "I want him to know me as his mother."

Jessica is unusually fortunate in going to school only three hours away from home and in having a mother who is willing and able to care for a grandson. This circumstance makes all the difference in her being able to finish college and support her son as she would like. Millions of other young women are not nearly so fortunate as Jessica and the young teen moms from Arizona. Without a special program or a relative available to help, many will barely survive month to month.

Other women struggle to put it all together. A dental hygienist who is the mother of a thirteen-year-old girl and has been divorced for nine years talks about raising her daughter alone on a limited income. Margot Johnson and her daughter live in a pleasant one-bedroom garden apartment in a very affluent suburb. The daughter has the bedroom; the mother sleeps in the living room and has done so for years. They must carefully choose how to spend their money. The father gives approximately $2,000 per year for child support; the mother's comment is "You can't get blood from a

stone." Mother and daughter have made the decision to live in a
small apartment in a high-rent area characterized by elegant, one-
family homes so that the daughter can attend a first-rate school
system. Margot feels that her daughter is reluctant to invite her
friends from school over because the friends live in "big, fancy
houses." When people in the community learn where they live, the
reaction is "Oh, you live in the apartments."

Margot went back to work when her daughter was sixteen
months old; when she separated from her husband, she was working three-and-a-half days a week. She says, "Dental hygiene has
been good to me," but she acknowledges that a central problem
has been trying to combine "nurturing and work." Margot tells a
poignant story to illustrate the conflict: recently there has been an
ad on television which talks about what a mother did for her child
when the child was sick. When Margot's daughter heard that ad,
her response was, "When I was sick my mommy used to go to
work." Margot's comment was, "My heart broke into little pieces.
No matter how hard you try, it's never enough."

Often women who are married also have difficult choices to
make. Women who have made enormous career commitments
sometimes find themselves torn by ambivalence upon the birth of
a baby. Claudia Palma recalls exactly when she decided to become
a physician. As a child she avidly read the Cherry Ames books
about nursing. One day her mother asked her if she wanted to be
a nurse. She responded immediately, "No, nurses take orders from
doctors, so I'll just be the doctor." Claudia was the oldest of three
daughters; her mother did not work outside of the home, and her
father was, and still is, a physician. "It was a given," she said. "I
was going to be a doctor."

She had difficulty being accepted to medical school but perse-
vered. When she thought she would not be admitted to a medical
school in the United States, she was prepared to go to school in
Mexico. At the last minute, however, she was admitted to a medical
school in New York state, and by the time of her graduation she
was, as she put it, the "top female student in the class."

She met her husband, also a physician, during a brief stay in
Mexico, and they were married at the end of her first year of medical
school. At the end of medical school she made what she calls a

"life-style" decision—to go into radiology so that she could have a nine-to-five job and therefore be able to have a professional life and a family life as well.

Her first child was born during her second year of residency, when she was twenty-nine. The hospital had no maternity-leave policy, so she took her month's vacation and was away a total of six weeks. She describes how she felt returning to work: "I hated leaving my baby. I had to leave for work before she was awake; if I was on call, I wouldn't see her for thirty-six hours. My mother was taking care of her, so I was comfortable with that, but I just didn't like leaving her. There was no longer any real joy in working; I was only getting through the day in order to get home."

A few months later she developed "fluid on both knees." It was so severe she had to take a six-month medical leave. "That," she said, "made my decision." After six months at home she knew she would never catch up—not with her medical work but with her daughter's "first smile, her first steps, her first words." She felt she wasn't there for her child and that she wasn't as good a physician, either. She was no longer reading medical books or journals; it was clear that her heart was elsewhere.

Since then Claudia has had two more children—her oldest child is now six, her son is four, and a baby girl is three months old. Her son has since birth had several bouts of severe respiratory illness. Often the only reason he has been able to stay out of the hospital has been because she has been there to care for him. "He vindicated me," she says. Initially she felt considerable guilt about her decision to stay home full time, but now she says she no longer feels much conflict over the decision.

Will she return to medicine one day? She doesn't think so. She is no longer up to date in radiology, and, in any case, medicine is not the profession she thought it was. When she was growing up, "people loved doctors, doctors had real rewards." Today, with the deterioration of the doctor-patient relationship, with the amount of malpractice litigation, and with the number of decisions taken out of the doctors' hands, she's not sure she wants to go back. Moreover, she likes being home, likes decorating her house, likes being with the children. "I grew up with the old pattern," she recalls. "Mom was there for milk and cookies at the end of the day. I like that. I used to believe in 'quality time,' but now I know that's crazy. There's no such thing as quality time with an infant."

Many of her working friends are what she calls "guilty mothers." They are the mothers who rush around on their days off or on vacations trying to make up to their children for working. They are the mothers who out of guilt "take the kids to the zoo in January." She feels that the conflicts will never go away but that, above all, "women must do whatever makes them comfortable within themselves."

Joanne Davidson is also the oldest of three daughters of a professional father (a professor) and a homemaker mother. She knew from the age of five that she wanted to be a doctor; she knew that she would be "something," and she felt that a wife and mother was not "something." But while she wanted to be a physician, she never seriously considered doing anything about it until her college years, when she met an older woman physician. This woman "opened the door" for her, helped her realize "I can do that." She says, "I grabbed on to that like a life jacket in the ocean." Since she had not taken any science courses in college, she had to take them all during the summer, "worked [her] butt off" and got straight As. "It was very important, proving to myself that I could do it."

One of the central problems for women of her generation, Joanne feels, is that there were two diametrically opposed role models—a successful, ambitious father who "worked all the time" and a mother who was at home. There was no intermediate role model. This becomes a particular problem when women enter traditionally male-dominated professions in which twelve-hour work days, often six or seven days a week, are the norm. Even before her son was born, Joanne was conflicted about working this grueling schedule. She felt it was not the life for her. She wanted to go to a museum now and then, or read a novel; she wanted occasionally to talk with friends, go shopping for clothes, have time to have her hair cut.

Joanne has recently arranged for a three-day schedule at work. Two days a week she spends the mornings with her two-year-old and the afternoons in the library doing research and writing. She feels there must be a middle ground between the traditional male model, which "completely devalues someone who doesn't devote herself completely to a career," and not playing the game at all. "Children *do* have to be raised," she states with feeling. She feels there must be a role for part-time professionals. Currently, she claims, there is resentment and hostility toward part-time physicians, particularly in hospital settings, as well as the feeling that part-time people cannot be relied on. This must change. "Top people need to work part-time to legitimize it. Part-time work must be institutionalized, entrenched in the system, so that those workers will not be punished."

Even with a more flexible schedule, Joanne says, it is hard going back and forth between a demanding profession and mothering. "I am less productive at work, but it is more enjoyable, and at home I constantly feel the pull to go back to work." But she recognizes that on this schedule when she does have time to work, she really works.

Joanne is fortunate: she lives near the hospital where she works. "Many women," she says, "work downtown and leave at six-thirty in the morning and don't return home until six-thirty or seven-thirty in the evening." These women must deal with "giving up the raising of their children to the baby-sitter. They must recognize their dependence on the caregiver and give her enough autonomy to do her job effectively." This, she feels, is very hard to do but essential for the well-being of the child. Joanne notes, furthermore, that many professional women have children but don't really want to raise them. "They make it tough for the rest of us."

"Young women," she believes, "think they can have it all, that they do not need to make choices. But," she states, "they *must* make choices, and making choices means leaving something behind." She has recognized that it is impossible to do everything well. She currently says no to many invitations to give talks, even though she thinks they should be given; she doesn't do as much "role modeling" for younger women, even though she thinks it certainly must be done; she's not as active in a physician's peace group to which she belongs, even though she strongly believes in its mission; and she feels her name is not as well known in her field as she would like it to be. But these are the choices she has made. They are painful choices; but because her priorities center around parenting, she has made them.

And what about the caregivers to whom Joanne refers—the "nannies," as they are often called these days in our endless desire to imitate upper-class life? Perhaps the title of a recent workshop for female executives tells us something of where we are: "How to Nurture and Maintain a Family Culture When You Work All Day, Your Mother Lives in Omaha, and Your Housekeeper Comes from Ethiopia." Kathy Dobie, in an insightful article in *The Village Voice,* points out that just as Omaha stands for "distance and for broken generational ties within white urban culture," Ethiopia is a metaphor for "blackness and foreignness." Dobie goes on to suggest that it is the caregiver who is often "holding the white families together, while striving mightily against the pressures of poverty, single parenthood, and institutionalized racism to hold their own families together." In New York it is often black women, many of them immigrants from Haiti, Jamaica, and the Caribbean islands, who are making it possible for many of our new doctors, lawyers, and bank executives to "have it all." In Boston, au pairs, young women who usually remain at the job for only a year or two, come from the American Middle West or from Ireland or England or Western Europe in order to help in the home. In Los Angeles, au pairs are often European while housekeepers are frequently Spanish-speaking women from Central or Latin America.

When these women are older with children of their own, one wonders who is caring for *their* children? As these women feed, bathe, comfort, and play with children of the middle and the upper middle class, who feeds, bathes, comforts, and plays with their children? Dobie points out:

the irony of having to support their own children by leaving them to bring up someone else's kids . . . She has trained her children to survive mother's absence. As she sits all afternoon in the park watching one tow-haired child play on the swings, her own kids are arriving home from school, where they will do their homework by themselves. If she has to work late, the older children will prepare dinner; the older ones will put the younger ones to bed.

One study of West Indian domestic and child-care workers in New York City indicates that many of these caregivers had never worked in this capacity until they came to this country to "better themselves." In the West Indies the majority of these women worked in "a range of jobs including primary school teaching, policy work, clerical and administrative assistant work . . . factory work, postal work . . . and servicing the tourist industry." One caregiver, a thirty-one-year-old Jamaican woman, indicates some of the humiliation so many of the West Indian domestic and child care workers feel: "I'm not looking for them to shower us down with money, with clothes, but with a little respect and feelings. . . . They want full respect from us and at the same time they want to treat us like nothing. . . . A lot of West Indians are very insulted, but we do it because we have no choice." These caregivers earn anywhere from $100 to $325 per week, or $5,200 to $16,900 per year. Salaries vary by city, by amount of experience and skill (in Los Angeles, being able to drive is a major asset), and by whether a woman "lives in" or not. Some employers pay social security and health benefits; others do not.

But where are the fathers—in the caregivers' families as well as in the employers'? Some of the caregivers have husbands or partners, either in this country or in their country of origin; others are their families' sole support. In either case, their income is crucial. Among the employers, many are two-parent families, and many are single parents who provide the sole or primary support for their children. In two-parent families, however, why is it the women who are leaving their professions, cutting back, working part-time, agonizing over choosing between work and children? Nancy Cameron, a Rhode Island physician and mother of two who shares child care and homemaking with her physician-husband, points out how difficult it is for men who want to be involved to integrate work and home: "Most jobs, especially medicine, exclude the family. You cannot confess to taking care of children. My husband never admits taking care of children. It is far better for a doctor to be on the golf course than to be with his children. Taking true responsibility for the family is viewed as nonprofessional. Your mind must be totally on the job. Certain 'male' responsibilities are acceptable—having the car repaired, having one's hernia repaired—you can take off time for those activities but not for traditionally female responsibilities. If a man says, 'I cannot attend that six p.m. meeting; I have to pick up my child,' the response would be, 'What's the matter with him?' They would think he is weak, not committed to his job."

Many would say that a physician has far more autonomy, more discretionary time than most male employees; but what is clear is that none of these male workers will either *be* free or *feel* free to participate in child rearing until it is recognized at the workplace that family responsibilities are important and legitimate. When picking your child up at the day-care center is at least as important as picking your car up at the repair shop, we will have moved a bit closer to legitimizing men's and women's responsibilities to children.

Even when these tasks are considered legitimate, it takes many years, perhaps generations, to alter people's attitudes. In Sweden, where all segments of society have been discussing sex roles for over a quarter-century, and where paid parental leave for both mothers and fathers at the time of the birth or adoption of a baby has been a right since 1974, only one-quarter of the fathers take any part of that leave. Swedish studies indicate that fathers who work in jobs where taking parental leave is viewed positively—in government jobs, in academia, or in other professional occupations—are more likely to take the option than fathers who work in occupations in which such behavior is frowned upon. Making parental leave a real option—for both men and women—is perhaps the easiest part of the task; making it acceptable is far more difficult.

There have been, of course, significant changes within many families in our society. Some fathers are already caring for their children more than could have been imagined a generation ago. It must be stressed, however, that many of them work in occupations in which this behavior is not only acceptable but considered praiseworthy, and many work in fields in which they have a great deal of independence and autonomy. In her optimistic book *Remaking Motherhood: How Working Mothers Are Shaping Our Children's Future,* Anita Shreve extols "the new working father." She points out that fathers used to be distant, almost sacred, and were rarely intimately involved in the often messy business of daily life—feeding the children, changing their diapers, doing the dishes and the laundry—but that now "the character of the American father has changed dramatically." She points out that fathers' involvement in parenting starts with books on pregnancy and childbirth classes, with being present at the birth; and then, "with some awkwardness, but with pride, they change diapers, bottle-feed infants, know where the T-shirts are kept and walk the floors at night to help settle colicky babies." To bolster these assertions Shreve quotes several men: an "independent producer of filmstrips and videotapes," a magazine editor, a journalist, and a sculptor. She then quotes several women who speak with pride of sharing child-rearing and household tasks with their partners. The first woman is a "university administrator"; Shreve does not tell us the occupations of the other women or their husbands. Do any of these people, men or women, punch a time clock? Do any of them work in a factory? Do any of them work in construction or as security guards or in one of the major insurance companies? Do any of them sell refrigerators at Sears or shoes at Macy's? Are any of them orderlies in a large city hospital? An independent producer, a magazine editor, a journalist, and a sculptor are hardly representative of "American fathers," and suggesting that they are is misleading. These are atypical members of the upper middle class, who probably have considerable control over their daily lives; assuming that they are representative distorts our understanding of the true problems of working women and men.

Shreve goes on to cite studies that give a very different picture of American fathers. In 1986 the Boston University School of Social Work did a study of employees at a Boston-based firm. They found that women work twice as many hours on child care and home-making as men, even when the woman's income is greater than the man's. They also found that women are more likely to stay home if the children are sick and that married female parents spend a total of eighty-five hours a week on work, in and outside of the home, while married male parents spend sixty-five hours. A 1982 study conducted by Joseph Pleck found that men spend an average of fifteen to twenty minutes a day in direct participation with their children (and two to four hours of indirect participation); women spend twice as much time. He found, moreover, that in families that share child care on a fairly equal basis, fathers are more likely to "play" with their children while mothers still carry out most of the "caretaking" activities.

A 1987 *New York Times* survey of 1,870 people nationwide indicates that men are still doing far fewer household chores than are women. Ninety-one percent of the married women surveyed said that they did most of the food shopping for the household; only 18 percent of the men said they did. Moreover, 90 percent of the married women reported that they did most of the cooking, as against only 15 percent of the men. As one observer of patterns within the American family stated, "I think most men feel a certain superiority because they are generally the ones in most marriages earning the higher income. There's a class distinction even in marriage." But as Joseph Pleck has pointed out, women help to maintain a traditional division of household chores, because they frequently feel these tasks are "their turf and the basis of their identity."

Kathleen Gerson, sociologist and author of *Hard Choices: How Women Decide About Work, Career, and Motherhood,* points out that

those who bear children still find it difficult to make fathers equal partners in the daily task of parenting. Whatever a couple's preferences, few men are able to withdraw from the workplace to care for a newborn. Given the pervasiveness of male-female earnings differentials, few families could afford to substitute male for female caretaking even if employers were willing. The organization of household labor has thus been slow to respond to changes between the home and the workplace while most men remain second partners in the private sphere.

Gerson continues by stressing the importance of the structure of the workplace and of programs such as day care to the structure and functioning of the family:

Workplace organization also still assumes a traditional family model, even though only a minority of American households now fits this pattern. Paternity leaves, flex time, job sharing, and other arrangements that might increase the options open to women and men are available to only a few. Day-care programs, whether public or private, are notable in the United States primarily by their absence. Employees and policymakers have done little to confront, much less alleviate, the dilemmas households face when women attempt to combine work and parenthood.

This is, I believe, a far more realistic picture of family interaction and role playing than the one supplied by anecdotal evidence weighted heavily toward a highly educated, privileged subgroup of the society. If we wish to formulate a social policy that will be relevant to the needs of most Americans, we must recognize the middle-and-upper-middle-class bias that charcterizes much of our thinking. It is only through an accurate assessment of family patterns and the needs of the majority of parents and children that we as a society can determine how we can best provide for our children and strengthen both individuals and families.

Recent Census Bureau data indicate that for the first time more than half of all new mothers are staying in the labor market. In 1987, 50.8 percent of new mothers were working or seeking employment within a year of giving birth. Older and more educated mothers are working in even larger numbers than younger mothers and those with less education. For example, 68 percent of women who had their first child after turning thirty remained in the labor market, compared with 54 percent of those ages eighteen to twenty-four. Sixty-three percent of new mothers with college degrees remained in the work force, compared with 38 percent of high-school graduates. Black mothers were most likely to work during the first year after giving birth; 53 percent were doing so. Fifty-one percent of white mothers and 36 percent of Hispanic mothers also returned to the workplace during that year. Widowed, divorced, and separated mothers were most likely to be working; 66 percent did so. Married women were next at 49.8 percent, then single women at 49.5 percent. One of the categories that has increased most in recent years is that of two-income families with children. In 1976, 8.3 million mothers in two-worker families returned to the labor force; in 1987 that number was up to 13.4 million. As the opening paragraph of yet another in the recent spate of articles about the day-care crisis in the United States noted:

> The figures are staggering. Ten million children under the age of six have two working parents or a single parent who supports the family. By 1995 two-thirds of all pre-schoolers will have mothers in the work force. And yet, in 1986, there were only 40,000 day-care centers and 105,000 licensed day-care homes watching over 2.1 million children. Every day, millions of other children are sent to unregulated facilities, where the quality of care they get varies widely.

The New York Times in a recent editorial points out that the "revolution" in the number of women in the labor force is

> not news to individual women and families. They've been adjusting in a host of ways—patching together day care by calling on grandparents, hiring illegal aliens, organizing nurseries. Yet society, from the local workplace to Washington, looks on blankly, fixed on romantic images of Mommy in the kitchen watching over Baby in the playpen. . . .

Studies show that the inability to find child care disrupts the jobs of parents, not to speak of the nearly unmeasurable anxiety it causes both parents and children. A recent government study, "Who's Minding the Kids?," states that some 450,000 parents each month lose time from work due to problems in their child-care arrangements.

Work and Family Resources of Minneapolis surveyed twelve

hundred employees at a major corporation and found that 65 percent of women under 35 with children who are part of dual-earner families are often affected by "child-care pressures." The same percentage say that they are often affected by "sick-child-care pressures"; 50 percent feel they have "no time for children"; 53 percent are "overwhelmed by family concerns"; 57 percent are "usually too tired for [the] family"; and an overwhelming 95 percent feel they have "no time for self." And these are women in dual-earner families! Imagine the responses if these questions had been asked of single mothers! Interestingly, nearly three-quarters of the men (72 percent) were affected by "child-care pressures"; over half (53 percent) were affected by "sick-child-care pressures"; and 60 percent felt there was "no time for self." But only 9 percent of the fathers felt "overwhelmed by family concerns"; 22 percent felt "usually too tired for [the] family"; and 31 percent felt they had "no time for [the] children." While men seem to be concerned about concrete issues such as child care and care for sick children as well about having too little time for themselves, they are far less concerned about more subjective feelings about parenting. In short, women may have higher expectations about parenting than men, or perhaps they feel guiltier about what they perceive as shortcomings in the quality of their parenting.

Recent research also points to an alarming shortage of preschool teachers. A 1988 study by the Bank Street College of Education found that almost half of New York City's Head Start and day-care classrooms are run by teachers who lack full qualifications. According to the report, "New York City's publicly funded day care and Head Start systems are being strangled by an inability to recruit and retain qualified teachers." The report continues, "This problem has reached a level where it presents disastrous consequences for both the supply and quality of these programs." Moreover, the turnover rate among preschool teachers and family day-care providers had reached alarming proportions. New York City, which in September 1987 had a teacher vacancy rate of 27 percent in day care and 13 percent in Head Start, has a turnover rate in preschool care of 20 to 25 percent. Nationally, the turnover rate is estimated to be 40 percent a year at day-care centers and a "staggering" 60 percent among family day-care providers. The

Bank Street report blamed the exodus of trained teachers on poor salaries; the average salary for teachers in Head Start and publicly financed day care is approximately $19,000.

In 1984 the estimated two to three million child-care workers in the United States were in the lowest 5 percent of American wage earners; they earned, on the average, less than parking-lot attendants. The median income for those employed full-time in centers was $9,204; for those employed in private homes, $4,420.

Among all the problems with child care in our society, none is perhaps more shocking than the instances of child neglect and abuse. When eighteen-month-old Jessica McClure fell into a well shaft at the unlicensed day-care program she attended, the country watched anxiously until she was finally lifted to safety. We could relate to little Jessica and her family and care deeply about her plight. When we hear shocking charges of sexual abuse in day-care centers, we react with anger and outrage. Why, then, do we as a society not react with equal anger and outrage when we read article after article, see program after program detailing the child-care crisis? It is clear that one of the richest countries in the world is not paying attention to the needs of its children. It is clear that we lack millions of urgently needed child-care places, that we have too few preschool teachers, and that many of those we have are inadequately trained. Some child-care centers, Ralph Nader has said, are nothing more than "children's warehouses."

In the winter of 1984–85, 22.3 percent of American children under the age of five were being cared for in a home other than their own by a nonrelative. Only a fraction of these family day-care homes are licensed. In 1986 a fire broke out in a Brooklyn family day-care home, killing two children and injuring six others. How many tragedies must take place before the society fulfills its responsibility and moves ahead to protect its children?

In recent years child abuse, particularly by parents and close relatives, has frequently been in the news. Headlines scream the latest tragedies; television anchorpeople tell us the stories in somber voices; editorials call for patching the system in an attempt to plug the holes in our inadequate child-welfare system. But what about societal neglect of children? Is it not neglect when an affluent society chooses not to provide desperately needed child care and after-school care? Is it not societal neglect when we permit existing centers to operate with inadequate numbers of teachers as well as teachers who are inadequately trained? Is it not societal neglect when we knowingly give parents of millions of children no choice but to send their children to unlicensed, unsupervised family day care?

While first-rate, accessible child care is essential for many working parents, for adolescent mothers it can mean the difference between a life of relative well-being and self-sufficiency on the one hand and a life of poverty and dependency on the other. As one researcher has pointed out, "The transition to motherhood can be an overwhelming experience for many adolescents, particularly for those with limited parental support." While it has become clear in recent years that "community programs which offer comprehensive medical, social and educational services both prenatally and postpartum . . . appear to have a greater impact on educational attainment, the acquisition of vocational skills, the delay of subsequent births, and economic self-sufficiency than programs which predominantly concentrate on prenatal services, or limited postpartum care," there has been relatively little attention paid to the provision of day care for adolescent parents and their children. If the young parents are to be able to support themselves and their children, it is essential that they at least finish their high-school education, obtain some specialized training or go on to college, and obtain some work experience. While some young parents do have child care available within their family networks, many do not; and the absence of child care or the ability to pay for it is frequently responsible for a high dropout rate from school, training programs, or work. Several recent programs have demonstrated the importance of child care in improving the life outcomes of both parent and child. As one observer has noted:

Each successful program model concentrates on education, employment, health, and fertility control, and parenting and child development, areas which have been identified as essential for the long-term goal of economic self-sufficiency and positive family outcomes for both mother and child. In each program the provision of day care is considered crucial for the successful provision of other services.

But preschool care is not the only out-of-home child care needed in the United States. Estimates of the number of "latchkey children"—school-age children between the ages of five and thirteen who are regularly left unsupervised some time during the day—range from two million to ten million. California alone, the acknowledged leader, has an estimated eight hundred thousand latchkey children. We generally think of latchkey children as poor children who live in dilapidated housing, a key literally hanging from a string around an eight-year-old's neck, but of course these children come from all classes, from all parts of the country, from cities, suburbs, and rural areas. Studies indicate, in fact, that a substantial number of these children are white and middle class and live in suburban and rural communities. They are children whose parents need to be working at jobs at which there is no flex time, living in communities in which there are few if any after-school resources and whose relatives are not available to take up the slack.

Despite the documented need for a massive influx of services to parents and children, and despite clear evidence that the issue is a popular one with the voting public, there is still considerable ambivalence about child care in the United States. This ambivalence is often fueled by experts who continue to question some aspects of day care. Dr. Jay Belsky, professor of human development at Pennsylvania State University, questions the effect of day care on children under the age of one. His research indicates, he maintains, that infants less than one year old who receive more than twenty hours of nonmaternal care are more likely to have insecure relationships with their parents and are more likely to have behavior problems later in childhood. Other researchers point to experience in other countries that, they say, indicates that if the care is first-rate there are no negative consequences. Belsky and other experts have issued a statement calling for additional infant and toddler care and stressing the need for better salaries and working conditions and more training for the workers.

One way of minimizing the necessity for infants to spend considerable periods of time in day care would be the passage of legislation mandating paid paternal leave after the birth or adoption of a baby. There has been, however, considerable hostility on the part of the business community toward parental leave. A bill finally approved in late 1987 by the House Education and Labor Committee provided only for a ten-week, unpaid parental leave and applied only to companies with fifty or more employees—"a level that exempts about 95 percent of the nation's employees, according to the General Accounting Office." The parental-leave bill, viewed by the business community as an encroachment by government on business, particularly on areas better left to collective bargaining or employer discretion, was killed by the U.S. Senate at the height of the 1988 presidential election. There was little discussion of the bill or the issue of parental leave in the remaining month of the campaign—indicating, perhaps, that those running for political office are more responsive to the business community than to the needs of infants and their parents.

Not only are the psychological aspects of infant day care questioned, but the illness rates of children in day care are routinely raised. Several studies have found that children in day care have higher rates of diarrhea, hepatitis A, and meningitis and that they are at higher risk for respiratory illness. Even assuming the best of hygienic practices—which is difficult, particularly if one is dealing with children still in diapers—children in day care are in close contact with many other children and are indeed likely to spread these illnesses more easily than if they were at home.

In addition to concerns about potential physical and psychological problems of children in day care, concerns about cost are omnipresent. One estimate indicates that quality care for infants (one year and under) with better-trained, better-paid workers and an appropriate adult-child ratio would cost $7,800 per year and that quality care for toddlers (two to four years) would cost $6,500. As economist Robert Samuelson warns, "Converting today's patchwork system into a subsidized network of centers run by the same strict standards would be horrendously expensive." Rita Watson of the Bush Center in Child Development at Yale University has estimated a cost of $62 billion for care for children under six and

$90 billion including after-school care for children between the ages of six and fourteen. As Samuelson comments, "If government paid only a third of the tab, the bill would be huge." Other estimates of the cost of preschool care are not nearly so high. According to *Children in Need: Investment Strategies for the Educationally Disadvantaged,* a statement by the Research and Policy Committee of the Committee for Economic Development, the cost for quality preschool care per child per year would range between $3,500 and $4,000. Providing for all "at risk" four-year-olds—those born into poverty, those who are poorly prepared for school, children of teenage parents, those with learning disabilities, emotional problems, physical handicaps, or language problems, those who are victims of racial or ethnic prejudice, and those who have access to only substandard schools—would cost between $2.6 and $3.1 billion. Any way we look at it, quality preschool care will be costly. But it may be far costlier—for parents, for children, and for the society—not to provide it.

As though these problems weren't enough, questions have been raised recently about the concept of "quality time." Claudia Palma, the physician who currently is caring for her children full time, questions whether quality time is a meaningful concept for infants. Anna Quindlen, writing in *The New York Times,* points out how children do not always cooperate when we want our limited time with them to be special and memorable:

> Since I've made a decision to be away from my children for a considerable portion of most days, I've got to make my peace with a couple of plain realities. One is that I'm going to miss some good stuff. There will be lots of fun had, questions asked, significant moments passed when I'm not there.
>
> The flip side is that when I am there, lots of the time is going to be the kind of just-hanging-around-doing-nothing-waiting-for-something-to happen time that constitutes a large part of a child's life.

The other "reality" is that "quality time" will happen when it is least convenient for the parent. Quindlen gives two all-too-real examples:

It is when you have just dropped a dozen eggs in the dairy aisle of the supermarket that suddenly a small voice will say, "Mom, do all people die? Will you die? Will Dad die? Will I die?" Luckily I've already answered those questions, and luckily I was merely in bumper-to-bumper traffic on Route 80 trying to change lanes to get around the stalled tractor-trailer when, from the back seat, I heard the dreaded words, "Mom, how does a baby get out of a mother's body?"

Not only might our infants who are away from their mothers too long become insecure, not only might our toddlers in day care get diarrhea or worse, not only are the potential costs for child care exorbitant, not only might parental leave undermine free enterprise—but even quality time, that concept which has lightened the burden of guilt for so many women, is being questioned.

Furthermore, many mothers are questioning the practice of leaving children in the care of others for prolonged periods of time. In a scathing op-ed piece in *The New York Times,* a Massachusetts mother of three discusses "a new form of neglect on the part of the rich: absence." Child abuse and neglect are often thought of as problems of the poor and near-poor. They are, of course, problems of families at all economic levels. As the Lisa Steinberg case indicates all tooo well, it is generally only the poor and near-poor who are singled out for societal intervention. "Nannies" of one form or another have been bringing up the children of the affluent for generations. One wonders why the practice is being criticized now. Is it somehow less legitimate for a mother to leave her children to deal with mergers and acquisitions than it is to leave them to play tennis, to go to bridge parties or the Bahamas? The op-ed piece criticizes dual-career couples who not only work full-time but are out every evening as well, parents who "work around the clock," have personalized Nautilus programs, getaway weekends in St. Thomas, and two full-time sitters, or nannies, or au pairs. The author is quick to point out that she is "not blaming mothers. Most of these women tell me their husbands want them to quit their jobs or reduce their hours so they can be with their children. Yet the men don't seem willing to take up the slack. So they both just buy more help."

Who indeed is going to parent? Who will care for the children—*really* care? If women in demanding professions must work a twelve-hour day and sometimes more, and men in the same professions must work at least that much, who will care for the children? There is a new track in law firms—the "mommy track." Although many law firms have recently begun to offer flexible working hours, child care, and maternity leave, taking advantage of these options is leaving many female lawyers on the bottom of a two-track system. According to the executive director of the Association of the Bar of the City of New York, "We are beginning to have two-tier law firms. The top tier is the full-time partnership track lawyer, who has all the perks and prestige, and the bottom tier is the part-time track made up largely of women." And, of course, "part-time" is often nine to five; "full-time" is being available around the clock.

And these are affluent families with many options. What about low-income families, who cannot simply "buy more help"? What about single-parent families, where the working parent often must do it all, without any outside help at all? Aren't we simply demanding too much of our parents and children? For not only are parents caught in the impossible conflict between work and nurturing but the children are caught as well. One working mother of two states, "Somebody has to be there—for the doctor's appointments, the music lessons, the Hebrew school car pools, the camp shopping. Something has to give somewhere. Some parent has to show up at the school assemblies, help out in the classroom. You can't just delegate your kids to other people all the time; somebody has to be a parent. Someone has to instill values."

Linda Jefferson, another mother of two, who teaches full-time, points out that the close, intense relationship between parents and children is "so fleeting." She goes on to say, "The reality is that we're creating a new generation and that many of them are not being supervised, loved, nurtured, and cared for. Society has to change. There must be ways of working and caring for children so that we will raise secure, emotionally complete individuals."

How, indeed, do we organize society so that women and men can play an equal role in the public sphere and so that our children will have the care, the nurturing, the protection that they need?

These are not insoluble problems. Ways can and must be found to enable parents to function effectively in the workplace and to provide for the well-being of their children as well, but finding those ways may involve significant restructuring of our places of work, our communities, our patterns at home, and our priorities as a society.

The young women I interviewed were certainly concerned about their roles as mothers, particularly about how they were going to be actively involved in work and still be the kind of mothers they wanted to be. Their role models for mothering were often their own mothers, some of whom work, some of whom do not, but few of whom work in the traditionally male-dominated professions to which many of their daughters aspire. As might be expected, the aspect of their future lives about which they are most realistic is the one with which they have had firsthand experience—mothering and child rearing.

Despite their concern, virtually none of the young women raised issues such as day care, parental leave, or the need to encourage the wider society to provide services for them and their children. They assumed that child care would be the responsibility of the nuclear family. If they anticipated that they would be married while raising their children, several young women, particularly among the New American Dreamers, hoped that their husbands would share in child care; if they planned to raise their children alone, they assumed they would have full responsibility for the support and the nurturing of their children. Most of the Neotraditionalists planned to take on traditional female responsibilities for children even if they had husbands who would "help," while most of the Outsiders assumed they would have virtually total responsibility for child care and possibly for their family's needs as well.

These young people have accepted an almost completely individualistic view of their future: that they as individuals will need to work out their conflicting pressures and demands, in some cases without the sustenance and support of the fathers of their children, and in virtually all cases without the support of their extended family, their community, or of the broader society.

Part III, "Choices," explores the implications and limitations of these young women's belief that they are truly on their own and suggests ways in which American society must change if we are to give young women—and indeed young men as well—genuine options and opportunities to lead productive, meaningful lives.

PART III

Choices

CHAPTER 9

Toward a More Caring Society

And when that child becomes sick or that employee becomes sick, we ought not to say to that family struggling to make ends meet: "Choose. Choose your child or choose your job."
SENATOR CHRISTOPHER J. DODD
Democrat, Connecticut

We have listened as young women have talked about their dreams: their dreams of work, of success, of affluence; their dreams of love, of child rearing, of intimacy; their dreams of affiliation and of independence. We have also heard their concerns: concerns about balancing work and family, about needing to be able to go it alone, about finding that close personal relationship so many seek. And we have heard their despair: the despair of those who cannot envision a future beyond tomorrow, of those whose lives have been shaped at a young age by personal circumstances and social and economic forces often beyond their control, of eighteen- and nineteen-year-olds who seem old before their time.

In listening to these young women it is clear that twenty-five years after the publication of *The Feminine Mystique,* much has changed and much has remained the same. Women are attending college and graduate school in greater numbers than ever before. In the area of work, women have made great strides: the vast increase in the number of women in the labor force; the once unimaginable increase in the number of women in high-status, high-income professions; the growing acceptance, both on the part of women and on the part of many men, that women are competent, committed workers who can get the job done and achieve a considerable amount of their identity through their work roles. In keeping with their greatly increased presence in the world of work, women are often pictured by the media, by the fashion industry, even by politicians as serious, significant members of the labor force.

In recent years women have also gained greater control over their bodies. Largely because of the feminist movement, women have far greater understanding of how their bodies work, more control over their own fertility, and far greater participation in the process of childbirth. As this is being written, some of that control is under siege, particularly the right to abortion; but there have been significant strides nonetheless.

And, perhaps most important, many women recognize that they must make their own way in the world, that they must develop their own identity rather than acquire that identity through a relationship with a man. Woman after woman detailed her plan for becoming a full-fledged person, able to survive on her own; and woman after woman recognized that she must be able to support herself and, if she has them, her children as well.

But in other areas over this quarter-century there has been very little change, and some aspects of women's lives have deteriorated dramatically. Women are still all too often depicted in advertising, in films, on television, and by the fashion industry as sex objects. Women are still encouraged to focus on their looks—their bodies, their clothes, their makeup, their image. How women are supposed to look may have changed; but the tyranny of physical attractiveness, compounded by the need to appear "fit" and youthful, is omnipresent. Even in an event such as the women's final of the 1988 U.S. Open tennis tournament, in which Steffi Graf was trying to win her fourth major tournament of the year, thereby winning the "Grand Slam"—a feat accomplished by only four other players in the history of tennis—the good looks of her opponent, Gabriela Sabatini, were mentioned numerous times by the male television announcers, who were otherwise scrupulously nonsexist. It is noteworthy that in the record-breaking four-hour-and-fifty-four-minute men's final, which pitted Mats Wilander against Ivan Lendl, there was no mention of Wilander's rugged good looks. It is not, after all, simply how well women play the game but how they look while playing that counts as well.

The area of sex is still extraordinarily problematic for young women today. Of all the mine fields women must navigate, sex is one of the most complex and treacherous. As we have seen, the pressures to have sex are enormous and the pressures not to plan for sex nearly as great. Many young women are caught in this incredible bind: some are caught by ignorance, others by the desire to be part of the group; some by fear, others by the need to be held or "loved." And many are caught by the notion that having sex is cool, sophisticated, a rite of passage somehow required in today's culture. But it is still widely seen as something you do inadvertently, almost as an afterthought, for as we have found, if a fifteen-, sixteen-, or seventeen-year-old plans for sex, goes to the local family-planning clinic for contraception, acknowledges her intention, takes responsibility for her actions, truly takes control, she is often seen by her peers, her family, even her community as deviant, as a "bad girl." To acquiesce is permissible; to choose clearly and consciously to embark on a sexual relationship is somehow reprehensible. One is reminded of many magazine advertisements that picture women being "carried away" by feeling or literally carried away by men, vignettes that are clearly metaphors for sex. Are we really saying that being carried away is appropriately feminine while being in control of one's actions is not?

But it is not only the objectification of women that remains a fact of life but the marginalization of women as well, particularly in the workplace and in positions of power. Contrary to the expectations of the young women I interviewed, female workers still occupy the lowest rungs of most occupations, including the prestigious professions they have recently entered in such large numbers. Women may have entered the labor market in record numbers in recent years, but they are still working predominantly in the lowest-paying jobs within the lowest-paying occupations.

In addition, it has become clear over the past decade that poverty dominates and determines the lives of millions of women in the United States. Today two out of three poor adults are women. Teen mothers, female heads of families, divorced women, many working women, elderly women, the "new poor" as well as those who have grown up in poverty are all at substantial risk of spending a significant part of their lives at or below the poverty line. And, of course, if women are poor, their children are poor. One out of five children under the age of eighteen and one out of four under the age of six live in poverty today. One out of every two young black children is officially poor. Perhaps most disturbing, moreover, are the sharp increases over the past decade in the number of children in families with incomes below the poverty line, a group that has been termed "the poorest of the poor." The vast majority of these families are headed by women.

Within this context, within the reality of women's true economic situation, what is surprising in talking with young women from various parts of the country—black women, white women, and Hispanic women; affluent, middle-class, and poor women; women who are headed for Ivy League colleges as well as high school dropouts—is the narrowness of their image of success, the uniformity of their dreams. The affluent life as symbolized by the fancy car, the "house on a hill," the "Bloomingdale's wardrobe," "giving everything to my children," was described yearningly time and time again. As if programmed, the same words, the same dreams tumbled out of the mouths of young women from very different backgrounds and life experiences. Success was seen, overwhelmingly, in terms of what they would be able to purchase, what kind of "life-style" they would have. The ability to consume in an upper-middle-class manner was often the ultimate goal.

The uniformity of responses is reminiscent of interviews with young people in China in the early 1970s. When they were asked what they hoped to do when they finished school, the answer invariably was, "Whatever my country wishes me to do." Why did they all respond, with minor variation, in the same manner? Were they programmed, "brainwashed," at the very least told how to respond to inquisitive American visitors? While all of these explanations may have some validity, the fundamental explanation, I believe, is that that was the tone of the time—that is what *everyone* said, and indeed on some level meant, during the late 1960s and early 1970s in China.

Today one hears a similar uniformity when young American women speak of their dreams for the future. Few spoke of becoming a reporter or a journalist, of teaching or entering the ministry. Rarely did anyone speak of caring for the sick or helping the poor; only occasionally did someone hope to make difference in the lives of others. Even those planning to become social workers or nurses (and there were very few) spoke mainly of their concern that these professions would pay enough to enable them to live the life-style they hoped for. Are these young women programmed or "brainwashed," or are they too reflecting the tone—and the economic reality—or their time?

Are young women focusing on material possessions in part because they are at least something to hold on to, symbols of identity and security in an era of fragmented family life, insecure, often transient work relationships, and a vanishing sense of community? In any case, young women are surely reflecting the omnipresent message of television. As Todd Gitlin has stated:

> With few exceptions, prime time gives us people preoccupied with personal ambition . . . Personal ambition and consumerism are the driving forces in their lives. The sumptuous and brightly lit settings of most series amount to advertisements for a consumption-centered version of the good life, and this doesn't even take into consideration the incessant commercials, which convey the idea that human aspirations for liberty, pleasure, accomplishment, and status can be fulfilled in the realm of consumption.

Given the reality of the job market for women, what will become of their dreams of affluence? Given the reality of the structure of work and the availability of child care, what will become of their image of mothering? Have these young women, in fact, been sold a false dream? Have young women become encouraged to raise their expectations, only to see those expectations unfulfilled because there has not been comparable change within society? Have the major institutions that influence public opinion—the media, advertising, the fashion industry, as well as the industries that produce consumer goods and parts of the educational establishment—fostered these rising expectations because it suits their purposes and, in some cases, their profits? Has the dream of equal opportunity for women and men, of at least partial redistribution of power both within the family and in the society at large, been coopted and commodified, turned into a sprint for consumer goods rather than a long march toward a more humane life for all of us?

Have we indeed over the last quarter-century persuaded women that they, too, are entitled to their fair share of the American Dream, in their own right, not merely as appendages to the primary players, without changing the rules of the game in ways that would permit them truly to compete and succeed? Have women, in short, been hoodwinked into believing that they can "have it all, do it all, be it all" while society itself changes minimally? And have we somehow communicated to them that they must make it on their own, recreating the myth of the rugged individualist seeking the American Dream—alone? The sheriff (or cowboy) alone but for his faithful wife (or horse); the prospector for gold, solitary and in competition with scores of others like him, obsessively searching for an often elusive fortune; the immigrant man or woman, arriving in this country without family or friends, unable to speak the language, but through backbreaking labor and determination managing to make it into the middle class—these images are familiar to most Americans. They have often been translated into memorable films that keep the ideology alive: *High Noon, The Treasure of the Sierra Madre,* even *Casablanca,* perhaps the only film whose lines millions of Americans know by heart. Rick is the quintessential American: a loner, cynical, but in the long run principled, the individual par excellence, who makes up his own mind, does his own thing, does not even tell his plan to the lovely Ilse until the last moment, and then walks off into the foggy night a hero, his own man.

One of the most illuminating and disturbing aspects of my interviews with young women was their often-stated belief that they are essentially on their own. Much of their sense of isolation is rooted in the realities of American life: the disintegration of the extended family, the deterioration of the nuclear family, the dwindling sense of community, and, over the past decade, the pervasive ideology of the Reagan era, which undermined the belief in societal responsibility for the needs of Americans while elevating individualism and materialism to new heights. Not only are the New American Dreamers quite convinced that they must be prepared to make their own way; the Outsiders, often surrounded by hopelessness, individual and societal neglect, and few supports in their lives, are convinced of that likelihood as well. Only the Neotraditionalists anticipate with any real certainty a life centered around the traditional nuclear family, a life in which with a man's help and support, both economic and emotional, they will be able to move in and out of the work force as their image of mothering dictates. Their vision of the future is based on the assumption that a breadwinner/husband/father will be ever present and able to provide adequately for the family. It is noteworthy in this era of high divorce rates, two-income families, and downward mobility that the New American Dreamers and the Outsiders were approximately equal and the Neotraditionalists were the fewest in number among the women I interviewed.

But what about the notion of going it alone? Is that belief on the part of young women an expression of hope or of despair? Is it a reflection of strength that stems from the recognition now emerging—at long last, some might say—that women must be complete human beings with their own identity, income, and independence, or is this an image of aloneness, of isolation that stems, rather, from the recognition that there are few supports remaining in American society and that one had better be able to survive alone? When a high-school student says fiercely "You can't count on a man!" and young teen mothers talk about all they want to provide for themselves and for their children—probably without a man—is it mature independence, is it an expression of a Rambo-like mentality, or is it simply the acceptance of reality? Is it that young women are beginning to recognize that they must be able to stand alone if they are to control their destinies? Is it a manifestation of the individualism that "lies at the very core of American culture" and at the very core of the American Dream? Or is it a recognition that self-sufficiency might be the only way left?

I suspect that this relatively recent sense of independence is based on a combination of all three factors: that it is in part recognition that women can and should care for themselves, in part a manifestation of mythic American individualism, and in part an understanding that there are indeed few supports today and that women, for self-preservation, must be prepared to stand alone. Few, if any, women even alluded to the need for external supports. They all spoke in "the language of individualism, the primary American language of self-understanding," which the authors of *Habits of the Heart* claim "limits the ways in which people think." Or, as Todd Gitlin has described the characters on prime-time television, "The happiness they long for is private, not public; they make few demands on society as a whole, and even when troubled they seem content with the existing institutional order." The extended family was seldom mentioned by the young women I interviewed; the community was rarely discussed. With the exception of marriage, which many acknowledged might not happen or might not last, many young women felt they must be prepared to be on their own with their children. But is self-sufficiency a realistic goal for women today? Is self-sufficiency possible or even desirable within the current structure of American society?

Much has been written about the difficult choices women currently have: how to balance marriage and career; how to balance motherhood and career; the timing of conception; the problems of a demanding job versus the demands and joys of motherhood. But these books, articles, television programs, and occasionally films put forth a largely false message: that the majority of women in late-twentieth-century America indeed have these choices to make. The illusion is abroad in the land that a young woman can simply "choose" to postpone pregnancy and marriage, acquire the education of her choice (which should, of course, be in a field in which jobs are available and well paying), and then step into the job of her choice. At that point, if she wishes, the man of her dreams will miraculously appear (and will be single and interested in "commitment"!), and, despite years of contraception and possibly even an abortion or two, she will promptly conceive, have a healthy baby or two, and live happily ever after. But of course we know life is not like that—at least not for the vast majority of women.

Most women do not have these magnificent choices. The education of many women is circumscribed by economics, by inferior schooling, and by the expectations of their social group. The jobs they will take are dictated far more by the economy, by what jobs are "open" to women, and by their own economic need than by individual choice. And, as we know all too well, controlling and timing fertility can be an extremely difficult and delicate task. Not only do many women become pregnant when they are unprepared for motherhood, but many cannot seem to have a child when they have been planning and longing for one for years. Moreover, many women grow up hungry, homeless, and hopeless, part of the underside of a society that is increasingly coming to resemble a third-world nation with its very rich and privileged and its very poor and despairing.

This illusion of choice is a major impediment to the establishment of conditions that would enable women—and indeed all people—to have real choices. Young women recognize that they are likely to participate actively in both work and home, in "doing" and "caring," but they fail to recognize what they must have in order to do so: meaningful options and supports in their work lives; in childbearing, child rearing, and the structure of their families; in housing, health care, and child care; and, above all, in the values by which they live their lives. Does emphasis on fashion, consumerism, and the lives of the rich and famous create the illusion of choice while diverting attention from serious discussion of policies that would give women genuine options? It is significant that during the 1988 presidential campaign legislation to raise the minimum wage, to provide parental leave, and to improve and expand the child care system—measures that would have significantly increased the life options of women and of all family members—were defeated, the latter two by a Republican filibuster. Despite the much-touted gender gap, little real attention was paid to policies that relate primarily to the well-being of women and children during the national campaign, a time when these issues could have been thoroughly discussed and debated. Do politicians really be-

228 · On Her Own

lieve that women are not watching and listening? Are women perhaps *not* watching and listening? Or have they given up on a society
that does not seem interested in addressing their needs?

For women to have real choices, we must develop a society in
which women and children and indeed families of all shapes and
sizes are respected and valued. Despite the mythology of American
individualism, it is clear that most women cannot truly go it alone.
The young women I interviewed know that they must be prepared
to be part of the labor force and still be available to care for others—
for children, for older family members, for friends, for lovers—
but these often mutually exclusive tasks will be possible only when
we develop a society that supports doing and caring. Men must
take on caring functions; the society must take some of the responsibility for caring and above all must be restructured to permit,
even to encourage, doing and caring. Women simply cannot do it
all and cannot do it alone.

To suggest that aspects of American society must be significantly
altered may seem to some to be utopian or at best visionary. In a
time of corporate takeovers, insider trading, and lavish levels of
private consumption, calling for fundamental restructuring of social and economic priorities may seem fatuous or at best naive. I
do not mean to suggest that such restructuring will be accomplished
easily or in the near future, but while many of these changes may
take years or even decades to accomplish, if we are to bring about
significant change in the twenty-first century, discussion and debate
must be ongoing and must involve all sectors of society. It must
be stressed, moreover, that most of these proposals have been out-
lined before and will be explored again and again. It is my hope
that this discussion will add to the debate and will thereby further
the process of developing a more humane environment in which
we can all live, work, and care for one another.

First, I believe that fundamental change must be made in the
workplace. Traditionally male-dominated professions cannot continue to expect their workers to function as if there were a full-
time wife and mother at home. Most male workers no longer live
in that never-never land; female workers surely do not. Alternative
paths to partnerships, professorships, and promotion must be de-

veloped that will neither leave women once again at the bottom of the career ladder without real power and equal rewards nor force them to choose between a demanding work life and a demanding personal life.

Nor should women have to choose a middle ground between work and mothering. One compromise has been described as "sequencing"—establishing a career, leaving it to bring up the children, and then resuming work in a way that does not conflict with domestic responsibilities. Isn't that what many of us did in the fifties? Most women, clearly, cannot afford to sequence. Try telling a stitcher in a garment factory to sequence—or a waitress or a clerical worker. In addition to the loss of income, status, and seniority, the problem with these upper-middle-class "solutions," which are often unsatisfactory even for those who can afford them, is that once again they give the illusion of choice. For the vast majority of American women, sequencing is not possible, or even desirable. What we must develop are options for the millions of women who must work and for the millions of women who *want* to work, not the illusion of options applicable only to that minority of women who are part of affluent two-parent families and are willing to sacrifice their careers, their earning power, and often the real pleasure they obtain from work because the larger society is unwilling to meet women and families even halfway.

Another compromise suggested recently is institutionalizing within corporations one track for " 'career primary' " women, who can "be worked long hours, promoted, relocated and generally treated like a man," and another for "career and 'family' " women, who will accept "lower pay and little advancement in return for a flexible schedule that allows . . . [them] to accommodate to family needs." This proposal clearly would legitimize the second-class status of any parent, mother, or father who wished to spend a significant amount of time on family responsibilities. Once again, we would be insisting that individuals and families bend to norms that are defined by employers and that primarily serve the needs of employers.

We must reevaluate our system of economic rewards. Do we really want our entertainers, our stockbrokers, our corporate executives, and our divorce lawyers making millions while our nurses and day-care workers barely scrape by? Do we really want the rich to get richer while the poor get poorer and the middle class loses ground? Do we really want to tell our young women that they must play traditional male roles in order to earn a decent living and that caregiving no longer counts, is no longer worth doing?

Robert Bellah and his colleagues call for nothing less than a "transformation of our culture and our society," a transformation of our "social ecology." They suggest that greater emphasis on "work as a contribution to the good of all and not merely as a means to one's own advancement" might begin to mend "the split between private and public, work and family, that has grown for over a century. . . ." They continue to develop this theme:

If the ethos of work were less brutally competitive and more ecologically harmonious, it would be more consonant with the ethos of private life and, particularly, of family life. A less frantic concern for advancement and a reduction of working hours for both men and women would make it easier for women to be full participants in the workplace without abandoning family life. By the same token, men would be freed to take an equal role at home and in child care. . . . *A change in the meaning of work and the relation of work and reward is at the heart of any recovery of our social ecology* [italics added].

Market forces cannot be permitted to rule in all spheres of American life. If our society is to be a caring, humane place to live, to rear our children, and to grow old, we must recognize that some aspects of life—the education of our young people, health care, child care, the texture of community life, the quality of the environment—are more important than profit. We as a nation must determine our priorities and act accordingly. If teaching, the care of young children, providing nursing care, and other human services are essential to the quality of life in the United States, then we must recruit our young people into these fields and pay them what the job is really worth. Only then will we be giving them, particularly our young women, real choices. If we want nurses to care for our sick, we must indicate by decent wages and working conditions that the job is valued by society. We must give nurses and other health workers real authority, a meaningful voice in the health-care system, and then, and only then, will some of our best and brightest and most caring women and men choose to enter nursing. Whatever happened to careers in community organizing, urban planning, Legal Aid, and public-health nursing? Young women and men will be able to consider these options only if they are decently paid, have a future and some degree of security and respect.

In this fin de siècle period of U.S. history characterized (in the words of John Kenneth Galbraith) by "private affluence" and "public squalor," it may be difficult to see our way clear to putting significantly larger amounts of money into health care, community organizing, education, or even a meaningful effort to deter young people from drug abuse, but we must recognize that these issues are central to the well-being of families and thus central to the very fabric and structure of American society. While the 1980s have surely been characterized by absorption with personal advancement and well-being (particularly economic and physical well-being), there are many indications that Americans are also concerned about the well-being of the society as a whole. Poll after poll has demonstrated that people *are* concerned about issues such as education and homelessness and *are* willing to make sacrifices to enable the society to deal more effectively with these problems.

Furthermore, it is often said that there is no money to truly make this into a "kinder, gentler nation" but we must remember that the United States spends $300 billion annually on arms, the U.S. Congress has approved the Bush administration's savings and loan bailout proposal that will cost nearly $160 billion over the next ten years, and the United States has one of the lowest tax rates, particularly for the wealthy, in the industrialized world. I suggest that the money *is* there. The issue is how we choose to allocate it.

What should our priorities be? Among them, parents must have some time at home with their children. Why can't parents of young children work a shorter day or week and not risk losing their jobs?

Why aren't parents at the time of the birth or adoption of a baby guaranteed some paid time together with that infant when virtually every other industrialized country has some statutory maternity or parental leave? The parental leave bill that was killed during the 100th Congress called for unpaid leave for the parents of a newborn or newly adopted child. It would have affected only 5 percent of all businessess and 40 percent of all workers (the firms affected would have been those with fifty or more employees). It was estimated by Senator John H. Chafee, Republican of Rhode Island, that the cost would have been $160 million per year, which averages out to one cent per day for each covered employee. The bill also would have provided unpaid leave for parents with seriously ill children. As Senator Christopher J. Dodd, Democrat of Connecticut, a sponsor of the legislation, stated:

Today fewer than one in ten American families have the luxury of having the mother at home with the children while the father is at work.

In this nation today there are 8.7 million women as the sole providers of their families. They are taking care of 16 million kids who have no father at home. And when that child becomes sick or that employee becomes sick, we ought not to say to that family struggling to make ends meet: "Choose. Choose your child or choose your job."

No, women cannot make it alone. They cannot work and parent and care for their elderly relatives as well without a caring society. They cannot work and care for others without sufficient income, parental leave, real flex time, and a work environment that recognizes and understands that a rewarding private life takes time and energy.

Furthermore, that work environment must make it possible for both fathers and mothers to care for others. It must become acceptable in the United States for fathers to take leave to care for a new baby, to stay home with sick children, to leave work in time to pick up a child from day care or after-school care; for sons to attend to the needs of aging parents. It must even become acceptable for fathers to attend a school play or a Halloween party during the work day. Changing male roles may take years of resocialization and structural change within the society, but we must attempt it nonetheless. Mothers can no longer play the solitary domestic role—not while participating in the work force as well. If women are to do and to care, men must also do and care.

Perhaps a vignette from the life of one family and one work site illustrates the need to humanize the workplace. On November 21, 1985, the U.S. Senate agreed not to cast any votes between seven and nine p.m. The following letter was the reason for this unusual action:

Dear Senator Dole:
I am having my second-grade play tonight. Please make sure there aren't any votes between 7 and 9 so my daddy can watch me. Please come with him if you can.

Love,
Corinne Quayle

What is particularly remarkable about this incident is that when the final version of the Parental and Medical Leave Act was being written by the Senate Labor and Human Resources Committee, Vice-President J. Danforth Quayle, then a senator, vehemently opposed it and, according to one observer, "offered an amendment in committee that would assure that an employer enjoys the right to fire an employee who takes as much as one day off to be with a seriously ill child." As Judy Mann, the *Washington Post* columnist who brought this incident to light, wrote: "Quayle lives by a set of special rules for the privileged and well-connected and doesn't hesitate to impose another set of rules and obligations, harsher and devoid of compassion, on those who were not to the manner born. Either he doesn't know anything about the reality of most workers' lives, or he doesn't care."

The United States must also finally decide where it stands on the care of preschool children. By 1995 two-thirds of all preschool children (approximately 15 million) and more than three-quarters of all school-age children (approximately 34.4 million) will have mothers in the work force. In addition, 3.7 million mothers receiving welfare with 3.1 million children under six and 2.9 million school-age children will with the passage of recent welfare legislation be required to enter the work force or to participate in education and job-training courses. Day care must be provided for those single-parent families for at least one year. Today only 23 percent of all children of working parents attend full or part-time centers, which vary enormously in quality; an additional 23 percent are cared for in family day care, most of which is unlicensed and unsupervised. As Edward Zigler, director of the Bush Center in Child Development and Social Policy at Yale and one of the founders of the Head Start program, has recently stated, "All over America today we have hundreds of thousands of children in child-care settings that are so bad that their development is being compromised. . . . We are cannibalizing our children. I know that sounds awful, but when you see 13 babies in cribs and one adult caretaker . . . you see children who are being destroyed right after birth."

How will 50 to 60 million children whose mothers will be in the work force be cared for during the 1990s? The New York–based Child Care Action Campaign, whose blue-ribbon board includes experts in child care from all over the country, has urged every level of society to become involved in solving this child-care crisis. It has urged the federal government to establish a national child-care office and a "new and separate funding stream" for child care, to expand Head Start, and to set federal regulations on minimum standards. It has urged state and local governments to establish school-age-child-care programs, expand resource and referral programs, and raise the professional status and working conditions of child-care workers. It has urged employers to adopt flexible work schedules, to support community efforts to expand day-care centers and family day care, to invest in on-site centers, to help parents to pay for regular day care and emergency day care, and to allow employees to use their sick leave to care for ill children.

Other groups have recently called for substantial societal investment in the well-being of families and children. The Research and Policy Committee of the Committee for Economic Development, an "independent research and educational organization of over two hundred business executives and educators," has called for "new partnerships among families, schools, businesses, and community organizations that can bolster the health, education, and well-being of the whole child. . . ." More specifically, it has called for "investing in the future," through increased prenatal and postnatal care for pregnant teens and other high-risk mothers, quality child care, quality preschool programs for all disadvantaged three- and four-year-olds, and a restructuring of the school system, again particularly for disadvantaged students.

We may indeed be approaching a proverbial "window of opportunity" with respect to many of these issues. Since the U.S. is moving into an era of labor scarcity, it has been estimated that women will comprise 60 percent of new workers between now and the year 2000. This is therefore a key moment to attempt to make work life more compatible with family life. Moreover, many corporations are concerned about the availability of a literate, skilled, and healthy work force; it is, therefore, a key moment to call for far-reaching reform of our health and education systems. The Committee for Economic Development states that "we know enough to act" and stresses the importance of federal, state, local, and business cooperation in the urgent matter of providing for our children. A consensus is clearly building: our families can no longer go it alone; our women and children can no longer go it alone.

One of the central components of all of these recommendations is adequate training, recompense, employment security, and status for caregivers at every level. By demeaning the role of caregiver, society demeans all women and indeed, to one extent or another, exploits all caregivers. It also sets up the exploitation of one group of women by another. The ripples are endless: from the middle- or upper-middle-class career mother who is "stressed out" by trying to do it all to the single mother who really *is* doing it all to the day-care worker who is working in inadequate conditions earning inadequate pay to the child-care worker/domestic who is often shamefully exploited in the home, society's fundamental disregard for caregivers and for raising children diminishes us all. Ultimately, of course, it is the children who suffer, but women at all levels suffer as well. And the poor, the nonwhite, those with least choice suffer the most.

Any society that really wants to enable women to be in control of their lives must provide a comprehensive program of sex education and contraception. Perhaps one of the most startling aspects of my interviews with young women and with relevant professionals was the sense that many young women are buffeted about by conflicting attitudes toward sexuality and indeed find it exceedingly difficult to determine what they themselves think and want. By the time they figure it out, it is often too late. They are pregnant and faced with a real Hobson's choice: to abort, or to have a baby at a time in their life when they are ill-prepared—economically, physically, socially, or psychologically—to care for a child. We know what it can do to both the mother and the child when the pregnancy is unplanned and the mother is unable to care for the infant properly. We must do everything possible to make every child a planned child, to make every child a wanted child.

We must learn from the experience of other industrialized countries, whose rate of unintended and teenage pregnancy is so much lower than our own. We must institute sex education in our schools at all levels. The ignorance on the part of young women is astonishing and serves no useful purpose. Moreover, in this era of AIDS and other sexually transmitted diseases, such ignorance can literally be life-threatening. We must increase the accessibility of contraceptives, whether through school-based clinics or community-based health centers. We should consider staffing these centers with midwives or other health professionals whose primary task would be to relate to young people, understand their needs, and help them to understand their choices. The empowerment of young women and men in the area of sexuality should be the central goal—empowerment through knowledge, empowerment through emotional maturity, empowerment through access to the health-care system. And teenagers must be assured of confidentiality whenever they are dealing with contraception or abortion.

As Lisbeth Schorr so forcefully points out in her recent book *Within Our Reach: Breaking the Cycle of Disadvantage,* "The knowledge necessary to reduce the growing toll of damaged lives is now available." We know what to do; we know what works. A school-based program in Baltimore, Maryland, illustrates what can be done. Starting in January 1982, professionals at Johns Hopkins

University and the Baltimore Health Department and School Board collaborated in bringing sex education, reproduction-related medical services, and counseling to students in the junior high school and senior high school closest to Johns Hopkins Hospital. Both schools had all-black student bodies. Many of the young people lived in nearby high-rise public housing, and in the junior high school 85 percent were poor enough to qualify for the free-lunch program.

A nurse midwife and a social worker were placed in one school; a nurse practitioner and a social worker were placed in the other. The same professionals were available every afternoon, with physician backup if necessary, to provide relevant medical services at a clinic across the street. The teams gave classroom presentations, counseled individuals and small groups, and made appointments for further consultation, education, and treatment at the clinic. Medical services, including physical exams and contraceptives, were provided during a single visit and at no cost. Every effort was made to ensure that the students would see the same professionals each time they came, "in the belief that consistency of relationships builds trust, helps youngsters to synthesize what they have learned, and makes it possible for them to share very private concerns."

The demonstration program continued until June 1984. During the two-and-a-half years of its existence, the proportion of sexually active high-school students who had babies went down 25 percent; the proportion of girls who became sexually active by age fourteen dropped 40 percent, and the median age at which girls became sexually active rose by seven months, from age fifteen and a half before the program was started to a little over age sixteen at the program's end. This experience is yet another piece of evidence that knowledge about reproduction and access to contraception and to caring people who can discuss a young person's options rationally, with concern and yet with objectivity, can and does lessen the critical problem of teenage pregnancy.

Michael Carrera and Patricia Dempsey, director and former program coordinator of the Teen Primary Pregnancy Prevention Program of the Children's Aid Society in New York City, claim that what is needed is a "holistic approach." "It is our belief," they state, "that the teen pregnancy problem is largely a symptomatic response to greater social ills and because of this, it must concurrently be attacked on several levels. For example, unintended pregnancies among poor, urban teens can be more effectively curtailed if we reduce the impact of the institutional racism that is systemic in our society; if we provide quality education for everyone; and if we create more employment opportunities for young people and adults. If we could accomplish this, we would probably impact, in a more meaningful way, on the lives of teens than can any school or agency sexuality program."

Continued access to abortion must be guaranteed. Efforts to overturn or limit women's right to abortion must be vigorously resisted. For many young women, abortion is the only barrier between them and a life of poverty and despair. Until we stop giving our young women mixed messages—that it is desirable and sometimes even de rigueur to have sex but not legitimate to protect against pregnancy—abortion remains the only resource. Saying that one is for adoption, not abortion, may sound reasonable and "pro life"; but once young women are pregnant and decide to have the baby, giving it up for adoption is a wrenching decision, particularly for those young women who see little opportunity to make another life for themselves. Indeed, among the women I interviewed those who were most despairing about their lives were often those who had babies at a young age and could see no way out of the trap in which they found themselves. I am not suggesting that any of these issues—particularly ones as personal and as controversial as sex education and abortion—are easy to resolve in our complex heterogeneous society, but we must somehow develop a public policy that will help our young people become mature before they are thrust into parenting roles. Other societies have developed such policies; we must learn from them and develop our own.

In addition to giving women greater choice over sex and childbearing, we must stop exploiting women as sex objects. As long as the message of jean manufacturers, cereal companies, automobile conglomerates, and perfume distributors is that women are for sale along with the product, that women are, in a very real sense, just another commodity to be bought, used, and traded in when the model wears out, both men and women will perceive women in this way. And until we enable young women to responsibly say either yes or no to sex, to understand their options and the risks involved, we are not permitting them to be in charge of their own destiny. But we cannot expect young women to take control of their own destiny unless they can see alternatives, pathways that will lead to a rewarding life.

It is ironic that young women, a group outside the cultural mainstream in at least two fundamental ways, age and gender, have internalized that most mainstream of ideologies, the American Dream. After examining the realities of women's lives today, it is clear that the American Dream, at least as conventionally conceived, cannot be the blueprint for the majority of women. The fundamental components of the American Dream—an almost devout reliance on individualism; the notion that American society, particularly at the end of the twentieth century and the beginning of the twenty-first, is fluid enough to permit substantial upward mobility; the belief that hard work will lead to economic rewards, even for women, a group that has always been at the margins of the labor force; and the determined optimism in the face of massive social and economic problems—will not serve women well.

We must recognize that even for most men the American Dream, with its belief in the power of the individual to shape his or her own destiny, was a myth. Men usually did not "make it" alone; they did not, as the image goes, tame the West, develop industrial America, and climb the economic ladder alone—and they certainly did not do it while being the primary caregiver for a couple of preschoolers. Most of those men who "made it" in America, whom we think of when we reaffirm our belief in the American Dream, had women beside them every step of the way—women to iron their shirts, press their pants, mend their socks, cook their meals, bring up their children, and soothe them at the end of a hard day. They did not do it alone. They *still* don't do it alone. How can women do it alone? Who is there to mend and press their clothes, cook their meals, bring up their children, and soothe them at the end of a hard day? How can women possibly make it alone when they earn 65 percent of what men earn, when housing is virtually unaffordable for millions of families, when child care is scarce and all too often second-rate or worse? And where did they get the notion that they *should* be able to make it alone? It may be progress that many young women now realize that they cannot depend on marriage and a man for their identity, their protection, their daily bread; but is it progress or is it illusion for them to believe that they can do the caring and the doing and do it all on their own in a society that has done very little to make women truly independent?

The American Dream cannot really work for any of the groups of women I interviewed. Yes, some women will accomplish their dreams and live productive, rewarding lives; but most of them will have to make substantial compromises, scale down their ambitions, not be quite the kind of parent they hoped they would be. How will the New American Dreamers make it in law, medicine, or oceanography when the rules were made for men with an elaborate support system? How will they get to the top of their fields when our image of authority is still someone who is six feet tall in a blue suit, striped shirt, and not-too-bold red tie? How will they afford the co-op, the BMW, and the trips to Europe when they must often choose between sequencing, the "Mommy" track, part-time work, or leaving their field entirely in order to parent? And how will they resolve their guilt about what they are likely to perceive as less-than-adequate parenting when they must work to remain competitive in their field, to contribute to the maintenance of the family, or to function as its sole support?

Nor does the ideology of the American Dream serve the Neo-traditionalists well. Many of them place their faith in a loving, lasting marriage and hope to spend much of their lives caring for others. But what happens if disaster strikes or the marriage fails? Will they be prepared to go it alone? Will they really be prepared and able to take care of themselves and their children—and possibly their aging parents—with relatively few societal supports? And what if they cannot be home at three o'clock for cookies and milk? How will they feel about themselves as mothers?

And finally, of course, the ideology of the American Dream fails the Outsiders most abysmally and most tragically. Those who are truly outside the system—the homeless and the hungry, the poor and the near-poor, who know that America as it enters the 1990s has largely forgotten them, the millions of nonwhites who feel permanently outside the culture, the young people who leave high school functionally illiterate, those who feel like a "circle within a square," those who try to forget their sadness and anger through alcohol or drugs or, tragically, through suicide—what can the American Dream mean to them? To many it means that their inability to find the path to success is their own fault; for imbedded in the ideology of the American Dream, inherent in that "I think I can" mentality, is the presumption that if we do not succeed in this land of milk and honey, in this world of infinite opportunity, it must be our fault. If everyone is so rich on "Dallas," "Dynasty," and "L.A. Law," if even blacks have made it on "The Cosby Show" and its spin-offs, if single women like Kate and Allie and married couples like Hope and Michael and rural/suburban people like Bob Newhart and his support group and urban people like Sam Malone and his gang at "Cheers" all live comfortable and relatively happy, contented lives, what must be wrong with those who feel like Outsiders, either temporarily or permanently? If the biggest problems are solvable in twenty-two minutes, what hope can there be for those of us so beyond the pale that we cannot think of solutions at all?

We must have the courage and the wisdom as a society to recognize that we need a new vision of America for the twenty-first century, perhaps even a new American Dream. We need a vision that recognizes that we cannot survive without one another, that families must have supports in order to thrive, that women cannot make it alone any more than men ever have.

We must provide many more paths toward a gratifying, economically secure life. Traditional male occupations cannot be the only routes to the good life; traditional female work must be restructured so that it too can lead to power, prestige, and a life of plenty. And the traditional male work style must give way, for both women and men, to the recognition that work is merely one aspect of life and that private concerns, family life, leisure activities, and participation in community life help to define who we are and must be seen as important both to the individual and to the society.

We must find ways of opening up American society to those who feel outside the system, to those who feel hopeless and despairing. We must educate all of our young people, not simply the most privileged. We must provide them with adequate housing, health care, nutrition, safe communities in which to grow, and, above all, a meaningful role in society. So many of them feel extraneous because so many of them are treated as extraneous, except, possibly, in their roles as consumers. Moreover, providing decent lives for the millions of young people who are Outsiders will provide decent jobs for millions of other Americans and, even more, the sense that one is participating in a worthwhile way in the life of the nation. But, of course, we will not make the society accessible to those who now consider themselves Outsiders unless power and wealth are distributed far more equitably. It has been said before, it will be said again, but it cannot be said too often: there is a greater gap today between the rich and the poor than at any point since the Bureau of the Census began collecting these data in 1947. In 1987 the wealthiest 40 percent of American families received 67.8 percent of the national family income, the highest percentage ever recorded, while the poorest 40 percent received 15.4 percent, the lowest percentage (along with that of 1986) ever recorded. Until we address these fundamental inequities, we cannot hope to enable our young people to become fully participating members of society.

These changes will not come about all at once or even, perhaps, in the near future. Changing our priorities is exceedingly difficult without strong national leadership pointing the way, but until we have representatives in Washington who will promote the public good rather than private gain we must develop leadership at the local level and work toward a more humane society step by step. We can raise these issues in our own communities and places of work. We can select one concern, such as child care or parental leave or flexible work hours, and together with others place that issue on the agenda of our employer, our union, or our local legislator. We can work with major national organizations to place family policy concerns on the national agenda. We must recognize that these concerns transcend the traditional barriers of class, race, gender, and age and form common cause with those who share our priorities.

Above all, we must develop a vision that recognizes that caring is as important as doing, that caring indeed *is* doing, and that caregivers, both paid and unpaid, are the foundation of a humane society and must be treasured and honored. We need a vision of

America that recognizes that we must reorganize our social institutions—our family life, our schools, our places of work, and our communities—to enable all people to care for one another, to enable all people to work and to participate in the public life of the nation. Our courageous, insightful, persevering, and often wise young women deserve no less. Our young men deserve no less. Future generations deserve no less.

NOTES

INTRODUCTION

page

1 "world is born": Elizabeth Ewen, *Immigrant Women in the Land of Dollars: Life and Culture on the Lower East Side, 1890–1925* (New York: Monthly Review Press, 1985), p. 264.

2 "of women's life": Mimi Abramovitz, *Regulating the Lives of Women: Social Welfare Policy from Colonial Times to the Present* (Boston: South End Press, 1988), p. 111.

7 " 'to get wealth' ": Richard M. Huber, *The American Idea of Success* (Wainscott, NY: Pushcart Press, 1987), p. 13.

"his own initiative": Robert N. Bellah, Richard Madsen, William M. Sullivan, Ann Swidler, and Steven M. Tipton, *Habits of the Heart: Individualism and Commitment in American Life* (Berkeley: University of California Press, 1985), p. 33.

"abilities and efforts": Huber, p. 43.

"and finished rich": ibid., p. 46.

"work and perseverance": ibid., p. 47.

8 "gold and safety": David M. Brownstone, Irene M. Franck, and Douglass L. Brownstone, *Island of Hope, Island of Tears* (New York: Penguin, 1986), p. 8.

"moment of birth": ibid.

11 "be really human": Felix Greene, "Free to Be Human," *Far East Reporter* (April 1973), pp. 4–11.

CHAPTER 1

17 "by a man": Rachel M. Brownstein, *Becoming a Heroine: Reading About Women in Novels* (New York: Penguin, 1984), p. xv.

20 "work commands": Nadya Aisenberg and Mona Harrington, *Women of Academe: Outsiders in the Sacred Grove* (Amherst, MA: University of Massachusetts Press, 1988), p. 3.

"to be universal": Michelle Zimbalist Rosaldo, "Women, Culture, and Society: An Overview" in *Women, Culture, and Society,* Michelle Zimbalist Rosaldo and Louise Lamphere, eds. (Stanford, CA: Stanford University Press, 1974), p. 19.

21 "activities of men": ibid.

most valued food: ibid.

"role as mothers": ibid., p. 24.

the two spheres: Joan C. Tronto, "Women and Caring: What Can Feminists Learn About Morality from Caring?" in *Body, Gender and Knowledge,* Alison Jagger and Susan Brodo, eds. (New Brunswick, NJ: Rutgers University Press, in press). See also Linda Imray and Audrey Middleton, "Public and Private: Marking the Boundaries," in *The Public and the Private,* Eva Gamarnikow et al., eds. (London: Heinemann, 1983), pp. 12–27.

23 traditional male route: *Glamour* (August 1988), pp. 208–9.

42 percent richer: Terry Arendell, *Mothers and Divorce: Legal, Economic, and Social Dilemmas* (Los Angeles: University of California Press, 1986), p. 2.

24 "out of control": Steven V. Roberts, "Poll Finds Less Optimism in U.S. on Future, a First Under Reagan," *The New York Times,* February 21, 1988.

more hopeful than women: ibid.

26 "for such careers": Therese L. Baker, "Rising Educational and Career Expectations of High School Women Since 1960: Baseline Comparisons with Men," unpublished article.

than were women: Karen Oppenheim Mason and Yu-Hsia Lu, "Attitudes Toward Women's Familial Roles: Changes in the United States, 1977–1985," *Gender & Society* 2, no. 1 (March 1988), pp. 39–57.

as for boys: Gerald Eskenazi, "Girls' Participation in Sports Improves," *The New York Times,* June 8, 1988.

27 "Be intense": Margaret A. Whitney, "Playing to Win," *The New York Times Magazine,* July 3, 1988.

"definitely not pretty": ibid.

28 "culture of the 1980s": Frank Rich, "Cutting to the Heart of the Way We Live Now," *The New York Times,* December 25, 1988.

CHAPTER 2

44 "on their children": Cynthia Fuchs Epstein, *Deceptive Distinctions: Sex, Gender and the Social Order* (New Haven: Yale University Press, 1988), p. 195.

50 "loved their love": Josephine Humphreys, *Rich in Love* (New York: Viking, 1987), p. 29.

"for some time!": ibid., pp. 77–78.

51 "end all house": Paule Marshall, *Brown Girl, Brownstones* (New York: Feminist Press, 1981), p. 12.

in the yard: ibid., p. 115.

"but nobody listened": ibid., p. 112.

"loved him more": ibid., p. 190.

52 "mothering seem natural": Kathleen Gerson, *Hard Choices: How Women Decide About Work, Career, and Motherhood* (Berkeley: University of California Press, 1985), p. 205.

CHAPTER 3

55 "she was afraid": Carson McCullers, *The Member of the Wedding* (New York: Bantam, 1975), p. 1.

56 "else except me": ibid., p. 6.

57 "preparation for it": Robert N. Bellah, Richard Madsen, William M. Sullivan, Ann Swidler, and Steven M. Tipton, *Habits of the Heart: Individualism and Commitment in American*

Life (Berkeley: University of California Press, 1985), p. 57.

"succession of identities": Kate Simon, *A Wider World: Portraits in an Adolescence* (New York: Harper & Row, 1987), pp. 19–20.

58 "she is the Other": Simone de Beauvoir, *The Second Sex* (New York: Bantam, 1961), p. xvi.

59 "minefield of sex": Isabel Huggan, *The Elizabeth Stories* (New York: Viking, 1987), p. 43.

65 rose 2 percent: James Barron, "Suicide Rates of Teen-Agers: Are Their Lives Harder to Live?" *The New York Times,* April 15, 1987.

suicide each year: "Community Planning Urged to Prevent Teen-Age Suicide," *The New York Times,* August 30, 1988. See also Donna Gaines, "Teenage Wasteland: Bergenfield's Dead End Kids," *The Village Voice,* July 14, 1987; Eva Y. Deykin, Chung-Chen Hsieh, Neela Joshi, and John J. McNamarra, "Adolescent Suicidal and Self-Destructive Behavior: Results of an Intervention Study," *Journal of Adolescent Health Care* 7 (1986), pp. 88–95.

"for the future": Barron.

"of those things": ibid.

66 of illegal drugs: Warren E. Leary, "Young Adults Show Drop in Cocaine Use," *The New York Times,* January 14, 1988; "Patterns of Drug Use," Institute for Social Research *Newsletter,* University of Michigan, Fall/Winter 1987–88, pp. 3, 6.

to age thirty-nine: Daniel Goleman, "Teen-Age Risk-Taking: Rise in Deaths Prompts New Research Effort," *The New York Times,* November 24, 1987.

with astonishing frequency: Eva Y. Deykin, Ruth Perlow, and John McNamarra, "Non-fatal Suicidal and Life Threatening Behavior among 13-to-17-Year-Old Adolescents Seeking Emergency Medical Care," *American Journal of Public Health* 75, no. 1 (January 1985), pp. 90–92.

"sooner, than men": "Drinking Problems Rise Among Young Women," *The New York Times,* October 13, 1988.

had attempted it: "Responses 'Dismaying' in Poll of Teen-Agers," *The New York Times,* August 10, 1988.

68 "our metaphysical condition": Toni Morrison, *The Bluest Eye* (New York: Pocket, 1974), p. 18.

69 "being torn asunder": W. E. B. DuBois, *The Souls of Black Folk* (New York: New American Library, 1969), p. 45.

72 was 23 percent: Joseph Caines, Marin City Multi-Service Center, unpublished paper, 1986.

74 "girl child treasured": Morrison, p. 20.

"adjustment without improvement": ibid., p. 22.

75 "positive male images": Patricia Hill Collins, "Learning from the Outsider Within: The Sociological Significance of Black Feminist Thought," *Social Problems* 33, no. 6 (December 1986), pp. S14–S32.

"smells like rain": Gary Paul Nabhan, *The Desert Smells Like Rain: A Naturalist in Papago Indian Country* (San Francisco: North Point Press, 1987), p. 5.

"at any time": ibid., p. 6.

79 "the schoolhouse door": Peter W. Cookson, Jr., and Caroline Hodges Persall, *Preparing for Power: America's Elite Boarding Schools* (New York: Basic, 1985), p. 15.

power and privilege: ibid., pp. 26–29.

"fresh cut flowers": ibid., p. 28.

"in my bedroom": ibid., p. 48.

80 "inadequate lighting": Elizabeth Kolbert, "Panel Finds New York Schools Poorly Maintained," *The New York Times*, December 28, 1987.

"and troubled men": Gregory Jaynes, "On Line for Hope and Knowledge in a Bleak Land," *The New York Times*, December 26, 1987.

"emergency intervention": Edward B. Fiske, "Carnegie Report Urges Crusade for 'Bypassed' Urban Schools," *The New York Times*, March 16, 1988.

three million people: "Families with Children Leading Ranks of Homeless, Study Shows," *The New York Times*, March 31, 1987.

the homeless population: ibid.

81 "might steal something": Sara Rimer, "In Suburb, Poor People in Despair at a Motel," *The New York Times*, April 5, 1988.

CHAPTER 4

91 "for her height": "Girls, at 7, Think Thin, Study Finds," *The New York Times*, February 11, 1988.

Miss America pageant: Steven D. Stark, "Miss America: For Women the Pageant Never Ends," *The New York Times*, September 16, 1987.

92 "to package themselves": ibid.

"please pageant judges": Anne Taylor Fleming, "The California Work Ethic: Be Beautiful," *The New York Times*, July 27, 1988.

"spike-heel shoes": Smirnoff advertisement, *Savvy*, February 1988.

93 "a lot less!": Diane Von Furstenberg advertisement, *Fashions of the Times: The New York Times Magazine*, part 2, February 28, 1988.

the late 1980s: Bernardine Morris, "The Sexy Look: Why Now?" *The New York Times*, November 17, 1987.

"like little dolls": Claude Montana describing his spring 1988 collection, quoted on "Style with Elsa Klensch," Cable Network News, October 24, 1987.

94 "bimbo chic": Ann Landi, "Bimbo Chic," *Manhattan, Inc.*, November 1987.

handsome brass handle: Guess jeans advertisements, *Vogue*, September 1987.

"form . . . of prostration": Erving Goffman, *Gender Advertisements* (New York: Harper Colophon, 1979), p. 40.

95 to resounding cheers: Guess jeans advertisements, *Vogue*, February 1988.

"outrage each season": "A Fashion Revolt," *Newsweek*, December 5, 1988, p. 60.

96 prehuman ape: Mimi Pond, "Dance with a Stranger," *Seventeen*, March 1988, p. 142.

"the secretary does": Ellen Hopkins, "The Office Star and How She Fell: 10 Hidden Career Killers," *Mademoiselle*, March 1988, p. 264.

97 of $1.5 million: Neil Chesanow, "Enterprising Women," *Working Mother*, March 1988, p. 30.

98 "not necessarily": Wendy Chapkis, *Beauty Secrets: Women and the Politics of Appearance* (Boston: South End Press, 1986), p. 10.

"we can succeed": Anne Summers, "Pleasing Ourselves," *Ms.*, March 1988, p. 6.

99 "single-minded succeed": Susan L. Taylor, "In the Spirit: Purpose," *Essence*, March 1988, p. 49.

"and our people": ibid.

100 "and dependent children": Linda Lee Small, "A Piece of the

Dream," *Ms.,* March 1988, pp. 36–41.

101 "much with us": Michael J. Weiss, "What Price the American Dream," *Ladies' Home Journal,* March 1988, pp. 109–11, 147–51.

102 "heart of Christmas": *Harper's Bazaar,* December 1987, pp. 118–25.

want pretty things: Donna Karan advertisement, *Vogue,* August 1988.

103 incomes under $20,000: Sally Steenland, "Growing Up in Prime Time: An Analysis of Adolescent Girls on Television," National Commission on Working Women of Wider Opportunities for Women, August 1988, pp. 1–25.

"do it all": ibid., p. 15.

104 on prime time: Patricia Lone, "TV's Nightingales—Or Birdbrains?" *The New York Times,* April 7, 1989.

"and sexual adventures": Ruth Rosen, "Soap Operas: Search for Yesterday," in *Watching Television,* Todd Gitlin, ed. (New York: Pantheon, 1986), p. 63.

105 "help from men": ibid.

for the season: " 'Thirtysomething,' a Chronicle of Everyday Life," *The New York Times,* February 24, 1988.

106 "The Cosby Show": Peter J. Boyer, "TV Turns to the Hard-Boiled Male," *The New York Times,* February 16, 1986.

"*man* on television": ibid.

107 "for something simpler": ibid.

"side of men": Joy Horowitz, "On TV, Ms. Macho and Mr. Wimp," *The New York Times,* April 9, 1989.

108 "really in control": Molly Haskell, "Sympathy for the Devilish," *Vogue,* March 1988, pp. 84, 92.

"all over again": Janet Maslin,

"Sexism on Film: The Sequel," *The New York Times,* February 14, 1988.

110 Amanda Cross books: See, for example, Amanda Cross, *No Word from Winifred* (New York: Ballantine, 1987).

with her husband: P. M. Carlson, *Rehearsal for Murder* (New York: Bantam, 1988).

of British mysteries: See, for example, Antonia Fraser, *Oxford Blood* (London: Methuen, 1986).

modern female sleuth: Liza Cody, *Dupe* (New York: Warner, 1983).

111 Chicago-based mysteries: See, for example, Sara Paretsky, *Bitter Medicine* (New York: Ballantine, 1987).

"desire for independence": Sue Grafton, *"D" Is for Deadbeat* (New York: Bantam, 1988), p. 1.

112 "the beach front": ibid., p. 29.

"swear to God": ibid., p. 237.

CHAPTER 5

117 "of his call": Alice McDermott, *That Night* (New York: Farrar, Straus and Giroux, 1987), p. 3.

123 were sexually active: *Teenage Pregnancy: An Advocate's Guide to the Numbers,* Children's Defense Fund, January/March 1988, p. 4.

127 in the United States: "Doctors' Group Acts to Aid Abused Women," *The New York Times,* January 4, 1989.

except Hungary: Elise F. Jones et al., *Teenage Pregnancy in Industrialized Countries* (New Haven: Yale University Press, 1986), p. 1.

of the Netherlands: ibid., pp. 25–36.

128 have spontaneous abortions: Cheryl D. Hayes, ed., *Risking the Fu-*

ture: *Adolescent Sexuality, Pregnancy, and Childbearing,* vol. 1 (Washington, D.C.: National Academy Press, 1987), p. 1.

fifteen to nineteen: *The Health of America's Children: Maternal and Child Health Data Book,* Children's Defense Fund (1988), p. 27.

all teenage births: *Teenage Pregnancy: An Advocate's Guide,* p. 18.

16.9 percent: ibid., p. 20.

are giving birth: ibid., p. 18.

teens under fifteen: ibid.

unmarried teen mothers: ibid., p. 12.

to unmarried women: ibid., p. 19.

129 of the U.S.: Gina Kolata, "Study Finds Rate of Abortion Is High Among U.S. Women," *The New York Times,* June 2, 1988.

12.5 to 13 years: Phyllis B. Eveleth, "Timing of Menarche: Secular Trend and Population Differences" in *School-Age Pregnancy and Parenthood: Biosocial Dimensions,* Jane B. Lancaster and Beatrix A. Hamburg, eds. (New York: Aldine de Gruyter, 1986), pp. 39–52.

130 "a baseball game": Robb Forman Dew, *The Time of Her Life* (New York: Ballantine, 1985), p. 27.

published in 1955: Vladimir Nabokov, *Lolita* (New York: Berkley, 1987).

years in 1984: Sara E. Rix, ed., *The American Woman 1987–88: A Report in Depth* (New York: Norton, 1987), p. 292.

131 "marriages are slim": Hayes, p. 85.

"never been married": William Julius Wilson, *The Truly Disadvantaged: The Inner City, the Underclass, and Public Policy* (Chicago:

University of Chicago Press, 1987), p. 70.

fewer financial resources: ibid.

poor "marriage market": ibid., p. 75.

"black men": ibid., pp. 104–5.

47 percent in 1985: *Teenage Pregnancy,* pp. 13, 4.

were sexually active: ibid., p. 22.

132 method of contraception: Hayes, p. 46.

133 than prime time: "Psssst! Wanna Watch TV?" *Hartford Courant,* February 9, 1988.

"outside of marriage": Ruth Rosen, "Soap Operas: Search for Yesterday," in *Watching Television,* Todd Gitlin, ed. (New York: Pantheon, 1986), p. 49.

"and sexual rivalry": ibid., p. 61.

"using birth control": "Psssst!"

136 "this contraceptive technique": Gina Kolata, "New Data on the Pill Find Breast Cancer as a Possible Risk," *The New York Times,* January 5, 1989.

137 to give birth: *Teenage Pregnancy,* p. 25.

139 tested for AIDS: "Study Finds Students Ignorant on AIDS," *The New York Times,* December 29, 1988.

sexually transmitted diseases: Keith Haglund, "Teeners Hip on AIDS, Not Other STDs," *Medical Tribune,* September 8, 1988, p. 7.

"high-risk sexual behavior": Janet Fishbein, "Teenage Girls Know About AIDS, But Don't Act Accordingly," *The Nation's Health* (official newspaper of the American Public Health Association) 18, no. 12 (December 1988).

were using condoms: Gina Ko-

lata, "Use of Condoms Lags, Survey of Women Finds," *The New York Times,* July 28, 1988.
140 of low birth weight: *The Health of America's Children,* p. 28.

the least likely: ibid.

received such care: ibid., p. 4.

the white rate: ibid., p. 9.

of white infants: ibid., p. 4.
141 "their economic support": Hayes, p. 132.

of $16.6 billion: ibid., p. 133.
142 "by teenage parenthood": Frank F. Furstenberg, Jr., J. Brooks-Gunn, and S. Philip Morgan, *Adolescent Mothers in Later Life* (New York: Cambridge University Press, 1987), p. 76.

"from public assistance": ibid., p. 46.

"in later life": ibid., p. 47.

"ubiquitous vending machines": Jones et al., p. 217.

in the Netherlands: ibid., p. 232.
143 "in the United States": ibid., p. 233.

"in the United States": ibid., p. 234.
144 "births, and abortions": ibid., pp. 239–40.

"to the next": Hayes, p. 267.

CHAPTER 6

148 "their life's work": Mary Field Belenky, Blythe McVicker Clinchy, Nancy Rule Goldberger, and Jill Mattuck Tarule, *Women's Ways of Knowing: The Development of Self, Voice, and Mind* (New York: Basic, 1986), p. 48.

"love and work": Carol Gilligan, *In a Different Voice: Psychological Theory and Women's* *Development* (Cambridge, MA: Harvard University Press, 1982), p. 51.

"relationship of connection": ibid., p. 171.
149 "affiliations and relationships": Jean Baker Miller, *Toward a New Psychology of Women* (Boston: Beacon, 1976), p. 83.

"the dominant group": ibid., p. 38.

"of one's superior": Joan C. Tronto, "Women and Caring: What Can Feminists Learn About Mortality from Caring?" in Alison Jaggar and Susan Bordo, eds., *Body, Gender and Knowledge* (New Brunswick, NJ: Rutgers University Press, in press). See also Tronto, "Beyond Gender Difference to a Theory of Care," *Signs* 12, no. 4 (Summer 1987), pp. 644–63.

"isolated from others": Ruthellen Josselson, *Finding Herself: Pathways to Identity Development in Women* (San Francisco: Jossey-Bass, 1987), p. 23.

"achievement and independence": ibid., p. 26.
150 "is all about": Francine Klagsbrun, *Married People: Staying Together in the Age of Divorce* (New York: Bantam, 1986), pp. 21–22.
156 best-selling books: Dr. Connell Cowan and Dr. Melvyn Kinder, *Smart Women, Foolish Choices: Finding the Right Men, Avoiding the Wrong Ones* (New York: Signet, 1986); Dr. Kevin Leman, *The Pleasers: Women Who Can't Say NO— and the Men Who Control Them* (New York: Dell, 1988); Robin Norwood, *Women Who Love Too Much: When You Keep Wishing and Hoping He'll Change* (New York: Pocket, 1986); and Dr. Susan For-

ward, *Men Who Hate Women—and the Women Who Love Them* (New York: Bantam, 1986).

157 "most men away": Cowan and Kinder, p. 263.

"self-validation": Norwood, pp. 272–73.

"and women will": Jessica Benjamin, *The Bonds of Love: Psychoanalysis, Feminism, and the Problem of Domination* (New York: Pantheon, 1988), pp. 186–87.

160 "late twentieth century": Willard Gaylin, M.D., *Rediscovering Love* (New York: Penguin, 1987), p. 124.

161 "of early infancy": ibid., p. 122.

"by being approved": Rachel M. Brownstein, *Becoming a Heroine: Reading About Women in Novels* (New York: Penguin, 1984), p. xv.

162 "probably means 'never' ": Sara E. Rix, ed., *The American Woman 1988–89: A Status Report* (New York: Norton, 1988), pp. 271–72.

163 "and 23 percent": ibid., pp. 272–73.

"it a thought": ibid., p. 275.

at least once: ibid., p. 73.

is increasing significantly: William Julius Wilson, *The Truly Disadvantaged: The Inner City, the Underclass, and Public Policy* (Chicago: University of Chicago Press, 1987), p. 68.

non-Hispanic white women: "Marriage Is Chancier 2d Time Around," *The New York Times,* September 1, 1988.

164 and child-rearing: Terry Arendell, *Mothers and Divorce: Legal, Economic, and Social Dilemmas* (Berkeley: University of California Press, 1986), pp. 1–8.

after a divorce: Rix, p. 92.

female-headed households: U.S. Bureau of the Census, Current Population Reports, Series P-60, No. 161, *Money Income and Poverty Status in the United States: 1987 (Advance Data from the March 1988 Current Population Survey)* (Washington, D.C.: U.S. Government Printing Office, 1988), p. 4.

of white men: Wilson, p. 95.

been well documented: ibid., p. 83.

"likely to remarry": Rix, p. 78.

165 has risen dramatically: ibid., p. 353.

female-headed families: *Money Income and Poverty Status,* pp. 13–14.

is very great: ibid., p. 27.

CHAPTER 7

170 of the story: Louis Uchitelle, "Making a Living is NOW a Family Enterprise," *The New York Times* Career section, October 11, 1987; Louis Uchitelle, "Top Labor Issue: Jobs for Single Mothers," *The New York Times,* August 5, 1987; Jill Abramson, "For Women Lawyers, an Uphill Struggle," *The New York Times Magazine,* March 6, 1988, pp. 36–37, 73–75; Renee Loth, "Jobs Go Begging in Human Services," *Boston Globe,* February 26, 1988; Perri Klass, "Are Women Better Doctors?" *The New York Times Magazine,* April 10, 1988, pp. 32–35, 46–50; Michael Freitag, "New York Is Fighting Spread of Sweatshops," *The New York Times,* November 16, 1987; Anita Merina, "More Women in Top State Posts," *Women's Political Times* (a publication of the National Women's Political Caucus), Spring/ Summer 1988; "Women Gain Little in Academic Jobs," *The New York Times,* July 23, 1987; and Michel

McQueen, "Despite Job Gains, Sexual Segregation Remains, U.S. Says," *Wall Street Journal,* September 4, 1987.

the labor force: Barbara Bergmann, *The Economic Emergence of Women* (New York: Basic, 1986), p. 21.

171 students were women: "Women MDs: Changing the Ranks of Medicine," *Medical World News,* April 25, 1988, pp. 57–68.

pediatrics, and psychiatry: Klass.

more egalitarian way: ibid.

172 had female chairs: ibid.

173 only one-third: Lawrence Farber, "Why Women Doctors Don't Have a Lot of Money," *Medical Economics,* November 23, 1987, pp. 62–75.

the previous year: "Among Career Choices, a Booming Year in Law," *The New York Times,* June 1, 1988.

of many lawyers: "Law School Applications Up Sharply," *The New York Times,* March 31, 1988.

more than $50,000: ibid.

174 to 40 percent: Abramson.

private law firm: ibid.

"you stay single": ibid.

"from your soul": Tom Goldstein, "Women in the Law Aren't Yet Equal Partners," *The New York Times,* February 12, 1988.

are white males: Abramson.

175 "have it all": ibid.

"very conservative profession": Eric N. Berg, "The Big Eight: Still a Male Bastion," *The New York Times,* July 12, 1988.

176 been no discrimination: "Promoting 'Femininity,' " *The New York Times,* May 6, 1989.

"work at night": Sandra Salman, "Top Tiers Still Elude Corporate Women," *The New York Times,* August 17, 1987.

177 "combating sexual harassment": "20 Corporations That Listen to Women," *Ms.,* November 1987, pp. 45–52.

off-site child care: "20 Corporations."

"but no parity": Larry Rohter, "Women Gain Degrees, but Not Tenure," *The New York Times,* January 4, 1987.

significantly lower salaries: See for example, Carla Rivera, "Blacks, Women Charge UC Irvine with Prejudice," *Los Angeles Times,* December 18, 1988.

178 "outside the academy": Nadya Aisenberg and Mona Harrington, *Women of Academe: Outsiders in the Sacred Grove* (Amherst: University of Massachusetts Press, 1988), p. ix.

"of professional authority": ibid., p. xii.

"prepared for autonomy": ibid., p. 20.

15.5 percent in 1988: "Women and the Vote, 1988: A Fact Sheet," National Commission on Working Women of Wider Opportunities for Women (Washington, D.C.: 1988).

Kassebaum of Kansas: "Women Make Few Gains in November Elections," *National NOW Times,* October/November/December 1988.

179 all the jobs: "Work Force 2000," U.S. Department of Labor, Washington, D.C., pp. 1–19.

180 is considerably smaller: ibid., pp. 202–28.

earned only $11,000: U.S. Bureau of the Census, Current Population Reports, Series P-60, No. 161, *Money Income and Poverty Status in the United States: 1987 (Advance Data from the March 1988 Current Population Survey)* (Washington,

D.C.: U.S. Government Printing Office, 1988), pp. 19–20.

181 "sense of purpose": Katherine S. Newman, *Falling from Grace: The Experience of Downward Mobility in the American Middle Class* (New York: Free Press, 1988), p. 23.

females under thirty (26.0 percent): Clifford M. Johnson, Andrew M. Sum, and James D. Weill, *Vanishing Dreams: The Growing Economic Plight of America's Young Families* (Washington, D.C.: Children's Defense Fund, 1988), p. 76.

low of $1,092: ibid., p. 46.
182 57 percent: ibid., p. 58.

income for rent!: ibid., p. 59.

married-couple families: ibid., p. 78.

falling into poverty: ibid., p. 79.
183 nursing was declining: David C. Anderson, "Roots of the Nursing Gap Are Economic and Social," *The New York Times*, May 29, 1988.

as a career: ibid.

pursue other careers: Martin Tolchin, "Health Worker Shortage Is Worsening," *The New York Times*, April 18, 1988.

$27,000 a year: Anderson.
184 "has just died": Stacey Okun, "For Bronx Nurses in Protest, Staying Home Is Painful," *The New York Times*, February 20, 1988.

New York City alone: Bruce Lambert, "Visas Extended to Help Keep Foreign Nurses," *The New York Times*, May 27, 1988.

"from their homes": Tolchin.
185 "own old age": Lise Lederer, "New OWL Report Examines Plight of Chronic Care Workers," *OWL Observer* (national newspaper of the Older Women's League), November/December 1988.

is $28,300: "Teaching: Surge in Popularity?" *On Campus* (newspaper of the American Federation of Teachers), March 1988.

and developing countries: "Teacher Shortage? Recruit Abroad," *The New York Times*, June 1, 1988.
186 "ten worst careers": Holloway McCandless, "The 10 Worst Careers for Women," *Working Women*, July 1988, pp. 65–66.

65 percent were women: Hilary Stout, "The Economics of the Minimum Wage: Propping Up Payments at the Bottom," *The New York Times*, January 24, 1988.

families live in poverty: Sar A. Levitan and Elizabeth Conway, "Shortchanged by Part-Time Work," *The New York Times*, February 27, 1988.

are laid off?: Louis Uchitelle, "Reliance on Temporary Jobs Hints at Economic Fragility," *The New York Times*, March 16, 1988.

"Federal poverty level": Uchitelle, "Top Labor Issue."
187 "or illegal conditions": Kendall J. Wills, "Rise Is Seen in Garment Sweatshops," *The New York Times*, September 6, 1987.

fire of 1911: Freitag.

"on the floor": Wills.

country as well: Freitag.

all clerical workers: Sara E. Rix, ed., *The American Woman 1988–89: A Status Report* (New York: Norton, 1988), p. 384.

and nurses' aides: Rhonda M. Williams, "Beyond Human Capital: Black Women, Work, and Wages," Working Paper No. 183 (Wellesley, MA: Wellesley College Center for Research on Women, 1988), p. 10.
188 "low wage firms": ibid., p. 9.

"low-wage black women": ibid.

Hispanic females, $6,611: *Money Income and Poverty Status*, pp. 19–20.

work part-time: Sara E. Rix., ed., *The American Woman 1987–88: A Report in Depth* (New York: Norton, 1987), pp. 134–35.

189 "164 percent, respectively": William Julius Wilson, *The Truly Disadvantaged: The Inner City, the Underclass, and Public Policy* (Chicago: University of Chicago Press, 1987), p. 26.

190 "isolation and poverty": Grace K. Baruch, Lois Biener, and Rosalind C. Barnett, "Women and Gender in Research on Stress," Working Paper No. 152 (Wellesley, MA: Wellesley College Center for Research on Women, 1985), p. 4.

stress for women: ibid., p. 10.

CHAPTER 8

199 "own families together": Kathy Dobie, "Black Women, White Kids," *The Village Voice*, January 12, 1988.

200 "ones to bed": ibid.

"the tourist industry": Shellee Colen, " 'With Respect and Feelings': Voices of West Indian Child Care and Domestic Workers in New York City," in *All American Women: Lines That Divide, Ties That Bind*, Johnnetta B. Cole, ed. (New York: Free Press, 1986), p. 48.

"have no choice": ibid., p. 46.

201 is frowned upon: Jan Trost, "Parental Benefits: A Study of Men's Behavior and Views," *Current Sweden* (Stockholm: Swedish Institute), June 1983, pp. 1–7.

202 "has changed dramatically": Anita Shreve, *Remaking Motherhood: How Working Mothers Are Shaping Our Children's Future* (New York: Ballantine, 1988), p. 194.

"settle colicky babies": ibid., p. 195.

or their husbands: ibid., pp. 196–97.

203 the "caretaking" activities: ibid., p. 199.

"of their identity": Marian Burros, "Women: Out of the House but Not of the Kitchen," *The New York Times*, February 24, 1988.

"the private sphere": Kathleen Gerson, *Hard Choices: How Women Decide About Work, Career, and Motherhood* (Berkeley: University of California Press, 1985), p. 221.

204 "work and parenthood": ibid.

205 to 13.4 million: "Working Mother Is Now Norm, Study Shows," *The New York Times*, June 16, 1988.

"varies widely": "Who Cares About Day Care?" *Newsweek*, March 28, 1988, p. 73.

"in the playpen": "Mothers with Babies—and Jobs," *The New York Times*, June 19, 1988.

child-care arrangements: "Jobs and Child Care Studied," *The New York Times*, May 11, 1987.

206 "no time for self": Katharine Macdonald, "Who Cares for the Children?" *San Francisco Examiner*, May 15, 1988.

of their parenting: ibid.

"of these programs": Joseph Berger, "Teachers in Day Care Questioned," *The New York Times*, May 23, 1988.

20 to 25 percent: ibid.

day-care providers: Tamar Lewin, "Day Care Becomes a Growing Burden," *The New York Times*, June 5, 1988.

207 approximately $19,000: Berger.

in private homes, $4,420: Macdonald.

"children's warehouses": ibid.

by a nonrelative: Lewin.

208 and their children: Fern Marx,

The Role of Day Care in Serving the
Needs of School-Age Parents and
Their Children: A Review of the Literature, Working Paper No. 174
(Wellesley, MA: Wellesley College
Center for Research on Women,
1987), p. 4.
209 "of other services": ibid., p. 19.
to ten million: "Among
Latchkey Children Problems: Insufficient Day-Care Facilities, Data on
Possible Harm," *Journal of the American Medical Association* 260, no. 23
(December 16, 1988), pp. 3399–400.
800,000 latchkey children:
Robert Reinhold, "California Tries
Caring for Its Growing Ranks of
Latchkey Children," *The New York
Times,* October 4, 1987.
and rural communities: Glenn
Collins, "Latchkey Children: A New
Profile Emerges," *The New York
Times,* October 14, 1987.
later in childhood: Sandra
Evans, "Psychological Risk of Day
Care Told," *The Washington Post,*
November 7, 1987.
for the workers: Glenn Collins,
"Day Care for Infants: Debate Turns
to Long-Term Effects," *The New
York Times,* November 25, 1987.
210 "General Accounting Office":
Linda Greenhouse, "Despite Support,
a Child Care Bill Fails to Emerge,"
The New York Times, June 6, 1988.
for respiratory illness: *To Your
Health!* (The Lahey Clinic [Burlington, MA] Health Letter), Fall 1986;
Larry J. Anderson et al., "Day-Care
Center Attendance and Hospitalization for Lower Respiratory Tract Illness," *Pediatrics* 82, no. 3 (September
1988), pp. 300–8.
211 "would be huge": Robert J.
Samuelson, "The Debate over Day
Care," *Newsweek,* June 27, 1988,
p. 45.

"and $3.1 billion": *Children in
Need: Investment Strategies for the
Educationally Disadvantaged* (New
York: Committee for Economic Development, 1987), p. 34.
212 "a mother's body?": Anna
Quindlen, "Is 'Quality' Time Really
as Good as a Good Time?" *The New
York Times,* June 9, 1988.
"buy more help": Sally
Abrahms, "Parents in Absentia," *The
New York Times,* January 20, 1988.
213 "largely of women": Jennifer A.
Kingson, "Women in the Law Say
Path Is Limited by 'Mommy Track,'"
The New York Times, August 8,
1988.

CHAPTER 9

223 "realm of consumption": Todd
Gitlin, *Inside Prime Time* (New
York: Pantheon, 1985), pp. 268–69.
226 "which people think": Robert
N. Bellah, Richard Madsen, William
M. Sullivan, Ann Swidler, and Steven
M. Tipton, *Habits of the Heart: Individualism and Commitment in
American Life* (Berkeley: University
of California Press, 1985), p. 290.
"existing institutional order":
Gitlin, p. 268.
230 "*our social ecology*": Bellah et
al., pp. 288–89.
231 "annually on arms": Andrew
Rosenthal, "Panel Endorses Cheney's
Spending Plan," *The New York
Times,* June 21, 1989.
"next 10 years": Nathaniel C.
Nash, "Bush Savings Plan Is Passed
by House!" *The New York Times,*
June 16, 1989.
232 "choose your job": Irvin Molotsky, "Fewer Businesses Affected by
Parental Leave Bill," *The New York
Times,* September 28, 1988.

233 "seriously ill child": Judy Mann, "Some More Equal Than Others," *The Washington Post,* September 21, 1988.

"he doesn't care": ibid.

234 in the work force: *Child Care: The Bottom Line* (New York: Child Care Action Campaign, 1988), p. 52.

unlicensed and unsupervised: ibid., p. 30.

"right after birth": Carol Lawson, "For Architect of Child Care, Small Gains," *The New York Times,* June 22, 1989.

235 "executives and educators": *Children in Need: Investment Strategies for the Educationally Disadvantaged* (New York: Committee for Economic Development, 1987), p. vi.

"the whole child": ibid., p. ix.

"enough to act": ibid., p. 14.

236 "is now available": Lisbeth B. Schorr, *Within Our Reach: Breaking The Cycle of Disadvantage* (New York: Doubleday, 1988), p. xix.

237 "very private concerns": ibid., p. 52.

at the program's end: ibid., p. 53.

238 "agency sexuality program": Michael A. Carrera and Patricia Dempsey, "Restructuring Public Policy Priorities on Teen Pregnancy: A Holistic Approach to Teen Development and Teen Services," SIECUS Report (January/February 1988), pp. 6–9.

242 ever recorded: "Analysis of Poverty in 1987" (Washington, D.C.: Center on Budget and Policy Priorities, 1988), p. 4.

SELECTED READING

Mimi Abramovitz, *Regulating the Lives of Women: Social Welfare Policy from Colonial Times to the Present* (Boston: South End Press, 1988).

Nadya Aisenberg and Mona Harrington, *Women of Academe: Outsiders in the Sacred Grove* (Amherst, MA: University of Massachusetts Press, 1988).

Maya Angelou, *I Know Why the Caged Bird Sings* (New York: Bantam, 1971).

Terry Arendell, *Mothers and Divorce: Legal, Economic, and Social Dilemmas* (Los Angeles: University of California Press, 1986).

Grace K. Baruch, Lois Biener, and Rosalind C. Barnett, *Women and Gender in Research on Stress*, Working Paper No. 152 (Wellesley, MA: Wellesley College Center for Research on Women, 1985).

Simone de Beauvoir, *The Second Sex* (New York: Bantam, 1961).

Mary Field Belenky, Blythe McVicker Clinchy, Nancy Rule Goldberger, and Jill Mattuck Tarule, *Women's Ways of Knowing: The Development of Self, Voice, and Mind* (New York: Basic, 1986).

Robert N. Bellah et al., *Habits of the Heart: Individualism and Commitment in American Life* (Berkeley, CA: University of California Press, 1985).

Lourdes Beneria and Catharine R. Stimpson, eds., *Women, Households, and the Economy* (New Brunswick, NJ: Rutgers University Press, 1987).

Jessica Benjamin, *The Bonds of Love: Psychoanalysis, Feminism, and the Problem of Domination* (New York: Pantheon, 1988).

Barbara Bergmann, *The Economic Emergence of Women* (New York: Basic, 1986).

Rachel M. Brownstein, *Becoming a Heroine: Reading About Women in Novels* (New York: Penguin, 1984).

259

David M. Brownstone, Irene M. Franck, and Douglass L. Brownstone, *Island of Hope, Island of Tears* (New York: Penguin, 1986).

P. M. Carlson, *Rehearsal for Murder* (New York: Bantam, 1988).

Wendy Chapkis, *Beauty Secrets: Women and the Politics of Appearance* (Boston: South End Press, 1986).

Child Care: The Bottom Line (New York: Child Care Action Campaign, 1988).

Children in Need: Investment Strategies for the Educationally Disadvantaged (New York: Committee for Economic Development, 1987).

Kathleen Christensen, *Women and Home-Based Work: The Unspoken Contract* (New York: Holt, 1988).

Liza Cody, *Dupe* (New York: Warner, 1983).

Johnnetta B. Cole, ed., *All American Women: Lines That Divide, Ties That Bind* (New York: Free Press, 1986).

Patricia Hill Collins, "Learning from the Outsider Within: The Sociological Significance of Black Feminist Thought," *Social Problems* 33, no. 6 (December 1986), S14–S32.

Amanda Cross, *No Word from Winifred* (New York: Ballantine, 1987).

Robb Forman Dew, *The Time of Her Life* (New York: Ballantine, 1985).

W.E.B. DuBois, *The Souls of Black Folk* (New York: New American Library, 1969).

Marian Wright Edelman, *Families in Peril: An Agenda for Social Change* (Cambridge, MA: Harvard University Press, 1987).

Lee R. Edwards, *Psyche as Hero: Female Heroism and Fictional Form* (Middletown, CT: Wesleyan University Press, 1987).

Cynthia Fuchs Epstein, *Deceptive Distinctions: Sex, Gender and the Social Order* (New Haven: Yale University Press, 1988).

Elizabeth Ewen, *Immigrant Women in the Land of Dollars: Life and Culture on the Lower East Side, 1890–1925* (New York: Monthly Review Press, 1985).

Eva Figes, *Patriarchal Attitudes: Women in Society* (New York: Persea Books, 1987).

Antonia Fraser, *Oxford Blood* (London: Methuen, 1986).

Frank F. Furstenberg, Jr., J. Brooks-Gunn, and S. Philip Morgan, *Adolescent Mothers in Later Life* (New York: Cambridge University Press, 1987).

Irwin Garfinkel and Sara S. McLanahan, *Single Mothers and Their Children: A New American Dilemma* (Washington, D.C.: Urban Institute Press, 1986).

Willard Gaylin, M.D., *Rediscovering Love* (New York: Penguin, 1987).

Kathleen Gerson, *Hard Choices: How Women Decide About Work, Career, and Motherhood* (Berkeley, CA: University of California Press, 1985).

Naomi Gerstel and Harriet Engel Gross, eds., *Families and Work* (Philadelphia: Temple University Press, 1987).

Carol Gilligan, *In a Different Voice: Psychological Theory and Women's Development* (Cambridge, MA: Harvard University Press, 1982).

Todd Gitlin, *Inside Prime Time* (New York: Pantheon, 1985).

Sue Grafton, *"D" Is for Deadbeat* (New York: Bantam, 1988).

Cheryl D. Hayes, ed., *Risking the Future: Adolescent Sexuality, Pregnancy, and Childbearing,* Volume 1 (Washington, D.C.: National Academy Press, 1987).

The Health of America's Children: Maternal and Child Health Data Book (Children's Defense Fund, 1988).

Carolyn G. Heilbrun, *Reinventing Womanhood* (New York: Norton, 1979).

Arlie Russell Hochschild, *The Managed Heart: Commercialization of Human Feeling* (Berkeley, CA: University of California Press, 1983).

Bell Hooks, *Talking Back: Thinking Feminist, Thinking Black* (Boston: South End Press, 1989).

Richard M. Huber, *The American Idea of Success* (Wainscott, NY: Pushcart Press, 1987).

Isabel Huggan, *The Elizabeth Stories* (New York: Viking, 1987).

Josephine Humphreys, *Rich in Love* (New York: Viking, 1987).

Linda Imray and Audrey Middleton, "Public and Private: Marking the Boundaries," in *The Public and the Private,* Eva Gamarnikow et al., eds. (London: Heinemann, 1983).

Clifford M. Johnson, Andrew M. Sum, and James D. Weill, *Vanishing Dreams: The Growing Economic Plight of America's Young Families* (Washington, D.C.: Children's Defense Fund, 1988).

Elise F. Jones et al., *Teenage Pregnancy in Industrialized Countries* (New Haven: Yale University Press, 1986).

Ruthellen Josselson, *Finding Herself: Pathways to Identity Development in Women* (San Francisco: Jossey-Bass, 1987).

Louise J. Kaplan, Ph.D., *Adolescence: The Farewell to Childhood* (New York: Simon & Schuster, 1985).

Maxine Hong Kingston, *The Woman Warrior: Memoirs of a Girlhood Among Ghosts* (New York: Vintage, 1977).

Francine Klagsbrun, *Married People: Staying Together in the Age of Divorce* (New York: Bantam, 1986).

Ethel Klein, *Gender Politics* (Cambridge, MA: Harvard University Press, 1984).

Kathleen Gregory Klein, *The Woman Detective: Gender & Genre* (Chicago: University of Illinois Press, 1988).

Jonathan Kozol, *Rachel and Her Children: Homeless Families in America* (New York: Crown, 1988).

Jane B. Lancaster and Beatrix A. Hamburg, eds., *School-Age Pregnancy and Parenthood: Biosocial Dimensions* (New York: Aldine de Gruyter, 1986).

Carson McCullers, *The Member of the Wedding* (New York: Bantam, 1975).

Alice McDermott, *That Night* (New York: Farrar, Straus and Giroux, 1987).

Catharine A. MacKinnon, *Feminism Unmodified: Discourses on Life and Law* (Cambridge, MA: Harvard University Press, 1987).

Paule Marshall, *Brown Girl, Brownstones* (New York: Feminist Press, 1981).

Fern Marx, *The Role of Day Care in Serving the Needs of School-Age Parents and Their Children: A Review of The Literature,* Working Paper No. 174 (Wellesley, MA: Wellesley College Center for Research on Women, 1987).

Jean Baker Miller, *Toward a New Psychology of Women* (Boston: Beacon, 1976).

Toni Morrison, *The Bluest Eye* (New York: Pocket, 1974).

Gary Paul Nabhan, *The Desert Smells Like Rain: A Naturalist in Papago Indian Country* (San Francisco: North Point Press, 1987).

Vladimir Nabokov, *Lolita* (New York: Berkley, 1987).

Gloria Naylor, *The Women of Brewster Place* (New York: Penguin, 1983).

Katherine S. Newman, *Falling from Grace: The Experience of Downward Mobility in the American Middle Class* (New York: Free Press, 1988).

Sara Paretsky, *Bitter Medicine* (New York: Ballantine, 1987).

Sara E. Rix, ed., *The American Woman 1987–88: A Report in Depth* (New York: Norton, 1987).

Sara E. Rix, ed., *The American Woman 1988–89: A Status Report* (New York: Norton, 1988).

Michelle Zimbalist Rosaldo and Louise Lamphere, eds., *Women, Culture, and Society* (Stanford, CA: Stanford University Press, 1974).

Ruth Rosen, "Soap Operas: Search for Yesterday," in *Watching Television,* Todd Gitlin, ed. (New York: Pantheon, 1986).

Marlene Sanders and Marcia Rock, *Waiting for Prime Time: The Women of Television News* (Urbana, IL: University of Illinois Press, 1988).

Lisbeth B. Schorr, *Within Our Reach: Breaking the Cycle of Disadvantage* (New York: Doubleday, 1988).

Anita Shreve, *Remaking Motherhood: How Working Mothers Are Shaping Our Children's Future* (New York: Ballantine, 1988).

Kate Simon, *A Wider World: Portraits in an Adolescence* (New York: Harper & Row, 1987).

The State of Black America 1988 (New York: National Urban League, Inc., 1988).

Teenage Pregnancy: An Advocate's Guide to the Numbers (Children's Defense Fund, January/March 1988).

Joan C. Tronto, "Women and Caring: What Can Feminists Learn About Morality from Caring?" in *Body, Gender and Knowledge,* Alison Jagger and Susan Bordo, eds. (New Brunswick, NJ: Rutgers University Press, in press).

Rhonda M. Williams, *Beyond Human Capital: Black Women, Work, and Wages,* Working Paper No. 183 (Wellesley, MA: Wellesley College Center for Research on Women, 1988).

William Julius Wilson, *The Truly Disadvantaged: The Inner City, the Underclass, and Public Policy* (Chicago: University of Chicago Press, 1987).

INDEX

Hispanics, 165, 205
  income of, 181, 187–89
  as Neotraditionalists, 38–39, 41, 49
  as New American Dreamers, 17, 18
  sexual activity of, 131
  teenage births of, 128
  wages and working conditions of, 187–89
homelessness, 80–81
homemaking:
  full-time, 20, 21, 44–45, 99–101, 190, 196–97
  male vs. female participation in, 202–3
home ownership, decline of, 181–182
"Hostos, Tory," 70
House Education and Labor Committee, 210
House of Games (film), 108
Huggan, Isabel, 59
Humphreys, Josephine, 50
Hunter College, 38–40

identity, 220
  of adolescents, 60, 62
  group, 60
  intimacy and, 17, 149–50
  loss of, 155
  of Neotraditionalists, 40
  of New American Dreamers, 17, 20, 40
  through marriage, 17, 40
immigration, 7–8, 57, 68
income, *see* economics and income
independence, 57, 67, 224–26, 239–40
  of Neotraditionalists, 40, 42, 44
  of New American Dreamers, 27–33
individualism, 27–31, 114, 115, 224–26, 228, 239
infant mortality, 140
infants, low-birth-weight, 140
insecurity, sex and, 122
interviewees, diversity of, 4–5

intimacy, 10, 86, 147–68
  acceptance and, 159–61
  adolescents' need for, 59
  caring for others and, 148–49
  dangers of, 154–55
  defined, 150
  domination and, 154–59
  identity and, 17, 149–50
  separation vs., 119
  sex vs., 119–21
  uncertainty and, 167–68

Jackson, Jesse, 58, 179
"Jackson, Wendy," 33–34
"Jefferson, Linda," 193, 213
Jews, in youth groups, 61–62
Johns Hopkins University, 139, 236–37
"Johnson, Margot," 194–95
"Jones, Laurie," 41–42

Kanter, Rosabeth Moss, 176
Karan, Donna, 102
Kassebaum, Nancy, 178–79
Klagsbrun, Francine, 150
Klass, Perri, 171
Koop, C. Everett, 127
"Kovak, Dorothy," 63–64, 66–67

Labor Department, New York State, 187
Labor Department, U.S., 179
labor force, women in, 170, 179, 205, 221, 235
Ladies' Home Journal, 96, 101
"L.A. Law" (TV show), 103–4, 173, 241
Lauren, Ralph, 74
law, women in, 173–76, 213
leaving home, 50, 57, 60
Lendl, Ivan, 221
lesbianism, 152, 159–60
Levine, Ethel, 135
"Levy, Lynda," 169, 184
Lewis, Ann, 179
Lincoln Hospital, 183–84
Lolita (Nabokov), 130
Long, Shelley, 101

as mothers, 41, 76, 81, 186–87,
205, 206, 213
"sluts," 1980s image of, 134–35
Smart Women, Foolish Choices
(Cowan and Kinder), 157
"Smith, Linda," 55, 67
soap operas, 133
social change, 10–11, 213–15,
219–43
American Dream and, 239–41
child rearing and, 231–35
repetition of familiar patterns vs.,
46
work and, 228–34
socialization, marital assumptions
and, 2–3
social problems, personal problems
vs., 99, 114
Souls of Black Folk, The (DuBois),
69
sports, 26–27, 220–21
"squeal rule," 136
"Stark, Sarah," 169, 172–73
status, 22, 24, 31, 115
decline of, 180–81
professional, 173, 174
relationships and, 126
"Stein, Janet," 151–52
"Stein, Peter," 151–52
Steinberg, Lisa, 212
"Steinberg, Stacy," 32
stereotypes:
gay, 160
about teenagers, 49, 128
television, 103
"Stern, Mallory," 43
stress, work and, 189–91
success, 90–91, 101
education and, 30–31
love vs., 96–97
narrow definition of, 115–16,
222–23
New American Dreamers' emphasis on, 15–18, 27, 29–31
occupational choice and, 22–23
suicide of teenagers, 64–65
"Sullivan, Shawn," 42
Supreme Court, U.S., 176

surgery, 171
sweatshops, 187
Sweden, 127, 142, 143
male child-care role in, 201

Tate, Sheila, 179
teaching, 185–86, 206–7
teenage pregnancies, 2, 6, 66, 67,
72, 76, 86, 117–18, 124, 127–
129, 235
blaming the victim and, 129
child care and, 194, 208
holistic approach to, 237–38
risks of, 139–44
statistics on, 127–28
teenagers:
birth control and, 131–32
black, 131, 137
grades pressures of, 30–32
Neotraditionalist, 49–52
sexually active, 120, 123, 131–32
stereotypes of, 49, 128
substance abuse of, 31
television, 226, 241
mixed messages of, 102–7, 113–
116, 133
sexual references on, 133
see also specific shows
That Night (McDermott), 117–18
"Thirtysomething" (TV show),
105–6, 115
Time of Her Life, The (Dew), 130
"Today" (TV show), 23
Tronto, Joan, 21, 149
two-income families, 2, 6, 200,
205–6, 225
"type A" personalities, 190

Unbearable Lightness of Being, The
(film), 108
unemployment, 75–76, 131, 181
marital instability and, 164–65
United States:
pregnancy rates in, 128–29
teenage pregnancy in, 127
upper middle class, 4, 114–16, 180,
199, 229
Neotraditionalists as, 39